Conversations in Jazz

Conversations in Jazz

■

The
Ralph J. Gleason
Interviews

■

EDITED BY

TOBY GLEASON

Foreword and Introductory Notes by Ted Gioia

Yale

UNIVERSITY PRESS

NEW HAVEN AND LONDON

Published with assistance from the Louis Stern Memorial Fund.

Yale University Press books may be purchased in quantity for
educational, business, or promotional use. For information,
please e-mail sales.press@yale.edu (U.S. office) or sales@yaleup
.co.uk (U.K. office).

Designed by Sonia Shannon.
Set in Electra type by Integrated Publishing Solutions,
Grand Rapids, Michigan.
Printed in the United States of America.

Library of Congress Control Number: 2015954409
ISBN 978-0-300-21452-9 (paper over board: alk. paper)

A catalogue record for this book is available from the British
Library.

This paper meets the requirements of
ANSI/NISO Z39.48-1992
(Permanence of Paper).

10 9 8 7 6 5 4 3 2 1

Contents

Foreword

DID RALPH GLEASON REALLY leave us forty years ago? It certainly doesn't feel that way. Even today, you will find Gleason's name on the masthead of each issue of *Rolling Stone*, the magazine he helped launch back in 1967. His trademark trench coat hangs in the Rock & Roll Hall of Fame, almost as if Gleason just stopped by a moment ago to check out the scene. The Monterey Jazz Festival, a bright idea Gleason had back in 1958, continues to thrive even as other music events and venues come and go. Every day, a music fan somewhere reads his liner notes to some classic album, whether Miles Davis's *Bitches Brew* or Frank Sinatra's *No One Cares* or Simon & Garfunkel's *Parsley, Sage, Rosemary and Thyme*.

I know that a car company has already usurped the motto "Built to Last" to sell pickup trucks, but I insist that Ralph Gleason has a better claim to the phrase. He might have earned a living writing for a daily newspaper, but he disdained the ephemeral and championed the timeless. And Gleason's knack for tapping into the zeitgeist went far beyond the jazz world. Even today, anyone probing the great causes and upheavals of the mid-twentieth century—the Civil Rights Movement, Vietnam War protests, Summer of Love happenings, beatniks, censorship trials, Altamont, you name it—will eventually encounter his name and legacy. In many instances, Gleason not only reported on the scene, but helped shape it.

Yet Ralph Gleason will always be remembered, first and foremost, as a jazz writer. Jazz was his first love and, like many early attachments, remained the most passionate. And that sense of intimate attachment comes across again and again in these pages. Gleason may be interviewing a jazz legend, John Coltrane or Duke Ellington, but the conversations come across as uninhibited tête-à-têtes between familiars. "I feel like I'm on the same level as you," Duke Ellington tells Gleason a few minutes into their dialogue. Quincy Jones, midway in their conversation, asks, "Do you want me to be frank?," and proceeds to talk the way jazz musicians usually do only among themselves.

Ralph Gleason discovered jazz back in 1934, when he was a youngster recuperating from the measles. Confined to bed in a dark room, he experienced contact with the outside world via the radio. "I lay there, wide awake in the night," he later recalled, "picking up those strange sounds in the night—Duke Ellington, Louis Armstrong, Cab Calloway, Earl Hines, Fletcher Henderson."

Gleason was soon writing record reviews for his college newspaper while a student at Columbia University. At this stage in American music history, serious jazz writing hardly existed. But around the time he graduated, Gleason launched his own music periodical, *Jazz Information*, one of the very first jazz magazines in the United States. The magazine's leading rival at the time, the *HRS Society Rag*, adopted a more playful attitude to jazz—a lighthearted approach that Gleason and his colleagues scorned. Even at this early stage, he stood out for his thoughtful and incisive criticism and his unflagging belief that the popular music of the day possessed deep historical and cultural significance.

World War II interrupted Gleason's jazz advocacy, but after a stint with the Office of War Information he relocated with his wife, Jean, to the West Coast. During the postwar years, the San Francisco jazz scene was decidedly old-fashioned. The most popular bands played traditional jazz of the Dixieland variety, and anything outré or experimental struggled to find an audience. Gleason catered to the local preferences by producing concerts by New Orleans trombonist Kid Ory, but also looked for ways to expose the public to the hipper new sounds they might otherwise miss.

This would be Gleason's modus operandi for the rest of his life. You can call him a music critic, but he might be better described as an evangelist for cutting-edge artistry and social change. He praised the greatest artists, and usually before most of the public even knew who they were. Readers looked to him for guidance whenever anything new or controversial emerged—whether Elvis Presley's rock 'n' roll or John Coltrane's modal music, Bob Dylan's protest songs or Lenny Bruce's edgy comedy routines. Gleason knew all of these individuals, and was one of the very few cultural critics of his day who was equally at home in conversation with Duke Ellington, Joan Baez, Hunter Thompson, or Miles Davis. (After one early encounter with Davis, he learned that they both used the same type of hypodermic needle—although Gleason used his only to treat his diabetes. Davis, for his part, had never scored insulin.)

Gleason's first platform for improving the musical tastes of the West Coast was the *San Francisco Chronicle*, where he started out as a freelancer at $15 per article and got hired full time in 1950. But Gleason soon found a way to shape the global conversation on contemporary music via his widely read articles for *Down Beat*, the leading jazz periodical of the day. And those who missed his write-ups in newspapers and magazines got a dose of Gleason's opinions in the countless liner notes he penned for the leading jazz albums of the day. To serious jazz fans, he was as familiar and as formidable as the famous musicians he interviewed and reviewed.

In 1954, Gleason purchased a small home on Ashby Avenue in Berkeley, which would serve as the epicenter of his activities for the next quarter-century. He even found that he could work on his articles at his home office and deliver them to the *Chronicle* via the trans-bay bus that conveniently stopped near his front door. The great and not-so-great jazz musicians of the day would visit this humble residence as an important stop on their West Coast itineraries.

There's a well-known photograph of Barack Obama standing in the White House looking at a framed image of John Coltrane—that picture of the saxophonist was taken in Gleason's living room. The photographer Jim Marshall recounts a conversation with Coltrane after a 1960 nightclub performance in San Francisco—the musician had one pressing question on his mind: How could he get to Berkeley to meet with Ralph Gleason? Marshall gave him a ride, and got that now-famous portrait photo in return. Many others would follow in Coltrane's footsteps and make the pilgrimage chez Gleason.

Yet Ralph Gleason was an unlikely jazz cat. He never adopted the pose of a hipster, instead dressing like a cross between a TV detective (think Peter Falk in *Columbo*) and a tenured Ivy League academic. Facial hair was on prominent display in the Bay Area during the 1960s and 1970s, but Gleason's handlebar moustache seemed like a carryover from the Taft administration. When he went to jazz clubs, he drank milk—another consequence of his diabetes—but this struck onlookers as just one more sign that Mr. Gleason operated by different rules from the rest of the audience. "He might partake of your world," jazz record producer Orrin Keepnews later recalled, "but he lived in his world."

The interviews included in this volume, almost all of them captured on tape at that Berkeley residence, date back to a decisive juncture in jazz history. Even today, many jazz fans look back to the year 1959 as the most glorious moment in the genre's history. If you asked experts to compile a list of the greatest jazz albums of all time, a surprising number of them would come from this period: Miles Davis's *Kind of Blue* (the best-selling mainstream jazz album of all time), Dave Brubeck's *Time Out* (which included "Take Five," the most popular jazz single of the era), Ornette Coleman's *The Shape of Jazz to Come* (which defined the avant-garde movement of the day), Charles Mingus's *Mingus Ah Um*, John Coltrane's *Giant Steps*, Thelonious Monk's *Thelonious Alone in San Francisco*, Art Pepper's *Art Pepper Plus Eleven*, Ella Fitzgerald's *Ella Fitzgerald Sings the George and Ira Gershwin Songbook*, and many other now classic releases.

How fortunate we are that Ralph Gleason pushed ahead at this key moment on a project to interview the leading jazz musicians of the day. He had no grant to create an archive of jazz oral histories (no one got stipends of that sort back in the 1950s). He had no editor badgering him to write lengthy Q&A articles. Except for the Duke Ellington interview included here, which took place as part of a TV broadcast, these conversations happened simply because of Gleason's personal passion to learn, document, and spread the good word.

He proved to be the right man at the right time. Gleason invited John Coltrane to his Berkeley home for a casual conversation when the saxophonist was in the early stages of launching his career as a bandleader—that very month, he initiated his influential partnership with the Impulse! label—and got the best interview Coltrane ever gave. Gleason talked to Sonny Rollins just weeks before the tenorist took a controversial sabbatical from the jazz world, abandoning night-clubs in favor of playing the horn on the Williamsburg Bridge. This is the most famous moment in Rollins's seven decades of music making, and Gleason was there to probe his thinking right before it happened. He interviewed Philly Joe Jones during the most productive period in the drummer's career. Gleason talked to Bill Evans less than a year after the recording of *Kind of Blue* and when the pianist was working with his most influential trio. Again and again, Gleason's instincts lead him to the musician that everyone else would soon be discussing and debating.

Yes, these are built to last—both the music discussed here and Ralph Gleason's revealing dialogues with a handful of artists who were in the midst of changing the sound of the twentieth century. While other jour-nalists were looking for their next article, he was documenting history, on his own exacting standards, and that comes across on every page of this volume. I'm grateful, but I'm hardly surprised. After all, that's what Mr. Gleason always did, and why we still care so many years later.

TED GIOIA

Editor's Note

FROM 1959 TO 1969, MY father, Ralph J. Gleason, the longtime jazz critic for the *San Francisco Chronicle*, decided to tape-record interviews with musicians he knew who made their way to San Francisco on tour. He intended the talks to provide invaluable background information for his work as a journalist, and tape-recording the conversations would make this background easily available. Conducting interviews is an art. A good interviewer must be, first and foremost, a good listener: patient, interested, knowledgeable, and engaged. Duke Ellington considered listening to be the single most important and meaningful thing he did as a composer. He called my father "a great listener."

All of these interviews—with the exception of the Ellington talk, which was done in the inaugural year of my father's public television show, *Jazz Casual*, on KQED-TV, which aired from 1960 through 1968—were conducted in the living room of our family's Craftsman home in Berkeley, California. Every inch of available wall space was filled with records on shelves, there were piles of records on the floor, and books and magazines on and about music were scattered every- where. Of course, the warmth and music-related clutter of the place put most of the artists at immediate ease (it didn't hurt that most were already friends with my father and also with my mother, Jean; in fact, she was the West Coast campaign manager for Dizzy Gillespie's write-in run for president in 1964). Our home was a relaxed and comfortable environment.

The musicians would settle themselves in an overstuffed leather chair, my father sitting opposite them, and the tape recorder and microphone sat on a coffee table between them. The sounds of outside traffic and other ambient noises can be heard in the background of many of the recordings.

Editor's Note

Some of the material in the interviews would later be used by my father in some of the liner notes he wrote, as well as in some of his articles and other writings. He also played clips from the tape recordings on various subsequent radio appearances. After his death in 1975, the tapes were stored on shelves in the basement of the home in Berkeley. For a long time, they languished and were all but forgotten. Then, in the early 1990s, they were rediscovered by the family, and an effort to have the tapes digitally archived was begun. This publication represents the first time that transcripts of these interviews have been made publically available in their complete form.

Acknowledgments

I WOULD LIKE TO THANK Cyndy McClay for her invaluable help in typing these transcripts, which were mostly in carbon copy form and thus impossible to scan, and getting them into computerized form. Thanks also are due to my sister Bridget and a succession of my father's secretaries for making the original transcripts from the tape recordings in the first place. Thanks also to my wife, Vera Blackwell, and to Paul Yonemura, Susan Muscarella, and other friends for helping to make me believe this project was worthwhile. Thanks, too, to Andy Ross, my agent, and Steve Wasserman, my editor at Yale University Press. And most of all, thanks to my father for having conducted and recorded the interviews and for being a pack rat and saving everything he ever did.

Conversations in Jazz

John Coltrane

MAY 2, 1961

■

S axophonist John Coltrane was at a turning point in his career when he visited Ralph Gleason's Berkeley home in May 1961. Just a year earlier, Coltrane had left trumpeter Miles Davis's group—although not before participating on the classic *Kind of Blue* album—and was now in the early stages of establishing himself as a bandleader. The same month as the Gleason interview, the newly launched Impulse! record label acquired Coltrane's contract from Atlantic Records, initiating a partnership that would produce some of the most treasured jazz albums of the decade, including the best-selling *A Love Supreme, Ascension*, and *Ballads*, and collaboration projects with Duke Ellington and Johnny Hartman.

But even in 1961, before these impressive achievements, many jazz fans already saw Coltrane as the leader of the new thing in jazz, the latest in a lineage of horn heroes dating back to Louis Armstrong in the 1920s. Critic Ira Gitler had recently coined the term "sheets of sound" to describe Coltrane's virtuosic saxophony, and fans now lined up outside the jazz clubs to experience this musical phenom in the flesh. In 1961, Coltrane took top spot in the tenor sax category in *Down Beat's* readers poll and critics poll. He was still evolving as a musician, challenging himself and advancing in his craft. But if the jazz world were a monarchy, this would have been the moment when fans gave him the crown.

Sad to say, Coltrane would live only another six years. In July 1967, he succumbed to liver cancer. He was just forty years old. Although he left behind many outstanding records, Coltrane gave us no memoir, and most of the interviews published in his lifetime were short journalistic efforts. This conversation with Ralph Gleason stands out as one of the most important and revealing documents in the literature on this iconic figure.

■

RJG: *It must have been quite a musical experience to work with Johnny Hodges and with Dizzy and with Miles, something like going to a couple of different colleges.*

JC: Yes, it sure was. I was lucky, I think, to get those kinds of jobs. I really heard music.

RJG: *Did you learn a lot of things from guys like Dizzy and Miles and Monk and Hodges that you can use now?*

JC: Oh yeah, definitely. Like every band I was in something came off.

RJG: *Was Dizzy's big band the only big band you played in?*

JC: Well, I played in King Kolax's big band. This was years ago. He was out of Chicago, he played trumpet with Billy Eckstine back when Dizzy was there and I played in Jimmy Heath's big band around Philadelphia. That's the only three that I've played with, but Dizzy's was the only one that was on the road, making the circuit.

RJG: *Do you ever think about having a big band or working on recording with them or anything?*

JC: Well, I feel the sound better with a big band. Some of these things that I like I think would really sound better with a big band but whether I could get one or not, I don't know. I plan to do a large band date for Impulse and I don't have the experience that I feel I need to do a date like that. I'd really like to do a real good big band thing, and I haven't had any experience. I haven't had any place to try these ideas with the men. You can't do it. If I was playing with somebody's big band I could get all the guys together, come in one day to rehearse and say here, let's try this one. I got no place to try this stuff.

RJG: *That's one of the things that's a drag the way it's set up now.*

JC: Sure, that's the trouble. Now when I was with Kolax or Dizzy, there was opportunity to go further in that kind of thing because you could bring your music in and you could get it played. But I'm going into this thing, I plan to do some head arrangements, that's the only way I think I could do it. I've got this last tune I wrote, we're going to try that, and we're going to probably do "Greensleeves" and maybe "Drinking Gourd" out of the folk book. I've got an idea how I'm going to do . . . I have it sketched, you know, set up, the framework, and I'm going to get a bunch of instrumentalists and bring them all into the studio and I'll get my experience in there if I can. But I'm paying for it.

RJG: *You'll have your own school.*

JC: That's right. We'll learn right there. It might take us two or three weeks, but that's the only way I can do it. I'll have an arranger there and if you have to write anything you can just write it and we can hear the sounds right then.

RJG: *How about Gil Evans?*

JC: Well, I've talked to Gil already. He said if he had the time . . .

RJG: *Was it fun working with him?*

JC: I never worked with Gil.

RJG: *You never worked with him at all?*

JC: No, I never did any of those dates.

RJG: *Were you on that TV show?*

JC: Yeah, that's the only time I ever played any of his music. I played alto because Cannonball was sick at that time. Miles never used a tenor on those so I never got a chance to play that music. Sure sounded good. He's got the sound, you know, he gets a good sound with those instruments. I'm probably going to get something like that instrumentation and as we go we'll just learn how. What I want is for the big band to be integrated with the quartet, you see, and I don't want it to be too pre-arranged. I want it to sound as though we're playing, just the group, and with the same feeling and get that big band in some way.

RJG: *In other words, when you come to places where you'd want to expand it to a big band then you'd be able to do that?*

JC: Yeah.

RJG: *It wouldn't have to be the big band all the time?*

JC: Yeah, that's right, that's the way I want it, something like that. So it might be easy . . . it might not be that much work, at least I don't think it will. That's why I feel that we can do it in head arrangements and I do know, too, that head arrangements used to be some of the best jazz arrangements. So try it, see what happens . . .

RJG: *Was the flamenco music with Miles your first experience with that kind of music?*

JC: I think so.

RJG: *Had you heard flamenco singers?*

JC: No more than on the radio sometime in the past, but I never actually consciously listened to it. At that time I probably heard quite a bit in Miles' playing and didn't know where it was coming from, because he had been listening for a few months. That's beautiful music, man, that's powerful music.

RJG: *And it lasts, it doesn't wear thin. It's like Duke. You can play it over and over.*

JC: Yeah, that's right.

RJG: *I was fascinated by the article that you did in* Downbeat *last year with Don DeMicheal. I read it again last night and I wanted to ask you, have you gotten back further than Sidney Bechet?*

JC: No, I haven't. Since then I haven't had that much time because the band has kept me so busy, busier than I thought I could be. I haven't had much time for listening, not since then. I'm going to find time soon because I've almost got my personnel like I want it. You know I had that difficulty in getting the right men last year, that's almost settled now so I'll have more time.

RJG: *Did you intend to go back and study the whole . . .*

JC: I've got to. Because there's so many things that I think I want to do that possibly have been done already. I know it. I know this because I find it happening. Every once in a while something pops up and I say, oh, man, that's just what I'm looking for and somebody did it. I notice a whole lot more back there so I might as well get it. If I had all those records that you were talking about, I could probably find a hundred things that I could work out something on, apply with the songs that we have today. It's just the thing that I got to do. I've looked into a lot of folk music and stuff like that, and also a few classical things, just to see whether they could adapt to jazz. There can't be no better source than just to go right back in jazz itself and get something.

RJG: *As much as you've already gone back, have you found similarities in the problems and approaches and ideas?*

JC: I haven't delved that much yet in what I've looked into to really compare it, not yet. I haven't gone far, I haven't done enough of this yet. When I got my soprano I went out and bought some of Bechet's things and that was the main reason I did that, to try to find out what he'd done on that instrument and see what kind of sound he was getting on it.

RJG: *Do you find that your own group is a greater responsibility in the sense that you're the only horn or does this really give you more freedom?*

JC: Well, it's the thing I like because I like to play long. I don't feel it too much. The only thing is I feel there might be a need now to have more musical statements going on in the band and I might need another horn. We went into the Apollo and the guy says, "Man, you play too long, you got to play twenty minutes." So now sometimes we play a song and I get up and play a solo maybe 30 minutes, or at least 20 minutes, we can look forward to a song being no less than twenty minutes long. How we going to do this? And, man, we ended up the third time we did it playing three songs in twenty minutes and I played all the highlights of the solos that I had been playing in hours in that length of time. So I think about it, what have I been doing all this time? What the heck have I been doing? It has made me think, if I'm going to take an hour to say something I can say in 10 minutes, maybe I'd better say it in 10 minutes and then have another horn there and get something else. I'm also planning to have some parts in there where we can have these interludes or bring in some other aspect of musical expression, which is what I wanted to find out when I got the group together. I wanted to expand myself musically because I've been soloing for years and that's about all and I feel a need to learn more about production of music and expression and how to do things musically. I feel a need for another horn for

that reason, to kind of offer more. I could really go on just playing just like I am now, I mean I enjoy playing that long, it does
me a lot of good to play until I don't feel like playing anymore.
Though I've found out I don't say that much more.

RJG: *On "My Favorite Things," which runs 14 minutes . . .*

JC: Thirteen minutes.

RJG: *Do you always play that about the same length?*

JC: Just about. Sometimes a little longer. Incidentally, that's one of
the things we played in this thing. I think we played that about
seven minutes long; cut it right in half.

RJG: *When you play this sometimes a couple of times a night and certainly
almost every night, does your solo on that follow a general pattern?*

JC: Just about. This is something I didn't want it to do, but it does it.
It has been following a general pattern. I don't want it to be that
way. The free part in there I wanted it to be just something where
we could improvise on just the minor chord and improvise on
the major chord. But I don't know, it seems like it gets harder
and harder to find something different on it. I've got several land-
marks there that I know I'm going to get to so I try to play something in between there that's different and keep hoping I hear
something different on it. But it usually goes almost the same way
every night, every time.

RJG: *Is that tune then an exception to the ordinary ones you do in the
sense that your solo follows a general pattern or do other tunes do
this too?*

JC: Well, actually, not as much as this tune. I think the 3/4 has something to do with this particular thing. I find that it's much easier

for me to change and be different in a solo on 4/4 tunes. I can play some tunes that I've been playing for five years and might hear something different on it, but it seems like the 3/4s got a kind of straightjacket on us. That meter, that feeling is just a little harder to be free on. And also there's just one chord, too. But that's the challenge, I'll just have to make myself do something else on that, or I'll have to think of more different ways to play. I'll have to think of rhythm and I'll have to think of substitutions and if I can think of more to build from then I'll be able to get in more.

RJG: *Dizzy remarked once that he thought of the rhythm first and then put the notes to it.*

JC: Is that right? That sounds good, sounds like Dizzy. Yeah, that sounds like Dizzy, man.

RJG: *Do you go back and listen to things you've done on record?*

JC: No, not much. The only things I listen to are the latest ones. When the record comes out, I'll listen to it for a while and after that, that's it, I don't listen anymore.

RJG: *Are you ever satisfied with anything you've done?*

JC: No, not a hundred percent.

RJG: *How about on the job when you're playing, do you ever get close to a hundred percent?*

JC: Well, I might. Usually, it's according to how a thing ends. If it ends well, you end feeling jubilant or you feel that relief which feels proper, and so that way it feels alright. If I could hear that back all the way down I'll probably hear something in there that I could have done without. I'll say, well, I could have done without that, or how did that happen. But not hearing it back, if you've managed to end well you get a feeling of release and relief and that's it, it feels good. I don't know whether to say that's just a momentary thing. I couldn't at the moment say, well, I just played something that I'm proud of, or I feel like it was swinging, something like that, it felt together.

RJG: *Do you ever play the other horns now, like alto?*

JC: No, I can't play it. I don't like my sound on that at all. Get a small sound on it.

RJG: *When you're picking a tune that you're going to use does this process take any length of time or do you just fall into a tune and go? Do you have to live with it a while? How does it work?*

JC: Sometimes we have to live with the tune quite a while and then again we just fall into it. "My Favorite Things" . . . fella told me about the tune, say, why don't you try this tune. I told him I wanted some music and so I bought the song sheet and we took it to rehearsal and just like that, fell right into it. We had the shape of it at the rehearsal but it took a little while for it to grow and get expanded and to really recognize the parts and know just how we were going to play it, but it was a very short period of time. Now some other songs, it takes quite a while. Like I had to sit around the house and think about a tune maybe a week or two weeks or a month before I even bothered to bring it in. I had to make sure that I really feel this thing, because I know if I don't feel it it's no need of me telling McCoy and everybody . . .

RJG: *When you're thinking about it, do you ever think in terms of soloing on it?*

JC: Hmmm, yeah, in fact that's the first thing, right now, that's the main thing that I'm thinking of, is soloing on the tune. Most of the songs we play recently, I try to pick a song that sounds good and a song that might be familiar, say, and then I try to have parts in the song where we can play solo. Seems like we are into this thing, we want to solo, on a modal perspective more or less, so therefore we end up playing a lot more vamps within a tune. I don't know how long we're going to be in that, but that's the way it's been for the last eight months. So the song is usually picked primarily as a vehicle to blow on.

RJG: *Do you think about it in the same sense when you're going to use the soprano or the tenor, or is there a different thought approach to it?*

JC: Well, there is a different thing. On soprano so far I haven't used much in 4/4. Most of the tunes I've played soprano on are 6/8 or 3/4. I don't know why, but that's the way it feels to me. It doesn't seem to have the power to really dig in on those 4/4 things, I don't feel that power there, which I do on tenor, see, so that's probably one reason we end up playing those kinds of songs. And then we play "Greensleeves," we do that sort of like "Favorite Things." It's one of my favorite things, did you hear it? We do that. It hasn't jelled completely yet, it's almost there. It's not as powerful as "Favorite Things," it doesn't have as much contrast because we're not going from a major vamp to a minor, it's all minor, but it does have a good mood if it's in the right tempo. I use soprano on that and it kind of gets that same feeling.

RJG: *Do you find tempo very important in mood?*

JC: Very important. I became aware of this thing about my last year with Miles. He was doing it all the time. He found out about it the last year I was there. I began to notice some of the tempos, he always took care to get them in the same place. Tempo is very important. I find that out more and more as I go.

RJG: *How about songs that you write yourself, your own tunes for the group? How do you work out a tune when you're composing?*

JC: Well, I've been going to the piano and working these things out.
       Now I think I'm going to move away from that. At that time I was
       working on these sequences which I ran across on the piano and
       I was trying to give all the instruments the sequences to play and I
       was playing them too and I was advised to try to keep the rhythm
       section as free and as uncluttered as possible and if I wanted to
       play the sequences or run a whole bunch of string chords, do it
       myself but leave them free. I thought about that and I've tried
       that some and I think that's the way we're going to have to do
       it. I won't have to go to the piano anymore, not for them, so I
       think I'm going to try to write for the horn from now on, just play
       around on the horn and see what I can hear.

RJG: *The tunes you're writing yourself, before you play them, before you
       work them out, do you run them through your mind?*

JC: Well, I'll tell you, I have yet to write a song that has a melody. I've
       written very few songs. I've just been going to the piano, getting
       chords and then I'll take a melody somewhere out of the chords.
       I think I've done enough of that and in the future I'm really going
       to try to sit and think of these things, of the song. I've got to take
       it more musically, and maybe some other ways too, and then
       maybe I'll be able to write real melodies, think for melodies and
       write melodies and then I might be able to do some arranging
       for another horn. That's why I haven't had another horn. That's
       something I've been doing since I've had the band, I got away
       from the piano song because I had to think of more than my-
       self. All the time I was with Miles I didn't have nothing to think
       about but myself so I stayed at the piano and chords, chords,
       chords, I ended up playing them on my horn. I've been thinking
       of rhythm since I've had the group and with Elvin Jones in there,
       he's such a rhythm fanatic, just about any kind of rhythm I think
       of he can take it and go even further with it. So it's interesting.
       Now the last tune that we got together, we just played it around
       three times. I have an African record at home, they're singing

these rhythms, some of that native rhythm, so I took part of it and gave it to the bass and Elvin plays the part. McCoy managed to find something to play, some kind of chords, I didn't tell him no chords, I said I'm through with it and so he's on his own and I'm kind of on my own. It's a little different from what I've been doing, still no melody, though. I had to make the melody as I went along, but at least I'm trying to think of a melody, I'm not referring to the chords to get the melody, I had to think of it myself, from just what I felt or heard. I'm trying to force myself to go in that direction, where I'll try to hear the melody of a song.

RJG: *What other plans do you have, things that you want to explore?*

JC: At the moment I really don't know.

RJG: *That doesn't mean that you're satisfied now, does it?*

JC: No, it doesn't mean that, it just means I don't know. I don't know what I'd like to do. I know I don't want to stop. I don't want to stop here. I'll tell you one thing, I have done so much work from within, now what I've got to do is go out and look around me some and then I'll be able to say, well, I want to do some work on this or some work on that. But actually I've been within myself. I got so I'm fooling around at the piano and trying to look at musical structure and trying to find a way that I feel about certain things and trying to work on that, and I've just run into a blind alley on this stuff. Like I get a bunch of changes, I'll change "Body and Soul" or I'll change this song, or . . . well, it's just so far you can go with that. I don't think I want to continue to do that because I don't see any other place . . . I don't think it's going to get me into as many things and as broad a field that I need to get into.

RJG: *Are you still practicing a great deal?*

JC: Not too much, now. The quartet has taken quite a bit of my time and recording, too, because I got to make three records a year. I'm always walking around trying to keep my ear open for another "Favorite Things" or something. I can't go up in the closet, I can't get in the woodshed and just stay in there all day and practice and that was all there was to it, I didn't have to worry about making a good record, because that wasn't important. Maybe I should just go back in the woodshed and just forget it.

RJG: *The whole business of playing jazz and why people play jazz has always fascinated me. What's been the biggest kick to you in playing jazz?*

JC: Well, anytime that feeling is there, anytime that the band that I'm with is really clicking. That's it. No matter if I'm playing or somebody else is playing, those are the moments.

RJG: *What is it that makes it really click?*

JC: When everybody's in good shape and they're really feeling . . . it's when that teamwork is there, that's the only thing I can say.

RJG: *Can this happen just on your own or does it take the whole thing?*

JC: It takes the whole thing, and that's the reward in playing because it's something that everybody up there feels and everybody really gets into it and it usually goes on out to the audience, too. It's a genuine feeling, it's an honest feeling because you know that you three or you four or how many of you are there, you're giving all you have honestly and they appreciate it and if they appreciate it, there it is, that's it.

RJG: *Do you find that true on record dates?*

JC: Well, live, that's the best way. On the record dates you might feel it, but still you're thinking about when the people hear this, they might like it because we did our best and we felt that we made or reached our objective on this.

RJG: *That's why I think records ought to be made in clubs on jobs.*

JC: Some of the best ones have been made there, recently, on the job. I know the things we've done in clubs always sound better to me than what happens in the studio. Maybe not in the sound or reproduction, but as far as the feeling of it.

RJG: *Have there been any particular moments that you can look back on that have been outstanding in those terms for you?*

JC: There have been quite a few. The Jazz Gallery, when the group started there, there were moments something like that. We really got into it pretty well. And with Miles' group it happened quite often. Usually in Chicago, the band really played Chicago. Sometimes it happens and you feel that it really wasn't, that the people were maybe a little overenthusiastic. It has to be just right, the right ingredients. Also, you have to feel that something is happening to you that hasn't happened before. You have to be finding some new ground instead of just playing the things which you know and which you've done over and over. That doesn't happen to me as often as I would like it to.

RJG: *But when it does happen . . .*

JC: That's when it's really rewarding and you feel . . . those are really the moments, the real honesty. It's a little out of your hands because there's more than you. It's something that's just happened once, just now, and the audience, they're receiving this and sort of participating in it.

RJG: *What makes that thing happen?*

JC: That's the spontaneous thing. I don't know what makes it happen, it's just like getting something in orbit after you reach a certain spot at a certain speed, it's go, like a chain reaction. Something like that.

RJG: *Is it an entirely different thing with Miles and with Dizzy?*

JC: Yeah, a lot of differences. It has just one thing that remains constant and I guess that's the tension of it, electricity, that kind of feeling about it, it's sort of a lifting feeling. No matter where it happens you get that feeling. It's a happy feeling.

RJG: *Do you think, then, about what you're doing, in a conscious sense?*

JC: Maybe momentarily, I don't know. The sort of a thing that you're here and you're not here. But it's easy. It gets easy because it's more natural, sort of a natural thing.

RJG: *Doesn't that almost always get through to the audience when it's that way for you?*

JC: If it doesn't, man, pack up!

RJG: *Have you studied harmony formally?*

JC: No. Oh, I started a formal study of harmony, but I didn't get into it as much as I would have liked to. I only stayed in this school about two months and then I got a job with Dizzy and I just couldn't turn that down and I quit school.

RJG: *That was your first trip out here with Dizzy, wasn't it?*

JC: Yes.

RJG: *That little club up on Geary Street, Ciro's.*

JC: That was 1950, yeah, I'd just left school then because I wanted to play with Dizzy. I wouldn't dare turn that job down.

RJG: *Do you feel a sense of responsibility to all of these guys that are digging every note you're recording and playing these days? Do you think about this at all?*

JC: Well, I don't know. There is a standard, you know. Like Horace and Miles and Dizzy, they have a certain standard of musicianship and presentation that is in their music. Sure, I feel a responsibility. I would like to be able to do as well as they do. When they're around I feel I'm not at ease too much because I don't feel I've got my music up to par, yet, and it makes me feel a little uncomfortable.

RJG: *There is another question I want to ask you, too, which is kind of a vague thing, but I've always been curious about it. If someone were to come from a foreign country and say what does this music mean to you that you are devoting your life to, how would you answer them?*

JC: That's a very good question. That's a question which I've asked myself too, and when I can fully answer that question, if I'm ever able to do it, maybe you would be able to get my answer from just listening to the music, because it just started as a thing that I heard around me. Like everybody in this country, you can grow up and you hear this music all the time and it's really a part of you from the time you're just a baby because it's being played all day in some form. It just happened to be a thing I liked at first, then it happened to be a thing that I felt that I had some of it in me to do this, and then it came to the point where I wanted to be very good at it and I wanted to excel and now it's reached the point where I'm asking the questions, what does it mean. In order to really try to get down and present what I honestly feel is really the way I look at the music and really what it means to me, it is my only means of expression. I don't voice opinions much about anything because I'm usually in the middle, I never make up my mind on anything, which is the way I am except in music and sometimes I'll vacillate in that. But I usually have to say something and I will get it together and eventually come out and say something about it. I don't know, someday I'm going to answer this for you.

RJG: *This began as fun?*

JC: Yeah, and it still is, it's sort of a thing where I get the fun. With playing I have a good time, have a ball.

RJG: *But it's more serious now?*

JC: Yeah. Now I'm wondering about the things like you say, responsibility to this and that. Also I've found that sometimes just me having a good time isn't enough for people at all times. There are some other things that have to be considered, too. Maybe I get a kick out of staying up playing the hardest song I can find or doing some things that are to me very clever where this man here don't know nothing about it. It might not touch him, he don't know up here what it is, it might not mean anything at all to him. So I've had to think about those things, too. As to what I want to actually convey, what I really want to say with the music, I haven't got it together yet. It's something that's coming. I know that whatever I begin to think about, that is going to influence the melodies I'm going to write or lack of melody or the rhythm or the lack of rhythm or the harmony or lack of that, because it's going to have to be more than just academic or exercises.

RJG: *When you listen to music, what do you listen to?*

JC: Well most recently I've been listening to folk tunes and been try-ing to find some meaning in that. I feel that basically the music should be dedicated to the goodness in people, the good things in life. Although we have the other things, I don't know whether I'm ready to start playing about the other things because I don't ad-vocate nothing that's not good so I better stay with what's good at the moment. Actually, I guess that is what I should, what I would like to learn to convey, just the good things in life. Folk tunes usually spring from these simple things and good sources and maybe I can work on this, listen to them and learn to combine what's done around the world with what I feel here and what is being done here and use any technical thing that I can learn.

RJG: *Do you ever feel that you're preaching in a way?*

JC: Sometimes it seems like that. There was a time when I went through a personal crisis, and I came out of it, so I was saying that I felt so fortunate to have come through it successfully that all I wanted to do if I could, would be to play music that would make people happy. That's basically all I want to do. But so many other things come in along the way and I often forget that. I let technical things surround me so often that I kind of lose sight . . . I can't keep them both together. Maybe if I think of it more I may be able to find a way, a path to follow.

RJG: *You were speaking before of the way you felt at times when the audience may have felt otherwise. I was curious to know how you felt about your performance that afternoon at Monterey? Did you like that afternoon?*

JC: Well, it was just an average performance. It wasn't much excep-tional as they usually go. The PA system was a dream . . . beautiful.

RJG: *McCoy has really gassed me playing with you.*

JC: McCoy is a beauty, isn't he? I felt like calling him up yesterday. I didn't do it, though. I got a tape at home and I just sat up here and listened to him. There's so many things that he does and I don't tell him to do. I couldn't tell him because when I hear it I say, man, that's just like I would want it, I would have done it myself if I'd have thought of it. And it happens so often until it's just, I don't know, he's just that sensitive, he's very sensitive.

RJG: *He seems to have blossomed with you.*

JC: Yeah, man, he's sensitive. Like "Favorite Things" the whole sound of the song is his sound. The way he's got the voicings. All the songs that we play, the whole sound of the thing is the way his voicings are because he picks his own voicings.

Quincy Jones

MARCH 19, 1959

■

Quincy Jones's fame transcends the jazz world. As producer and musical mastermind behind Michael Jackson's best-known recordings, most notably the 1982 megahit album *Thriller*, Jones racked up sales of more than 100 million units worldwide. He produced and conducted the 1985 single "We Are the World," one of the most star-studded collaborations in music history, which sold 20 million copies and was the fastest-selling pop single of all time. Along the way, Jones has taken home more than two dozen Grammy awards and has worked with everyone from Frank Sinatra to Steven Spielberg, in one of the most celebrated music careers of modern times.

But all of that was in the future back in 1959, when Jones participated in this interview. At this juncture in his career—the Gleason conversation took place five days after his twenty-sixth birthday—Quincy Jones was an up-and-coming jazz composer, arranger, and bandleader. The big band may have already fallen out of favor in the jazz world and among the general public, but Jones was a hot new talent who was convinced that he could take this traditional jazz sound and turn it into a platform for a celebrated music career.

Years later, Jones described this period as a turning point in his own musical development: "We had the best jazz band in the planet, and yet we were literally starving," he recalled. "That's when I discovered that there was *music*, and there was the *music business*. If I were to survive, I would have to learn the difference between the two." In this conversation with Ralph Gleason, Jones shows how deeply he has already grasped both ends of the equation—the music *and* the economics. You might not have been able to predict, back in 1959, all the future successes Quincy Jones would attain, but you could definitely tell he had an abundance of ambition and vision, and they would take him places.

■

RJG: *Why can't they pick up a big band and make it sound like a big band really sounds in person?*

QJ: With that earthiness in it. I don't know.

RJG: *Well, you're going to face this problem.*

QJ: I know it.

RJG: *What are you going to do about it?*

QJ: Well . . . I hope that Bob Fine [engineer] will stretch out a little bit, you know. He's been doing—Bob Fine's been doing pretty nice, though, so far. Of course we been doing more commercial-type things, you know. The jazz things. That's when I miss it the most. On pop things I don't mind them boosting it, you know. But the jazz things, it is a problem. You know, to get that real present feeling. That's like the band's across the room, you know. That's what I like.

RJG: *With Dizzy's band, for instance, the LPs never sound like the band.*

QJ: Oh no! Well, you know what happened in that first LP piece. We cut seventeen sides in an hour and a half. Dizzy's out of his mind. Norman [Granz] didn't show up for the date and so Dizzy says let's try something, fellows, and it was horrible. We set up one balance and just played straight through seventeen tunes. It sounds like it, you know.

RJG: *Sure it does.*

QJ: *Ridiculous!*

RJG: *What plans do you have for your band?*

QJ: Just to keep it working.

RJG: *How big a band is it going to be?*

QJ: Eighteen.

RJG: *That's a big band to work.*

QJ: That's why you have to really build up the thing first.

RJG: *Uh-huh.*

QJ: 'Cause really Basie's going good now but he's not going as big as the band can go. It takes many angles too, Ralph, you know that? I think that's one of the most important parts is stirring up and creating work for it, rather than just following the things that are already set. You have to almost create—like the Lambert singers—they made themselves a gig! There was no place for them to work, but they just made themselves a gig.

RJG: *Yeah.*

QJ: And they gave Basie something new to do, which is very delightful.

RJG: *I'd like to see them tour with him.*

QJ: Yeah. They fit. They just made a gig, that's all. Created one. And created another hole in jazz just for themselves.

RJG: *Do you think there is room for another big band?*

QJ: Definitely. There's room for *a* band now, I think, you know. Because Basie and Duke are institutions. Nobody's going to hurt or help that situation. They're there, man, and it's like granite. And it's—Nobody else is starting anything like this. Nobody else is building anything.

RJG: *Well, I don't mean to be discouraging, and you've obviously thought of this, but all the attempts to get another big band going in the last five years have been unsuccessful.*

QJ: But who's done it?—who's done it?—Not saying that I will do it right, but I don't think that any of the attempts have been right. I don't. I think that the Johnny Richards recording band—that's wonderful, man. But this is the most impractical thing you can do. You know, to try and take a band like this and build it on the basis of what Johnny was trying to build it on, because it's better, if you say you're not going to compromise, you don't work. But to go out and do it is masochism. To go out and just say that this is what I want, and I'm going to take it out and spend all the money. 'Cause I know we—in publishing, we gave Johnny a five grand advance, you know, to help with the band. Man, he went through that just like, boom! And the records didn't sell or anything. We didn't make all our money back. And neither did Johnny. And so why do it?

RJG: *Well, you're thinking of something that's going to be more commercial than a pure jazz band.*

QJ: No. I can't have a pure jazz band, right now. Maybe I could have a pure jazz band if I get some people that like the band first. We get the band, so we're playing half and half. Then maybe later on, when they get the kids now that like these idiotic things, we're not going to play those as idiotic as they want. But maybe they'll come in a little bit too, you know. And when they get older, then they'll be all the way with us and we can just, play. Really stretch out.

RJG: *What sort of things are you going to play?*

QJ: I'm going to try to get the ballad book, and I talked to Nelson [Riddle] and Gil [Evans]. But with just a little simpler things. 'Cause I think that they put a little bit too much emphasis on all these guitars and things. And a lot of things in the charts have proven that's not always right 'cause "Lisbon Antigua" came through and knocked everything out of the way. Things like that.

RJG: *And do you have plans for particular guys?*

QJ: Yeah. I wanted what I call a good musician. The guys that can bend. You know, like Benny Golson and those cats—they play everything. And they're experienced and mature enough to real-ize that we have to play a few things. 'Cause Basie did it the hard way. And boy, he broke his ass on it. 'Cause see, he scuffled for so long and by that time Willard [Alexander]—he owed Willard a fortune, you know. And because he started out playing just what he wanted. Because that's Basie's scope. He's always stood for that. And, see, you can't do it that way. A new band can't get away with that.

RJG: *He can't do it any other way, actually.*

QJ: No, Basie couldn't do it any other way. 'Cause that's the way he is. The first five years he really paid dues. And Willard, Willard got into him. He owed Willard so much money that when he finally got straight he was still so much in debt. And so now just the last year, Roulette has really helped him make some money. And now he's finally getting somewhere. I couldn't last that long. And I wouldn't be able to take it, to have the agency running the band.

RJG: *Who are you going to have in the band?*

QJ: Benny Bailey. I'm bringing him back from Sweden. And, very confidentially, Clark Terry. He's leaving Duke. A lot of cats want to come with the band. That's why I'm making sure that I protect them first and I'm trying to build up the thing of where we've got crazy work. And Willard's getting new rooms now, like the Waldorf, and Chez Paree and the Latin Casino, combined with a singer. With Sass [Sarah Vaughn] or somebody in the Waldorf. I think it's going to be a different type of business.

RJG: *He's going to book the band for you?*

QJ: Yeah.

RJG: *Are you planning on staying out a full year at a clip?*

QJ: No. Europe six months and the States six months. Because we got three months already in Monte Carlo every year.

RJG: *With the band?*

QJ: Yeah. In Europe we can play nothing but jazz. And that way, we can keep our jazz chops up and still play dances every now and then. Because I do want it, Ralph, to be a very—the band to be able to turn off the attitude if we have to play for that type of crowd. 'Cause it's a drag to go in a place where you know what you're fighting in the first place and have them put you down completely. I'd rather have them hear what they want to hear at first and then we say, OK now. You danced. Let's have a little hour's concert. And then, that way they'll go with you. But if you fight 'em, they'll put you down, and you'll never get back.

RJG: *Then it'll be six months in this country and six months in Europe?*

QJ: Yeah.

RJG: *Three months in the Riviera and three months of concerts.*

QJ: The folk parks—I talked to the director of the folk parks in Sweden. We got forty folk parks. The contract for the whole folk park circuit, and television things in Germany and Baden-Baden. And I'm sure that we could do film soundtracks because I was supposed to do some things over there with [André] Hodeir. You have to create a lot of things for them.

RJG: *So you have actually gone about doing this the other way around: you got the work first.*

QJ: Right. And I'm trying to create situations for the band and exploit —I hate to use that word—but exploit as many facets that a band can cover. It's a very important thing to keep all things going in a diversified thing, so the guys don't sit around and get bored. This is the one thing that Basie has trouble with. The guys get pretty bored. I want them to be—One night they're playing one certain kind of thing in a completely square crowd or something and—or show. Or we've had talk about a late television show in New York, with thirteen weeks. That would be nice.

RJG: *Sure.*

QJ: So if you get the European scene where you got the dances and jazz concerts, and so forth, that way I think you can really build a band.

RJG: *You can play here at clubs but can you do many one-nighters?*

QJ: The colleges. That's all I want is the clubs, the colleges, and maybe a few other things—a few television things. That'll be a good six months.

RJG: *That's wild. I sure hope it works.*

QJ: If you get, say, the three jazz clubs. I talked to [Frank] Holzfeind [owner of Blue Note, Chicago], Gene Norman [owner of The Crescendo, Los Angeles], and the fellas. Morris Levy, who's real drug because he wanted to record the band. He wants to own you.

RJG: *Of course.*

QJ: But Basie's on my side and so Basie's telling me. . . . And those three clubs [Birdland, Blue Note, The Crescendo], places like the Chez Paree, Latin Casino, Philly, and the Waldorf. And there'll be a few more of those things. The Flamingo wants to put Basie in a half-year and [Harry] James in a half-year. Twenty-six weeks, man.

RJG: Twenty-six *weeks?*

QJ: Yeah. Those things are growing. 'Cause the band is exciting. The bands, they love them now.

RJG: *Yeah.*

QJ: The guy at the Flamingo. And this is good, you know.

RJG: *Jeez, that's beautiful.* Twenty-six *weeks?*

QJ: Yeah. If Basie wants it. Twenty-six weeks a year. That's a little bit too much for a band but it's nice to know that it's there. And so Basie doesn't take twenty-six, he takes thirteen or something. I'll take the other thirteen. I think it can work out. I've thought about it for five years, Ralph. And I've never had the urge because I know that it's an uphill fight. I've watched guys like Maynard [Ferguson]. And I've seen guys make a lot of mistakes.

'Cause [Lionel] Hampton really gave me a lot to work with. This cat was something else. Regardless of how he plays. We saw every city in the country with Hamp. And you get to see how he approaches people. What he does psychologically can be done musically, too. And Hamp used to get away with playing what he called way-out things. He would just mess them up, that's all. The pacing is important. Basie plays a lot of things that are really just pop things, but the pacing is so nice that you just don't care. And I think it's a drag to be so narrow-minded that you just have to be— Because I'm not the kind of guy—I'm no Bach, nor Beethoven. I'm not an innovator. Maybe I'm just not born to be one. And I like to search the new things but I'm not going to blueprint 'em.

RJG: *Are you going to use any European musicians in the band?*

QJ: I'm going to try. 'Cause I was going to start it in Europe at first. 'Cause there are some crazy cats over there.

RJG: *Who's going to write for it other than you?*

QJ: Ernie Wilkins. Melba [Liston]'s going to be with the band too.

RJG: *Oh yeah? Great.*

QJ: And jump things, I don't know. 'Cause I have had to think about that. 'Cause Gil—I think his best groove is ballads, mood things, real atmospheric things. But swingin' things, I don't know. It's kind of rough.

RJG: *Do you know Cedric?*

QJ: Yeah. he's somethin' else. I'd like to try some of his stuff.

RJG: *'Cause he's done some good things. Really good things.*

QJ: He always did write good.

RJG: *He wrote some good things for a big rehearsal band [Earl] Hines had, and for Eddie Walker's band.*

QJ: They don't record him?

RJG: *I don't think so.*

QJ: I'd like to hear some of Cedric's things because I've been looking for guys. Different types of things. And then another guy, this guy's with Hamp right now, Eddie Mullins. He's fantastic. Well schooled. He's well trained and he knows everything. And man he's such a good arranger. Nobody knows anything about him. 'Cause he's such a pessimistic guy.

RJG: *"It isn't going to work."*

QJ: Yeah. He's the kind of guy that used to get off the bus (There's no women here, is there?)

RJG: *No.*

QJ: He used to get off the bus. One time in Atlantic City. He's always cryin' like everybody's after him. And a pigeon shit on his hat. He says, "That pigeon knew I was goin' to get off the bus!" Everything is like that. Everybody's after him. Wow! But he's a helluva arranger. He's got a fresh sound. It would be very great for the dance end of the band.

RJG: *When you go to Europe will you use any European guys to write for you, or anything?*

QJ: Well, there's not too many guys over there that really write that good. Really, they copy a lot. And I know mostly all of them. They really don't have too much to say. They've got good control and they're all technicians, fantastic technicians. But they don't really have a conception. They don't have enough authority to *lead* with a conception. They follow and really pussyfoot.

RJG: *This is true of their soloists, too, isn't it?*

QJ: In most cases, yes. Sweden is the only one that's trying to break out of that.

RJG: *What about that piano player in France?*

QJ: Who? Martial Solal? He's good. He's good. He's very daring. But I still feel a certain amount of taste is lacking. It feels a little too much honey.

RJG: *Is it maybe like learning a language, Quincy, where they haven't quite gotten used to thinking in it?*

QJ: Yeah. That's why the Swedes play better because they think like Americans almost. They live like Americans. And they use the same swear words, like the guys. They've really got American attitude towards life and they have less problems anyway, so they're uninhibited and they're sincere. It makes it easier for them to play. They don't try to act hip. They aren't self-conscious.

RJG: *Did you get to England at all?*

QJ: Yeah. A lot.

RJG: *Did you get to know those guys very much?*

QJ: Yeah.

RJG: *You know Woody's going to use a British band . . .*

QJ: He could get a crazy one, too, man. There's a lot of good musicians there.

RJG: *A baritone player and some other guys and a sextet from New York. He's going to take over a sextet from here and augment to a 17-piece band.*

QJ: I heard about that. It'll be very successful, too.

RJG: *I hope it is.*

QJ: 'Cause they read good. And if he takes his own rhythm section, he's in business, because, boy, those cats are really great.

RJG: *He's taking a lead trumpet player and Nat Adderley.*

QJ: I don't think Nat's going.

RJG: *Nat's not going?*

QJ: No.

RJG: *Well, that was three days ago he was going.*

QJ: Well, he had called Joe Castro two weeks before and asked the guy will he take a trumpet player because I would like to play with your band, your group. Leroy Vinnegar and that. I don't know. Who knows? He might be—

RJG: *The rhythm section was set and Vince Guaraldi was going to be piano. And Bill Harris was going. Then they were going to augment all the sections and get a whole saxophone section.*

QJ: He could get a helluva band over there. He really could

RJG: *That's why I was curious to know if you would, when you went to Europe, if you would use European musicians.*

QJ: Well, I hope that I get my band in its—It'll be almost like a military unit. You know, I mean, the army. It's together. Because that's the only way you can make it, is the same guys. And that's why I want every guy in the band to be happy. I want to get dates for them and bring them out more—guys like Clark, man, that have just been laying around for years unused, it's terrible. Benny Bailey, too.

RJG: *I remember him with Hamp.*

QJ: Yeah. Good lead man in a ballad. They're just misused. And if a guy's going to be a leader, that's one thing. Some guys just have the feeling of being in the band, like Marshall [Royal]. He'll always be loved, he'll never be a leader. But he's a good disciplinarian for a band. And that's why he's right at home with Basie, 'cause he loves that job.

RJG: *The Europeans' reception to jazz—did you find it vitally different than you do here?*

QJ: They think they know what they're listening for.

RJG: *In what way?*

QJ: Like we said yesterday, the cats, they are used to listening to good music anyway, whether it's jazz or classics. They've been indoctrinated from birth, to listen to good music. Where in the States it's something else.

RJG: *You think maybe after some time here, Quincy, if we have more classical programs on the air, a rise of FM, an increase of radio* *broadcasts of symphonies and things, that this will aid in appreciation of jazz too?*

QJ: Well, I don't know. This sounds strange, Ralph, but there's something funny about the American's outlook on life in the first place, and I think that that's the biggest problem. It's a certain amount of humility Europeans have. Maybe it comes from having so much culture and so much background that there's something in their character that's mellow. I don't know how to explain this. And it gives them a tremendous amount of sincerity and humility. Which I think is very essential for full appreciation of an art. In the States it's something else. It's so much rebellion, in so many ways, and frustration. And when you come back, you can see it. It's so unsettled, and there's the false sense of values in so many things. It's really true, though, and when you've been overseas a lot you can really see this. It's very obvious when you get back home.

RJG: *Then that raises an interesting cultural problem, which is: how come that a country that has these debits, so to speak, can produce this music, and that areas which have the credits for the reception of it, are not able to produce it?*

QJ: Well, they say conflict always produces this type of thing. It's always been conflict behind it.

RJG: *But historically, in music, your society produces music for itself.*

QJ: Reflects, you mean?

RJG: *Yeah. Reflects itself.*

QJ: Yeah, I think you're right. That's the funny part about it, and I don't know whether the Europeans see their own problems through jazz or what. And I can't understand why it isn't greatly the most, the most reception here. That's what I can't understand.

RJG: *Well, Duke wrote an article for my quarterly in which he discussed part of this question and said that jazz represented freedom to Europeans. Is this part of the reason why—*

QJ: It is. I think the very uninhibited nature of it—

RJG: *Do they look to this country still as a place they want to go?*

QJ: No. Not too many. No, not anymore. That's been a fallacy because I would say right now that the States right now is in very bad—Here's what it is—I think in some cases it's almost a question of 'em looking at jazz as the *underdog* in the United States. And they like this, too, they like *this* scene. And they don't really consider jazz—They won't accept jazz because it's so ostracized here. Because it really is, you know. And I think that might have a tremendous thing, too, to do with it. It's like a rich family, that might have a deformed child, and the poor people—It strengthens their fight and their attitude against these poor people if the poor people sort of look down upon this child as a black sheep of our family. It's for them to accept it.

RJG: *Do you see much hope here, for instance, coming back—How long were you in Europe? A year, wasn't it?*

QJ: Nineteen months.

RJG: *Nineteen months. Do you see any better situation here at all for jazz?*

QJ: I tell you what I don't see—In some areas I see some sincerity but I still think that the people are so far away from what really jazz is all about. And I don't know why in some cases where it's accepted, like Brubeck, for instance. I would go so far as to say that half of the Brubeck fans were accepting him because it was a vogue and not because they really understood or felt what he was doing.

RJG: *Sure. That's been true all along.*

QJ: And it becomes a fight, you know. So that the real pure love of jazz is not present in too many cases.

RJG: *Now, do you know, for instance, how many albums that Dinah Shore sells?*

QJ: How many?

RJG: *Well, less than 10,000 of the best ones she's had in the last 10 years.*

QJ: No kidding.

RJG: *Yeah. So I would be willing to wager that one of your two ABC-Paramount albums came either pretty close to that or went past it.*

QJ: Yeah.

RJG: *And this is also true of Rosemary Clooney.*

QJ: She sells like that?

RJG: *Miles Davis outsells Rosemary Clooney on albums. I don't say this means that Miles Davis is going to star in the next Paramount picture or be in a 13-week television thing, but as far as acceptance of albums is concerned it's true.*

QJ: Well, I'll tell you this now. This might not have anything to do with the music 'cause I'm sure Presley sells—outsells the whole jazz market combined.

RJG: *He outsells anybody, certainly. He sells 75—100,000, maybe, of an album.*

QJ: And so does Ricky Nelson and many more people like that.

RJG: *But then, so does Frank Sinatra.*

QJ: This is very encouraging. But there's a few rare instances. But they're worldwide favorites. Those talents like this, you really can't compare with anybody. Nat Cole and Sinatra and Ella. It's international acceptance.

RJG: *The three best-selling jazz artists at the moment, for instance — here as well as anywhere else — would be Erroll Garner, Dave Brubeck, and Ahmad Jamal.*

QJ: Jonah [Jones]?

RJG: *Yeah. I forgot about him. I actually don't think about him as a jazz artist most of the time, but anyway we would have to make it five. Erroll, Jonah Jones, Ahmad Jamal, Brubeck, and the Modern Jazz Quartet. To the market — now, if you make an album in France, a good jazz album and an album that would be considered a good-selling jazz album in France, how many copies does it figure to sell?*

QJ: Well, if it was made in France, it wouldn't sell too many. It really wouldn't, because they're very much like that. They figure, why buy European jazz.

RJG: *Well, I don't mean an album by French jazz musicians.*

QJ: You mean, just a jazz album there.

RJG: *Yeah. Quincy Jones' swingin' band is sensational and goes to Europe for six months and records an album in France and is issued on a French label. How many does it figure to sell?*

QJ: Well, I would say maybe 8,000, or something like that. Some-where in that vicinity—'cause those areas, you know, albums cost so much in the first place—about eight or nine dollars. And they sell most of their things on EPs. EPs are the biggest sales. Now, the Harry Arnold band thing that we did in Sweden—of course it got the gold record. In Sweden it sold 10,000 LPs and 50,000 EPs. Which is fantastic for Sweden. But it shows you—Sweden is a hipper country too. Where France, you could have 50 records in a store and 50 Frenchmen would go in and they would all buy a different record. 'Cause they're much more of an individual. Like in Germany, when one group buys it, everybody buys it. Because it's that type of thinking. Where the French are very—there's too much individualism there. France is rough!

RJG: *In other words then, your major jazz market still remains here?*

QJ: I think so. There's more people here than in any other country. I would say that, on a consistent level, that Sweden sells more jazz than pop, than here.

RJG: *Proportionate.*

QJ: Yeah.

RJG: *It may be that what you just said, the fact that there are more people here, is a clue to the other anomalies of the situation, such as Elvis and the rest of it. Because when he sells a million copies of a piece of junk, in the same six-week period or eight-week period Sinatra sells a million copies of a good song. They don't share any buyers—or very few.*

QJ: No, not at all. They're a split market.

RJG: *You actually have a dichotomy in the market.*

QJ: It's a very split market.

RJG: *Which means that you can appeal to a market that's potentially capable of purchasing a million copies of your album without expecting any of the purchasers of Fats Domino records to be hooked over to your side.*

QJ: Absolutely. Because of the completely different crowds. And where Sinatra is strong in albums, he doesn't sell the singles.

RJG: *Sure he does.*

QJ: No, he doesn't.

RJG: *Sinatra's never had a million-seller.*

QJ: Never. He doesn't sell any singles at all.

RJG: *Well how come his singles get on the Billboard chart?*

QJ: They do. But they bounce around 20 and 30, like "Witchcraft" and those things. They never did get into the top 20.

RJG: *But the albums do.*

QJ: Yeah, 'cause the albums are the older people's market and the singles are the kids.

RJG: *Did you ever try to appeal to those kids with your band?*

QJ: I think you can. Not the way that they've been—the things that have been appealing to them. I doubt that I could do that, because I don't think that I would follow it up. We could go into a studio and make those types of records, but I don't think I could really follow that up.

RJG: *You'd flip, wouldn't you?*

QJ: I'd go out of my mind. But here's what I think. I think that there's going to be a little change here. I don't know how it's going to come about. Now Hank Mancini told me he's really analyzing this hit situation, and I think it's very smart that guys with his capabilities do it. And so it's one thing to listen to the charts, and say this is horrible junk, we don't listen to it. But that's not always too smart. We're still in the record business and we're still concerned with the future of this. Now he's analyzing it. He's saying, what is it that appeals, basically? It's not lyrics or out-of-tune vocalists, and so forth. There's a certain element, the X element behind this, that is making these things sell. And he brought "Peter Gunn" to Ray Anthony. He asked Ray Anthony to record it with him. He says, *"This is a hit."* I mean, and not saying that he has any psychic powers or anything, but he's analyzed it very carefully. He says he's listened to the Top 40 all day, as unbearable as it might be sometimes. And he's trying to find the *elements* in there that they are going for. Now, "Peter Gunn" is—It's not a kind of a thing that I would just make for the pop charts. It's a step forward, I think.

RJG: *What does he figure is the thing that's behind the whole thing— beat?*

QJ: Authority in most cases. Extreme authority. And, not too complex.

RJG: *Oh, never complex.*

QJ: Yeah. But authority is one of the main factors, I think. And that's why they like all these clowns.

RJG: *Yeah.*

QJ: Like [Perry] Como is suave; he's very suave. And they don't understand taste yet. They don't understand what taste means, 'cause he's saying big words that they don't understand, and emotions that teenagers have never felt before. Like Sinatra, too. And it's things that you feel when you're older. Where they're rough and wild anyway. And I think that they like things that come from some kind of meeting ground to them. And they see these little teenagers with sideburns, and they act just like them. Act the same way. Now they're going to grow out of this.

RJG: *To change the subject back to Europe again—do you think that Europe is going to produce jazz musicians that will be good enough to compete over here?*

QJ: I definitely do. Because, see, here is the thing. In Europe they don't have to worry about this economical thing, 'cause they're starving anyway. The musicians pay dues anyway. So they figure, if we're going to pay dues, we'll pay the dues and just stick with jazz. So that's a good attitude, too—if you can afford to do that. Like in Sweden, why the guys can work because there's a hundred jazz bands there. In Stockholm alone. You know what I mean, bands—There's 1,200 bands in Sweden—

RJG: *My God!*

QJ: And man, they're all over the place. In every tiny burg you'll hear a little band play. And that's wonderful. And everybody takes it for granted. Every Swede, they know what's happening with the jazz artists. And they have broadcasts once a week with Harry Arnold's band. They let the kids out of school, and they get 5,000 of them in a big auditorium and they just go crazy.

RJG: *Is that essentially a jazz band, Harry Arnold's band?*

QJ: He plays everything. He's the staff man at the radio. And it's a pretty nice staff band. And the kids, Harry Arnold to them, that's their man; that's their Mitch Miller. And it's wonderful. And Harry doesn't sweat and try and figure out hits and everything. He just plays what he likes. They're very spoiled, I'd say. The guys don't worry about society bands or anything. The society bands are playing "Cutie Pie" and Ernie Wilkins' things. In the hotels. It's wonderful.

RJG: *Who in Sweden could give me a whole report on this situation?*

QJ: Carl-Eric Lindgren. You know him?

RJG: *Where is he?*

QJ: He's in Stockholm. He writes for *Estrad*. He's the editor of *Estrad*.

RJG: *He's editor of* Estrad. *I know that paper.*

QJ: He's a wild guy. He loves everybody. He loves Ray Charles. Beautiful imagination.

RJG: *Do they get the Voice of America there?*

QJ: Willis [Conover] could be president in each country.

RJG: *No kidding?*

QJ: They used to leave the concerts in Yugoslavia to go hear Willis when we were with Dizzy.

RJG: *No kidding?*

QJ: Willis is president, really. I started a fan club for him over there.

RJG: *What does he play on these shows?*

QJ: He gives education. He's beautiful, too. Like he tells the people where Stan Kenton stole "Intermission Riff" from. Or Ray Wetzel stole it—whoever stole it. And things like that. He just plays. He plays an evening of all Evans arrangements, and shows the developments. Oh, it's so enjoyable. No commercials. It's wonderful. And it's really an intelligent show. Well paced. Even his pop shows are wonderful. And, believe me, Ralph, when you're away from your own country you learn a lot more about it than you know about it when you're here.

RJG: *Of course you do.*

QJ: And your perspective—'Cause I would never attempt this if it hadn't been for living in Paris 19 months. And the perspective— Gee whiz! Everything seems to sift out, about what's important, all the politics involved in the music business.

RJG: *Well, can you beat that political scene here?*

QJ: I think so. You just have to get some politicians working with you, that's all. You can't fight them. You just have to get some nice politicians. And there are a lot around. Like Willard has been in the band business a long time and he's the biggest fan so far. He acts like a kid.

RJG: *You know what I think about him, above all other guys in the management and booking end of the business? He likes music.*

QJ: He does! He's like a kid.

RJG: *Stones me.*

QJ: The last date we did was on a Tuesday. So Willard had come into his office that morning, and Jack Tracy sent him copies of "Tuxedo Junction," and he was afraid that I was going to write some really way-out things for the pops dates and he would be helpless. He couldn't do a thing for me then, and I knew this. And so he came in that morning and listened and played them to the secretaries, and so forth. The other secretary was telling me this. And so he says, "Get Quincy Jones on the phone." And he calls my house, and my wife answered and said, "Well, he's at a recording date." And he says, "What? Nobody told me about this." And she said, "I saw the hat and coat hittin' the door." And 20 minutes later he calls up and he's in the booth, and he calls back to the office, and he says, "Get Irv, Dick, and Oscar over here immediately!" He says, "They're working." He says, "I don't care. Get 'em over here 'cause I want 'em to hear what they're selling." And believe me, he's our biggest fan. And that's wonderful.

RJG: *That's great.*

QJ: He's happy and he calls up all the club owners and raves. And that's wonderful. And the same thing's happening with Terry Gibbs in California now. All his guys, his politicians, they're behind him and they're raving about the band and bringing the guy from the Flamingo Inn, and the movie stars. This is healthy, 'cause Willard is not making a penny off the band yet, and when he does I'm sure he'll still like it if we got a good thing going—I think he will—he'll still have this enthusiasm and it makes it very enjoyable. It really does.

RJG: *And you're signed with Mercury?*

QJ: Yeah. I'm very happy.

RJG: *How many albums? Are they going to put out a regular series or just an occasional one?*

QJ: We're going to try to keep a very balanced thing, with the commercial LPs and the jazz LPs. 'Cause this sounds like I'm going to be a schizo, but I think I can make it. I really do. Because I love music, man, and I'm not going to say that I have to play

"Cherokee" all night. I love music. And it covers a lot of scope. I would love to have a band that could just play everything. But I dig playing all kinds of stuff.

RJG: *When did you get back from France?*

QJ: November 23rd. I went to Stockholm and did another concert with Harry Arnold before I came back.

RJG: *That's a good album.*

QJ: Beautiful band.

RJG: *I like the one they do with Ernestine [Anderson], too.*

QJ: Yeah. They're so happy and straight ahead. They're so unpretentious it's amazing.

RJG: *Well Sweden's the hope then, to you?*

QJ: Oh, it's wonderful. And they get their rock and roll things, too. Like they get pretty upset with Tommy Steele, the young girls, 'cause—Little young kids swingin' a guitar around. And that's always been the case. And Willard had the Waldorf for us, but I want to get out in the sticks for three months. Nobody can hear us and we can get our chops together. Because it takes time to build this thing.

RJG: *You're not going to debut in Newport?*

QJ: No. I think it would be the most foolish thing we could do. Because there's too much pressure and publicity there, Ralph. And you're playing bands that have been together too long.

RJG: *Why don't you debut at Monterey?*

QJ: That's October?

RJG: *That's right.*

QJ: That sounds good.

RJG: *That's three months later.*

QJ: That sounds good. Now that might be a more feasible thing. 'Cause you can get hung like that, with the guys—There's too much pressure on the band and I don't want them to be under any pressure. I want them to always play—Like Terry Gibbs started, which is great. Nothing was expected of him at first. So they got all the guys together on every Tuesday night and they rehearsed, man, and the spirit start going and the guys start having section rehearsals and for six weeks they did Tuesdays and then they finally—the guys said, "Well, what the hell!" The kids were just going crazy—every Tuesday night, just raving over the band, and cheering and everything. So they opened it up full scale now. I hope it lasts. And now the guys, there's no pressure and they have just accidentally grown into something. It's like making a kid practice eight hours a day on piano when she's four years old. She hates the piano after a while.

RJG: *Sure. Was France fun?*

QJ: Yeah.

RJG: *Is it better for jazz than Sweden?*

QJ: Oh, no. Not at all. France is good because the people there love to ball, they love to party, and they drink their good wine and eat their good food and—They swing. The place is constantly balling. Nobody stays at home. You're never invited to French homes much. Some Americans have been there 12 years and never been invited to a French home. 'Cause they all believe in going out. "Let's go out." Nobody's at home on Saturday nights. Everybody's out dancing, and listening to records or movies or something. That's nice. Everybody's out. And the clubs—Every club is packed, every club.

RJG: *How do the jazz groups really do when they go there? You get so many conflicting reports of what actually happens in Paris.*

QJ: I know. Well, when they give concerts they get in trouble sometimes. There's a split sense of values now, about the guys. Some guys can come over and be starving to death in New York, and go to Europe and get straight. And things happen for him. Like Donald Byrd and the guys. Donald works good in New York, but not like he did in Europe. In Europe he did very good. They gave him a chance to get his chops together, and confidence together. And he did movies and they had a lot of articles on him and they made all kinds of things. And it was—So they just stayed over after the festival at Cannes and got tremendous exposure. And more fans.

RJG: *Do they still go for traditional jazz there?*

QJ: Not so much. Really. I mean, there's a few moldy figs around, but the guys that play good, yes. They respect them. But it's not too big there.

RJG: *Then [Hugues] Panassié doesn't enjoy the status that he used to?*

QJ: No, not at all. He has his glory when Duke comes to town, and they talk about 1920 or something, and Pops. But he's running out of clients.

RJG: *Yeah. I bet he is.*

QJ: Because some of the other guys are getting modernized. Like Basie, he doesn't feel too much at home with Basie anymore. 'Cause Basie is smoking, and he can't talk about the old days. 'Cause Frank Foster doesn't know what he's talking about. I saw Mezz [Mezzrow] a lot over there, too, you know.

RJG: *Oh yeah? What does he do over there?*

QJ: Everything. Writes books. He's a nice guy.

RJG: *Does he play over there?*

QJ: Sometimes, he gets a few gigs going. He goes to Morocco. See, some of those places are so hungry for things like Kenny Clarke one night he'll call up and say, "Do you want to go to Morocco on the weekend?" And they'll give him a grand for two nights, and fly him down, and it's good. They make money on him, too, which is very good. Boy, jazz is taking off. It's really being felt. It's taking its grip. It kills me how the French are experimenting with movies. Which is very good. They're really jumping all the way out on that. And in Germany. In many ways they're growing more than we are. Like in Germany they did a whole ballet on Fontessa.

RJG: *Yeah, I know about that.*

QJ: That's beautiful. John Lewis is a great guy. John Lewis is a very quiet guy and he's helping jazz a lot, believe me.

RJG: *That radio station that Berendt—*

QJ: Joachim Berendt, yeah. He's a wild cat.

RJG: *I've had lots of letters from him.*

QJ: He's a nice guy, too. He really knows what's happening.

RJG: *He may come over this year, he says, on another trip.*

QJ: Good. They've been doing some very good things down there for jazz. And they keep the scene moving because it's State funds. They're very fortunate, that they get guys in the State to think that way. That's more than we can say. 'Cause when we went to Pakistan they told USIS [United States Information Service] that Dizzy Gillespie was coming. You know the hot clubs from Calcutta were hiring planes. They chartered a plane to come up and see the band and everything. And they said, "Isn't it thrilling that Dizzy Gillespie coming?" And they said, "Yeah." One of the guys at USIS, he say, "Yeah, that's one of our best baseball players." Really. That happens all the time. They don't have no idea—They think that jazz—the epitome of jazz—is the "St. Louis Blues." That's all they can call. And if you can play all those other things, boy, they really don't know what's going on. But they were very funny because most of the Americans in these places had never—This was the first time that this had ever happened. And most of the Americans in these places, they clocked the audiences—and they sat there with a neutral look, and before they would be pro or con—and see where the audience was going, and when it got good, they'd rear back and start clapping, like "my boy." And in Greece, well we had a little trouble. We didn't have trouble but USIS was in trouble when we got there.

RJG: *Yeah I know.*

QJ: They stoned them. By the Cyprus situation.

RJG: *Well, isn't this all getting a lot better because of what Dizzy and you guys did down through that area and what, for instance, Woody just did in South America after Dizzy? It was twice it hap-*

*pened down there. And Teagarden and Louis and Benny all went
to India, and Brubeck.*

QJ: This is great. Really is. But, see, here's the thing now where they
get hung up sometimes. This has nothing to do with Benny's stature or anything else. But, frankly—Do you want me to be frank?

RJG: *Of course.*

QJ: Frankly, Benny's tour didn't raise that much sand, believe me.
There's a lot of Benny Goodman fans around but this didn't really do it. There were a lot of bad reports about it.

RJG: *The band stunk.*

QJ: That's what I mean.

RJG: *The album was lousy.*

QJ: Well the band was bad. And the people knew that they did not
enjoy playing together. So this proves nothing. Didn't prove a
thing. Brussels, it was a flop. It really was. And so this is not the
kind of thing they could send to Europe—See, here's where the
Americans are brainwashed. In D.C. they could send a completely unknown band over there, and if the guys played good
they could do more than Benny did. Believe me. 'Cause we
played with the Harry Arnold band, with a local band in Stockholm a week before Benny did. And I was scared to go up there
'cause I said, "No. I don't have any name for the crowds. We
sell records, sure, but I can't do anything at a concert." And
we had 4,000 people. We did two concerts and had 4,000 people
at each concert. With just Harry Arnold's band and I. I only did
five numbers. And Benny had 2,800 people. A week later, with
Jimmy Rushing!

RJG: *See here's what happens, Quincy. I wrote a column raising hell about the State Department and George Wein being involved in that Brussels situation with the pick-up band with George on piano, and also sending over the International Youth Band to appear at Brussels, which I thought and still think is utterly ridiculous. I mean, pick a rehearsal band from any major city, for Christ's sake, and send it over instead of the International Youth Band. And yet, they come back at you immediately and say that it was a success. Well, you weren't there and you can't prove it.*

QJ: I was there.

RJG: *Yeah . . . This is the answer that George Wein wrote a long letter in Nat [Hentoff]'s magazine [Jazz Review] about how I was out of my nut for saying this. Because they want to cover that up.*

QJ: We have the biggest problems with the Americans, really. The Americans in charge have been the biggest problems in most of these because, Ralph, believe me, when I go to a country I don't sit there—The places like in Beirut and these places—the government personnel, they know the least about the country than anybody involved. We go to a country—and like Ambassador Heath, he told us in Beirut—he was honest—He says we found out more about these people in the time you've been here than we have since the whole . . . our job is 100 percent easier now. Like the guy in Athens, a cultural attaché, he hangs out with Mrs. So-And-So who's a patron of the arts or something. And they hang out with the snobs in each country. They don't feel the pulse of the country. And we get out immediately and we are with the guys, the people that make the country tick. The heartbeat of the country, really. The students and the people that pay dues. This is what makes a country tick—not the people that sit around in the best homes and everything. You don't learn a thing about that. And when I go to Morocco and Casablanca I want to go to the Casbah and feel the breath of the country. And they don't do that.

RJG: *Do you want to take your band on a tour like that?*

QJ: Oh, definitely. I'd just love to stay on it. Because I love the feeling of them learning and us learning, too. It's a wonderful feeling, you know. And it's a challenge and it's beautiful. I'd like to go to Russia very much, you know. And we've got a bid in with ANTA [American National Theater and Academy] to try to take the band over, but they say, "You need a name." So I'm going just have to get a name. You can't move, you know. It's so many obstacles. And I know how the Europeans think. We sit around and have conversations like this 'cause we don't have television to keep us occupied. You have to talk to people and get to know each other. And you talk to many different facets, types of people. The writers, novel writers, very intelligent people. They've watched their countries, and they have very strong national spirit and you learn a lot from them. The bookers—They don't talk to these people. They talk to another promoter that's thinking of, "Let's make some money." And there's a human element in everything, I think, that solves the problem.

RJG: *And you'd like to do it?*

QJ: I sure would. Tokyo, all of them. Even in the places if we don't make—I'm hoping that—I'm this kind of a thinker that if we make it up and that we make more than we should in some places, I don't mind not making enough in another place. I would like to play a place for nothing if we make a lot in one place. It's very idealistic, but you can't make it if you don't.

RJG: *Are you still going to do commercial dates for that French company?*

QJ: No. If I get the band going, I'd just like to think about that and working with the artists that I like then. Write for Basie.

RJG: *Where is Ernestine [Anderson] at this point?*

QJ: New York.

RJG: *I haven't heard a word from her since—*

QJ: Well, she sends her regards to you. She's always talking about you.

RJG: *I talked to her about sometime in January. One hysterical night.*

QJ: Yeah. Well, Ernestine, she won't write, but believe me, she's with you.

RJG: *Oh, I know that. I know she just won't write letters.*

QJ: Some people just don't write, no.

RJG: *Have you heard her second album?*

QJ: Yeah. I have the dubs at home. "Heat Wave" and those things? "Social Call"? Yeah.

RJG: *Well some of those are very good. In fact, I don't think Pete Rugolo is the guy to back her on albums at all.*

QJ: He didn't write any of those, I don't think.

RJG: *Who wrote them?*

QJ: Somebody else.

RJG: *Yeah. [Jack] Tracy couldn't tell me who did them. They didn't want to mention anybody on the album at all.*

QJ: Well, Marty did the big band thing. Buddy Collette did the little things for the flute.

RJG: *But she would sound better—She doesn't need to be bolstered up with stuff. She's strong enough to stand on her own feet.*

QJ: Yeah. Ernestine's got a very rich voice and she should really be sparsely written.

RJG: *Yes, definitely.*

QJ: Leave her holes. Because when you fill her up there's too much richness.

RJG: *Yeah. It's too busy on a lot of those things.*

QJ: Yeah.

RJG: *What's impressed you since you came back in music?*

QJ: Well, I was surprised. I expected to find much more. 'Cause all the while you're over there, you feel like you're being left out of everything, and all these new things are happening. You feel like you're so far behind, and you listen to all the records and everything that comes out and you read everything. But I was surprised. There was not too much happening while I was gone. Stereo was about the only thing that really changed, because everybody was playing about the same. And I was happy to see that a lot of people that I know really scuffled and made it now, like Ernestine. It's nice to see.

RJG: *Where is Sam Woodyard? Is he back with Duke?*

QJ: I think so.

RJG: *He played in France a while.*

QJ: I didn't know that. Oh no, they just stayed a couple—him and Jimmy Woode stayed over a couple weeks, I think.

RJG: *Was that it? Because he had a television show and there was Gus Johnson.*

QJ: He had a cold that night, though.

RJG: *Oh, he did? I couldn't believe it. Gee, he sure changed. Face got fat.*

QJ: Playing different.

RJG: *What other plans do you have?*

QJ: I think this band is going to take up a lot of time. I would like to get more contact with—to help more people like music more. And that's why we want to work a little closer with schools. Like Marshall Brown's thing—Marshall, he's accomplishing a lot because he's getting people behind these things. I heard the Youth Band, this Newport Youth Band. And this is a good thing for these kids. This keeps a lot of guys out of trouble, 'cause when they have this they don't have to lean.

RJG: *Well, that may be. But I must say for a guy—If he's doing a good thing—and I don't know whether he is or not because I haven't heard it—but if he is doing a good thing, he sure is getting a lot of adverse reaction.*

QJ: From whom?

RJG: *All sorts of people are beefing about it.*

QJ: Marshall?

RJG: *Yeah. All the time.*

QJ: What do you mean—in the music business or—

RJG: *I don't mean agents and bookers but I mean guys in the business.*

QJ: Yeah. I don't know. I haven't heard too much about it. But it's a good thing to see these kids have some place to go. I wish we had it.

RJG: *You haven't been at Lenox, have you?*

QJ: I went up one year.

RJG: *That might be a place for your band sometime, too.*

QJ: Yeah. Well, if you watched the patterns of what a lot of the commercial bands have done—and I'm speaking only in terms of just processes, you know, and procedures, that they go through—there's a lot to be learned. Especially when the business is in this kind of shape, where no jazz band can make it and Stan [Kenton] loses all his money on a business venture. Somebody is doing something wrong when Lawrence Welk can go to the Corn Palace and get 40,000 dollars for three nights. That's fantastic.

RJG: *But then Stan has always been doing something that's basically unpalatable.*

QJ: You mean the music?

RJG: *Yeah. For instance, Kenton is still in the business and still playing one-nighters and still scoring now and then with the music that fundamentally has been difficult for the people to accept— extraordinarily difficult for the people to accept.*

QJ: But since he got accepted at one time—See, the consistency is the most important thing in these things. This has been what's been killing everybody. Because they get on top and they make the big money. But then there's other things that you have to do to keep this going. You watch the machines with guys like, say, just the process of business procedures, you know of guys—What happens to a guy like Eddie Fisher. Or Jimmie Rodgers. The guys that happen. They get managers that think, "Okay, now, you've opened the door. Let's fix it so that you don't fall out so easy. Let's put a few chains around it." So they work on the television things 'cause if they don't have the talent to sustain their position, get something else that they can hold on to. The jazz artist should think more about this. We've been very fortunate in the past three years, to get groups to break through on a national basis. John [Lewis] is doing this. And I admire him very much for it. And some guys, they make it and they say, "Yeah, let the good times roll in." Start finger-popping and all and get in new clothes and homes and everything else. And in three years it's gone, and they've had it.

RJG: *Well now, Erroll's got a good thing going for him in this Sol Hurok concert.*

QJ: Absolutely. And he's climbing, he's building. And they retain the stature, they can't drop. And Ella's been doing it too, which is good. And Norman's been doing some good things for her.

RJG: *The best thing that ever happened to her was Norman Granz.*

QJ: It was. Norman really put her into a different bracket. And boy, I'm very happy to see. It gives you faith to see like in any other profession the best people are in the best positions. And that's the way it should be. But to see a lot of idiots making it and the best people scuffling, like Ben Webster and those guys. To see them scuffling around—

RJG: *Now what are you going to do with guys like Ben Webster? How do you fix it so that they make it?*

QJ: Well—it's what they do on the way up. I mean, it's more than just playing now. Dizzy's a cat that's taken care of business. Dizzy realizes that one of these days his chops fold up. They haven't yet. But he realizes that when his chops fold up, and he's thinking about other things. He's thinking about clubs. He was thinking about getting a club once in Spain, where he owned the club and bring in groups and play there himself when he wanted to. You got to think like this. I saw Artie [Shaw] in Spain and he—Well, I guess he had money enough to just retire, and cool.

RJG: *He's in New York now.*

QJ: Artie? Really?

RJG: *Yeah. He's going to be there for another three or four weeks. He's at the Hotel Windsor. You going back there?*

QJ: I sure would like to see him.

RJG: *He's at the Hotel Windsor.*

QJ: Crazy.

RJG: *Then he's going to Sweden where he's going to make some record dates for somebody.*

QJ: With Harry Arnold. I set that up.

RJG: *Is that what that is? And then he's going back to Spain.*

QJ: In fact, he's going to write for them. He's not going to play.

RJG: *Is that what it is? He doesn't want to play anymore?*

QJ: No. He's just going to write, he's been writing about that for about a year now.

RJG: *I just had a letter from a friend of his that saw him in New York. He's a pretty astonishing guy.*

QJ: Who? Artie? Yeah.

RJG: *He's at the Hotel Windsor.*

QJ: I'll write it down. He told some funny stories about the old days. It's interesting to get them from a guy like Artie 'cause Artie was one of the biggest, in his field.

RJG: *Did you ever read his book?*

QJ: No, I didn't. I'm sorry, but I didn't.

RJG: *You should read that book sometime. I think it's out of print now but it's in most of the libraries. The reason I recommend it is not for—It's for a very specific reason, actually. It's a textbook, it's a textbook for young bandleaders.*

QJ: That's the way you feel with him.

RJG: *It's too much. The first thing he tells you in the book is when he got the band the difference in personal relationships, how the personal relationships altered between from the time when they were all scuffling to when they started to make it. And when it became a problem who he had dinner with.*

QJ: Really—that's true!

RJG: *He couldn't have dinner with just anybody he felt like having dinner with. He had to think about it because he's upset—He'd do something wrong and some cat would get salty, and the whole thing altered, see?*

QJ: Yeah. And you'd establish things that can't really be sustained. That's a problem. This is the weird part about that. Because how could you fire a guy—you're buddies and you start together, and you work together, and there comes a time when he goofs, and really goofs. You get hung up. But I guess that's always been—

RJG: *I guess you've thought about all of these things?*

QJ: Oh sure. I used to watch it even when I was on the other side. And now that I'm thinking about—Not that you want to be a bandleader *or* Big Man or anything, but you end up being in that position. And the only way you can find if your ideas work is to be the boss. And then you have to start giving—carrying the ball. And you run into a lot of problems. Because people are—I've noticed this too, and this is what discourages me in a way, from getting in this. 'Cause see, when you're writing, man, you're free. You don't have to cater to this. You just hang out with the people you like. People test you. They constantly test you; the more the popularity grows, the people constantly test you. I mean that people that wouldn't care if you never spoke to them before. When you get bigger, they test you. And it's weird. I seen them do it to other people, and really give them pressure that they can't stand. Like, not understanding a guy's situation. That he can't have dinner with 20 different people. And putting the pressure on him just because he is big. Oh, that's natural.

RJG: *Quincy, is it really true that every band, no matter how good it gets, you can talk to them and it sounds like the worst thing that ever happened and it's going to break up in 20 minutes? I mean, I've talked to bands that are so good that I couldn't believe it.*

I've talked to guys. And yet they lay down a long story on you of things—that's wrong—the griping.

QJ: Yeah. They always do. They always gripe. It's just like the army. They've got to gripe because they don't have any—They don't have the last say about it. And the guys that have the say about it are the most optimistic. But the ones that—But Terry's band— Well, they're just organized, too.

RJG: *It's a baby with them. They're all working somewhere else.*

QJ: Right. Right. So they can afford to. They all feel part—

RJG: *They're benevolent—it's a philanthropy.*

QJ: Right. But I think that the bands, Ralph, can be—I don't think that anybody's approached it from this angle. Because the bandleaders have had to scuffle too hard and they—I don't know what it is. A certain amount of insecurity makes them either cold or too generous or something. But I realize that if the guys in the band aren't straight—and I know if they're going to be leaders then they should be leaders. But if they are going to be part of my band, I can make them the straightest sideman in the business. I can see to it that they're the most well-taken-care-of musicians in the business. I mean, 'cause it can be that kind of a thing. Like Les Brown's band—all those guys are straight. They all have their homes and everything, and they can learn different things and study different instruments and learn to write, and you can build each one as an artist. And so I'd like to try this kind of a thing. 'Cause I know in New York, without even having a band, you're still responsible for guys making 10 and 15 grand a year.

RJG: *Sure, sure.*

QJ: I mean, individually. You might as well do it for your band, and for the guys. They can make a pretty good living, in a band. It sounds like, well one-nighters and 15 dollars a night or something, but it's not that way. Because in many ways you can build up publicity and an appeal for each one. Like Duke did in a sense.

RJG: *Well, I sure hope you are successful with this.*

QJ: I do, too.

RJG: *I really do. It's a wonderful idea. It's a very exciting idea, actually.*

QJ: It is. It really is. And it's a thing I've given a lot of thought. By no means just jumping on a little—

RJG: *Well that's obvious. You've been thinking about it!*

QJ: Thinking about it a long time, between arrangements and it's something I've always wanted. So I just hope it comes off.

RJG: *Well, good luck.*

QJ: Thank you very much.

RJG: *If there's anything anybody out here can do to help, just let me know. I'd be glad to, any way at all. If you're going to come, just let us know you're coming.*

QJ: Good. It's nice to know that—it's nice to have that feeling. It really is. It's encouraging.

John Birks "Dizzy" Gillespie

MAY 11, 1959

■

Don't be misled by the nickname. John Birks "Dizzy" Gillespie was as steady as a gunslinger on the bandstand, where he made his mark as the hottest jazz trumpeter of the mid-twentieth century. As a key instigator of the modern jazz movement (or "bebop," as it came to be called) during the 1940s, Gillespie helped reinvent the jazz vocabulary. But unlike most of his modernist peers, he also demonstrated a rare skill for showmanship and onstage repartee. Gillespie emerged as the public representative of bebop, and even those outside the jazz world followed his moves and imitated his personal style.

But at the time of this interview, Gillespie still had a few unfulfilled ambitions—and the Gleason family played a key role in the boldest of them all. Perhaps it started out as a joke or publicity stunt, but Gillespie's decision to run for the president of the United States soon turned into something bigger. After all, the State Department had already enjoyed great success in reducing international tensions by sending jazz musicians around the world as unofficial ambassadors—so why couldn't a charming jazz musician in hip attire chill out the Cold War? Certainly the Gleason clan thought so—Ralph Gleason took on the role of unofficial campaign publicist, and his wife, Jean, served as campaign manager.

The couple had some "Dizzy Gillespie for President" buttons made, and they started showing up at political rallies and events all over the world. You could seem them in New York, Chicago, and Paris, even at the March on Washington. "By early 1964," Gillespie later related in his autobiography, "the campaign was definitely off the ground, and Jeannie Gleason had been contacted by people in 25 states about it. The drive began to place my name on the ballot. . . . There were pressures on me to withdraw from the race after the press began to show some interest, and they found out I was a serious candidate." Perhaps the cleverest move was the name given to the bebop party, which got dubbed "The John Birks Society."

Although the trumpeter never made it to the Oval Office, the Gleasons and Gillespie provided the most endearing moments of a 1964 race that had few to offer. Yet even if you didn't know about this remarkable interlude in American politics, you could tell how closely aligned the legendary trumpeter and the celebrated journalist are from the rapport in this interview.

■

RJG: *What was the first jazz music you remember hearing?*

DG: I guess it was when Teddy Hill's band used to come from the Savoy. We didn't have a radio at home, but the lady next door had one. We were pretty poor after my father died. I don't remember hearing music before he died 'cause I was only 10 years old. It was around 1931 that they used to come from the Savoy. I used to say, "Boy, how'd you like to play with that band?" So when I got to New York that was the first band I played with. What a break!

And then after I got that scholarship at Laurinburg School, we used to get Glen Gray, you know, "Casa Loma Stomp" and "Wild Goose Chase" and things like that. I was always interested in music, but we never had any records in my house.

I played piano when I was about two, three years old. My mother used to put me up on the stool. The funny part about it, my two older brothers — my father tried to *beat* music into them, and I'm the one that they didn't give music to and everything, and I'm the one that's a musician! My mother talks about that all the time.

I was always around with some kind of instrument and then when the boy next door got a trumpet, that's when I started playing trumpet. But before that, when they gave out all the horns in the school, when they got this junior high school band together, well, the bigger boys was the ones who got the instruments, and I was little so they didn't give me none, the only thing that was left was the trombone. Yeah, I started on the trombone, that's the first instrument. I can play trombone *now*. I know all the positions.

RJG: *But it was the guy next door that had the trumpet that got you interested in trumpet?*

DG: In a way. His father bought him one of them long trumpets, it wasn't silver, it wasn't brass . . . nickel plate. He was in the band but he didn't follow it up afterwards. Then after a while he moved to New York. By the time he got ready to move to New York, I had the trumpet! After I'd been playing around with his and they saw that I was interested in the trumpet and I would practice on it, then the school finally gave me one. Boy, I had a hard time getting an instrument 'cause I couldn't buy one, it was out of the question.

As a matter of fact, the first instrument I had on my own — that's when I did that hitchhike to Philadelphia — I got there and I didn't have no horn 'cause I'd been playing the school's horn, so my brother-in-law went into the pawn shop and bought me one for about eight dollars or something like that and then I went and had it in a paper bag. He was just outside. I came walking out with that paper bag, he called me "Dizzy."

RJG: *As soon as you got that trumpet, did you know you wanted to be a jazz musician?*

DG: Well, that the only thing I could play, because I couldn't read at the time, so there was nothing else to play. And then we got this little band together around home, B Flat band. Actually, Miss Alice Wilson was my first teacher, because she's the one who helped. We had little plays every year, like a minstrel, and they had a little band and I was in the band and my cousins were singing. They had a terrific trio, two of my cousins and another boy named Fred. Boy, they were singing harmony. Miss Wilson couldn't read music, that's what was so funny about it. And she could only play in B flat. And she'd teach us all the numbers and she'd write songs. I had to teach all the guys and I couldn't read. My cousin was a bass player. We only had one string on the bass and we only played in B flat. So therefore, this one string I marked, put a mark on the bass, on the neck of the bass where B flat is supposed to be and then you turn the thing up there and bring that up to make that B flat and then make another mark at F, you know, and then make another mark at C and then that was it and he played and he was slapping the bass and everything and he was playing on that bass. That was my father's bass. We had a terrific thing going there every year.

RJG: *Before you played an instrument, did you sing in church?*

DG: I was a Methodist at home, so I didn't do any singing in church. I used to go to Sunday school, but I didn't sing in the choir or anything. I was too small. I was pretty small and I left home to go to school, I was about 14 or 15, something like that. But I used to go to the Sanctified Church all the time. The Sanctified Church was only about half a block from my house. As a matter of fact, you could hear it from there and every Sunday night I'd go down and sit down in the back, sit way in the back and listen to those guys. Boy, there was some hell of a rhythm going on there!

RJG: *Who was the first jazz musician you met?*

DG: Well, after I'd been playing around home awhile, I became a little famous in my home town as a trumpet player who could only play in B flat, so the first jazz musician, the first professional jazz musician I met, was Sonny Matthews. Sonny Matthews is a pianist. He was a terrific pianist, he must have been 'cause his mother taught him music when he was a little boy. He was the big star from home, you know, he'd been away and he came back. I was nervous and he asked me, "You play?" I said, "Yeah, play a little bit." He say, "What do you want to play?" and I say, "Well, I don't know." I asked him what he knew and he knew all the numbers and everything and I could only play in B flat. "River Stay Away from My Door" and things like that, and so he said, "Well, you know 'Nagasaki'?" I said "Yeah." So he say, "OK, we'll play it." So he started on the piano and he started off in C and, boy, I'll never forget how embarrassed I was, 'cause every note I played was wrong, you know, no sharps. I couldn't find nothin.' I couldn't play nothin.' I was really embarrassed. Then right after that I started reading. A boy named Norman Poe, actually, was the cause of my reading. Norman used to play with Louis Armstrong. We grew up together. I had a cousin named Ralph Poe, he's a lawyer now in Brooklyn. Ralph was a trombone player and he could read and everything 'cause the other school over there had somebody teaching those guys how to read. They could read anything and play all the marches and everything, but they couldn't play no jazz. We got all the jazz musicians 'cause we had all these things going like country parties and things like that. Ralph was teaching Norman how to read (they were both of 'em named Poe, but they weren't any relation) and how to count and we'd get together, we'd sit down all day counting out these things, counting and counting, so finally we learned how to read.

There was a boy at home named Bill McNeil. He got killed, the white people killed him, killed him 'cause they said he was a Peeping Tom or something like that. I don't think he was, but they found him on the railroad tracks, nobody ever knew who did it or anything. And he was terrific! He was a trombone player like [J. C.] Higginbotham, that kind, and you know, he had never heard anybody! None of us there had any records or anything like that to go by, and so we just had to do what we could. Bill's brother Fred was in that little trio that Miss Wilson had singing, and Bill and I were in the band. We didn't have no saxophone player, there weren't no saxophone players at home. Nothing but brass. Bill never learned how to read, but, boy, he could play. He was just born with that trombone and I'm quite certain that if he had lived and if he had come up North and had done the same thing that I did, he'd a been a terrific trombone player, terrific. He had good chops and everything. But he got killed. It was terrible.

RJG: *When did you decide to be a musician?*

DG: I always wanted to be a musician 'cause I was pretty lazy in the first place. I was supposed to work, go to school in the winter and get my tuition and my board and room, and in the summertime I was supposed to work on the farm. The school that I went to grew all of their things to eat.

RJG: *What school was that?*

DG: Laurinburg Industrial School. I took agriculture for two years 'cause it was easy, you know, and I didn't have to study too hard. I was spending all my time on the instrument and I didn't have time to be messing around with books. I used to make my teachers so mad! I had a pretty good mind (only mathematics I wasn't too good at) and I didn't have to study much and I'd make good marks and pass. But Mr. Smith used to say "Gillespie"—now that's how they call you—"Gillespie, I'm so mad with you because you pick things up, you can get them right just like that, and if you spent the time . . ." And, man, I was so busy trying . . . and then I found out about football. I found out that the football students had the training table—boy, that food was awful good. Next day I was on the football field! There was a good teacher there at Laurinburg the second year I was there, Shorty Hall, terrific trumpet player. He was the soloist at the World's Fair in Chicago with the Tuskegee band. They had about the best marching band in the country at that time and he was the soloist. Little bit of a guy, but that guy could triple-tongue and everything.

RJG: *Dizzy, you mentioned before that these guys could all read, but they couldn't play jazz.*

DG: Yeah, they played marching music. None of those guys played jazz, not one of 'em, and even Ralph, the guy who taught Norman, he never played jazz but boy, he could get over that horn, he could play and read practically everything. And he worked his way through college down in Tuskegee. He played in the band. And then he worked his way through law school. He didn't have no people, no mother and father, anything like that. I admire that guy 'cause he pulled himself right up and now he's a lawyer, a really good lawyer.

RJG: *When you got to Philadelphia, you were looking for somebody to play with.*

DG: The first thing I did, my brother-in-law got me this horn. I just got a ride up there, so here I come through the door and they didn't even know I was coming. So this guy named Johnny, an alto player, got me a little job. I was there about two days and they got me a job at 12th and Bainbridge, a little bar over there, and they had a piano player and a drummer, a very fat drummer. Johnny got me this job for eight dollars a week. After that I went out to 59th and Market, someplace like that, and these jobs was twelve-dollar jobs. And then I think it's Frankie Fairfax.

Up to that time I had never seen any arrangements. In my hometown they used to bring me up to the dances and let me play with these bands. I could play a little bit, but when I got to Philly, Bill Doggett and those guys were with Frankie Fairfax. Bill was writing music and a boy named Calvin was writing music. Calvin was a very good arranger and Ted Barnett and all those guys, and Shadow Wilson . . . Anyway, I went to Frankie's rehearsal, they told me to come, so I went down there with my horn. There was a boy there named Joe Fishell, he played trumpet with the valve tops off, could play very good too. I knew I could read, but boy I wasn't used to looking at this manuscript like that, the stems looked like notes. I was used to reading printed music, you know, boy, I was messing up! I'd play rests and everything, the rests looked like notes. But those guys were used to that, and so finally I didn't get that job. Bill Doggett told 'em, he said, "No, we get Joe Fishell," so they got Joe Fishell instead. I was mad 'cause I wanted this job with Frankie, I wanted to play in a big band. Right after that, Bill Doggett quit and took all the musicians and they went down to Atlantic City to work.

About that time I was getting up a little name around Philadelphia, playing around there, and Frankie Fairfax came back for me and then I went with his band. Bill Doggett was working down at the Harlem Club with this band and he asked me if I wanted to go down there. He was coming up from Atlantic City all the time to see me and I was still mad with him and I said, "No, I'm not going." Finally Tiny Bradshaw took us over and we went down South and got stranded, and then we came back to Philadelphia. Jimmy Hamilton was in the band then, he was the trumpet player then. We called him Joe Trump, I still call him that, so anybody call him "Hey, Joe Trump," and he knows it's somebody from his early years in Philadelphia. He was playing trumpet in the band but he was practicing clarinet every day. After that Charlie Shavers and Carl "Bama" [Warwick] came to Philadelphia and then everything perked up 'cause they come from New York and Charlie played all of Roy's [Eldridge] solos. I didn't know Roy's solos, but Charlie had all these records and he knew 'em note for note and I'd watch him when he'd play and I'd get to do my solo and I'd play the same thing. So one day he says, "Why don't you play your own solo?" I say, "I'm getting it secondhand now!" Then Charlie and I became very good friends in Philly, that was about '36.

When I was with Frankie, the first arrangement I made for a big band was "Good Night My Love." Ella Fitzgerald made that record and boy, I must have spent six months on that damn arrangement, all the notes and everything. We had four saxophones and five brass and everything. We had a nice little thing going there. And I made that arrangement and everybody congratulated me. I didn't get paid for it or anything like that, but I just wanted to. Then right after that, Charlie and Bama went with Lucky Millinder. Lucky Millinder at that time had Charlie, Bama and Harry Edison, so they were going to get Lucky to get rid of Harry and get me in that band. Lucky came over to Philly, and Charlie and Bama started raving 'bout me. So they took me back to New York with them, Lucky Millinder's band, and they were working in the Savoy and I didn't have no card, so I didn't play, but he was paying me. Finally after a couple weeks, two, three weeks, Lucky finally decided not to hire me and then I was embarrassed because I didn't want to go back to Philly and everything—I'd been playing around, in the Savoy with Teddy Hill and Chick Webb, and they'd let me sit in. Chick used to like me, I don't know why he took a liking to me, and he let me sit in in Taft's place, Taft Jordan. He never let anybody else sit in, and I never see nobody sit in, but they just let me sit in. I'd just get up and play. I'd been reading music and everything 'cause I could read pretty good by then. I remember I was down to rehearsal, down at the Apollo once, and Teddy was getting ready to go to Europe. This was in '37. I'd just been there since March and he was going in May. So Teddy say, "Where can I find a trumpet player? We going to Europe." I say "Yeah? I am. Let's go!" Frankie Newton didn't want to go to Europe. Then the boys in the band like Dicky Wells and Shad [Collins] and them, they found out that I was young, I didn't have the finer points in music, and they told him, Dicky and Shad and them, "Well, if this guy's going to Europe, we're not going." So Teddy say, "Well, he's going." So they went too.

After I went over to Europe and got back, I still couldn't work in New York and I played with this guy Cass Carr. We used to play all them . . . didn't know they was . . . I think it was sort of left-wing dances and things like that, you know, the Communist dances, all that sort of stuff. That was some good gigs, you know, weekend gigs. I finally got my card together, I went with Edgar Hayes and then back to Teddy and then I got the job with Cab Calloway.

I remember when I first met with Cab. Milt Hinton and I used to have a good time, used to go up on the roof in the Cotton Club. Nobody else wanted to play, all the other guys talked about real estate and insurance and things like that. Paul Jones used to tell me, "Save your money and put it in dirt." I said, "Put it in dirt? What do you mean, put my money in dirt?" He say "Buy yourself some land somewhere." And that was all they'd talk about, they never talked about music. Talking about everything but music. I say, "Well, damn, maybe I'm in the wrong market. Maybe I should be in real estate or something." So Hinton and I used to go up on the roof in the Cotton Club and we played between sets and everything. That used to happen quite a bit 'cause he's a good bass player. But he didn't have it . . . you know . . . the *flyness*. He could play anything that you'd show him, so I used to show him all his choruses and things. And then Chu [Berry] was there and it was a little thing going there that year.

RJG: *When you got with those guys in Philly and started meeting trumpet players, guys who were already established as professional musicians, did they help you or was Bill Dillard the only one . . .*

DG: Well, Bill Dillard was my biggest help after I came to New York, but there was nobody helping me in Philly. There was one guy there, I see him around, I see him all the time now, he was good, he's from Charleston, South Carolina, and we use'ta come home together all the time. He was playing in Jimmy Gorham's band. They had all of Jimmie Lunceford's arrangements and they played the whole thing, they sounded like Jimmie Lunceford. Bill Doggett's band was Count Basie's band, see. They were writing . . . they weren't exactly like Count Basie's, but Bill was playing the piano like Count Basie and everything.

RJG: *You didn't run into Roy, then, for a long time, did you?*

DG: No, I didn't see Roy until . . . well, in Philly I had an interesting experience with Roy. All the bands used to come to Philly. When I got to Philly in '35, Roy was with Teddy Hill and Chu, and they used to jam downstairs in the Rendezvous up under the Douglas Hotel where the Showboat is now. Well, those guys used to play and I wouldn't dare play, you know, I'd just go and listen to those guys. So one time, I remember, Rex Stewart, Duke Ellington, and Teddy Hill were there at the same time and they had a session downstairs and Roy was down there that night. And Rex, you know, Rex was Roy's idol. Roy tells now about the time he first heard Rex play that high B flat. Roy finally found that B flat, I guess, 'cause when he come to Philadelphia that night they was jammin' round there and Roy started playing. Damn, Rex started crying and just tightened up and left 'cause Roy was in rare form that night. I didn't meet Roy until way later. I met him there, but he didn't remember me. You know who was nice to me there? The Lunceford band, 'cause I had an entrée in the Lunceford band. [Eddie] Wilcox, the pianist, his sister taught school in Laurinburg, Miss Wilcox was one of the teachers there, and when I told her I might go up North some time, she says, "Well, if you do, if you go up North, when you see the Jimmie Lunceford band, you go up and speak to the piano player, my brother." And I say, "Oh thank you, I will." So the first thing I did when Jimmie Lunceford came to Philadelphia, I was right there waiting. Then, you know who used to be nice to me? Sy Oliver and his wife, Billie. I used to go up there and sit in the room for hours. I was a little boy then and they'd spend a little time with me. An' now they say they can't believe it, you know, they can't believe that I'm really me!

Then I finally got to New York, my old gang was Charlie Shavers and lil Bobby Moore, the best trumpet player out of all of us. He was the best. He went with Count Basie. I was supposed to go with Basie then instead of Harry Edison when he got back to New York from that European thing. Basie offered me a job and it wasn't no money, but I didn't care about the money. Then I was supposed to take Bobby's place, something happened to his tooth. He had it fixed and then he couldn't do the same thing that he did before. But I wouldn't take Bobby's job and then Harry took the job later. I don't even know whether Basie remembers he offered me the job or not. But he did offer me the job to take little Bobby's place 'cause we played almost alike, we both of us were *fly*.

But little Bobby was the best out of all of us, like L'il Benny [Harris] and Charlie and Bama and Bobby and myself. We use'ta go down and play at all the joints, none of us were working too much, but we had this thing, we'd meet every night and we'd go down to the Village and we'd play in Ernie's an' the Yeah Man Uptown and the Brittwood and the Victoria an' we use'ta have a set thing and we'd play behind these singers. 101 Ranch, that's where I first heard the Savoy Sultans.

RJG: *That was a good band.*

DG: That's the swingingest band I ever heard in my life. I've never heard nobody with that much exuberance in a band. They use'ta blow and they didn't have nothing but three saxophones, two trumpets, and a rhythm section and they'd blow Benny Goodman, *anybody* out, they didn't care about nobody 'cause the rhythm that it had . . . one time I remember in the Savoy they start shouting so much up there one night the people was dancing, everybody was goin' on the same beat and one of them beams broke downstairs in the pool room. Them cats run out that pool room like rats out of a trap.

So, we use'ta play all the places and we ran across Roy a number of times in New York. Roy use'ta go around and blow . . . a guy would be playing on his bandstand and Roy walk in the place and take out his horn at the door and start the next chorus from the door.

RJG: *When did you first hear Louis?*

DG: In Philly, I heard Louis and Duke. I heard all the bands first in Philly 'cause I never heard no bands before. I use'ta hear bands like Jimmy Gunn, from Charlotte, North Carolina, Capitol City Aces, Billy's Jazz Hounds. Those were the bands that were traveling down South at the time . . . and Smiling Billy Stewart and Belton Society Syncopators, Johnson Happy Pals . . .

RJG: *What kind of bands were those?*

DG: Good bands. They had arrangements. I remember when I first started out, the bands had a brass section, they had three saxophones, two altos and a tenor and the third alto player doubled on baritone, and then they had two trumpets and a trombone. Then I remember when they added the third trumpet and had four brass and then I remember when they added another trombone, they had five brass, and when they added another trombone they added another tenor saxophone and then later on they started having five saxophones and six brass. That was way later, late '30s.

RJG: *Do you think the guys that come up today lose something by not having . . .*

DG: Oh, man, the experience they lose! It takes 'em longer. I see guys like Lee Morgan and Booker Little, Freddie Hubbard, and it amazes me how they can get experience and they don't have the facilities for that experience and yet they can get it. They scramble just like we did, they scramble around and do the same thing, but when I was coming up, you see, we would play in big bands, we could go all the places and sit in, just go and take out your horn and sit in. No money, you didn't have to have no money. But nowadays, it's terrible. They should start having some big bands and things like that so the guys can get experience at playing with different . . . especially the colored bands, 'cause most of the time I notice that the white bands, most of the guys phrase sort'a alike, you know, most of the guys have teachers and all the teachers teach certain ways, almost the same way. But in the colored bands . . . you play in Willie Bryant's band and you get a trumpet section there and them guys use a vibrato. Like some of 'em, the first trumpet player might use a vibrato, too, and don't shake his hand at all and use a lip. So you have to do the same thing he does. Then you get another band and those guys do this—shake their hands and you get that experience. You go in another band and they do some other kinda shit and you just keep goin' around in that circle and you get all that experience. When you jam every night, you gonna hear maybe six trumpet players and you get a couple of things from each one. But you can't get that experience nowadays.

RJG: *Does it help a soloist to have the discipline of working in a big band?*

DG: Oh, yeah. The discipline is very good for young musicians coming up, but a lot of musicians will never get the things that I got. I didn't get the same things that somebody else got earlier, you know, 'cause they had many, many big bands when I was coming up. You could go outta one, get right in another one. Dollar and a half more the guy pay you, you quit and put in your notice.

Lucky Millinder is the greatest conductor that I've ever seen, including Toscanini. Now I know everybody's gonna be mad, but Lucky was absolutely the greatest conductor that I had ever seen in my life and he can't read a note. He'd watch Chappie Willet. Chappie Willet would rehearse the arrangement and Lucky would say, "Play that part over." And we'd play it and play it and Lucky would get up there and, boy, you wouldn't have to read the music, all you have to do is look at Lucky, and he'd bring you in.

Lucky fired me, and my notice was given out in Philadelphia. Well, I was havin' trouble with my chops. Boy, they use'ta be sore. When I was with Cab [Calloway], I had terrific chop trouble. I went and bought one of them twenty-dollar mouthpieces, all-silver mouthpiece, and it cut into my lip and my lip was sore for years.

When I would find Roy, I use'ta play with Roy at that time. We used to jam together and Roy would start making them Gs and then B flats and I'd sneak my head down. I used to practice all the time, you know, with Monk and them. Roy used to get together and play all these things at Monk's and everything. Monk used to tell Roy, and this was before I even had made any kinda thing, Monk say, "Dizzy's the greatest trumpet player." They'd get mad, Monk tell him that.

Johnny Carisi was the only white boy that just stuck it out. He'd be right there every night, right there playing. He knew all the arrangements. You'd play any one of them weird tunes of Monk's, Johnny Carisi was right there with it. I like Johnny Carisi, Johnny's a terrific trumpet player and Johnny would play with anybody, Roy or Hot Lips . . . and boy, Hot Lips Page. I remember we used to go down to Monroe's Uptown House every night. They had a swinging little band down there, it was a terrific band too, and Charlie Parker was in it. That's when I first saw Charlie Parker down there and they had all these arrangements and not one note of music, none of 'em could read. They announced this guy, and Hot Lips would come out and he'd do his blues thing and he'd play for a hundred or so choruses on some and I'm telling you there's no trumpet player in the world that plays the blues like Hot Lips Page 'cause he'd *shout* the blues like you sing them. Then we'd play "How High the Moon" and things like that, we'd get all lit, all complicated, and everything down there. I loved Hot Lips.

RJG: *Today when kids are playing and they take long solos, what the hell do you suppose they think about?*

DG: You don't need that many choruses. Give me two and a half choruses and that's it. I wonder what they trying to prove, but I guess they are fishing. You don't need to play eight or ten choruses, you be playing the same thing all over again—if you record it, you hear the same things over and over.

RJG: *When you add a tune, start to do some new number, do you think about that tune when you're off the stand or consider ways to play it?*

DG: No, I don't. That's never crossed my mind. Unless it's something hard, you get them hard things and you have to figure certain things. It's only if it's difficult changes or something you figure . . . you practice or something like that. Then you go onstage and put it to use. But most numbers, man, you just go up and start playing.

RJG: *Does anything cross your mind when you're playing?*

DG: No, you just have a set of chords up there in front of your face you're trying to do. I don't ever think 'bout nothin'. You find numbers that give you a lot of trouble, you play 'em and you play 'em and finally you get into the groove of it and you know how things go from here to the other and then you do it.

I hate for a piano player to try to lead you. Young musicians, if they listen, that's another thing for experience. I've always had young musicians in the band and if anything goes wrong, you know, like a meter gets jumped or something like that, the piano player starts banging, banging, banging, to bring everybody back. I say, "Look, just relax, let it take its course." You know the loudest instrument, let him do that, let the loudest instrument do that and you just follow him if it gets off. Just the other night in the club, something was happening, the drum played a solo and we came back in and it was in the wrong place and the bass was doing something and the drums was saying ripicha, ripicha, you know, he was on the wrong beat. It's very easy to get with a drummer and a bass player, without the piano banging in there, all three of 'em on the wrong place. So you say "stroll" and they finally get together. But I see some guys, if something goes wrong on the solo or something like that, and the drummer maybe gets on the other meter, I see some guys play all the way through that chorus and the drummer's playing ripicha, ripicha, ripicha. I say, "How would you do it?" They just fight one another and I don't do it, I can't play. When something gets wrong like that, I just stop, I stop altogether, I turn around and say, "You all get together now, get together, yeah?"

RJG: *In all the various scenes that you've been in in music, what have been the biggest moments . . .*

DG: I've had some great moments, like when playing with Charlie Parker. Playing with Benny Carter. Yeah. We had a little band with Benny Carter down at Kelly's Stable when we had Kenny Clarke, Sonny White, Charlie Drayton, and Benny and Al Gibson, he was playing clarinet then—six pieces. Boy, we used to have some good times. But Benny, he's a terrific trumpet player. When I come with Benny's band he got on a different stick. Tenor, he went and got a tenor. Sounds like Ben Webster on the tenor . . . I guess Ben Webster sound like him . . . but on tenor they sound almost alike. Tenor . . . and that was his kick then. Every now and then he'd pick up his trumpet and the valves would stick, hadn't played in so long. Sometime in between sets I'd go take his trumpet and I'd go back in the back, take the valves out, clean the valves out and oil it up and come out and then we'd play for hours. Say "Come on," and he'd get his horn and we'd play and we'd have a good time. Oh yeah. Benny Carter. Boy, Benny's got a record now on trumpet, I caught him, I was listening in Hollywood. I don't really remember the name of the tune, but, boy it was beautiful and I knew it was Benny 'cause I don't know no trumpet player that thinks like that. Boy, he played the shit out of this thing. Oh, man, the slow thing he play, low, low, low Gs, way down there. I don't know the name of that thing, but it was good.

Dizzy Gillespie

RJG: *The name of the album was "Aspects."*

DG: Yeah, I had the album, I went and got it. Yeah. And another thing, another one of my thrills was playing with Larry Adler. This is here recently. I went down to the Village Gate. I did a television show with him and then we played along . . . I did a couple numbers by myself and everything. But it really was a thrill playing with that guy, him and Ellis Larkins. That Ellis Larkins is a master pianist. Oh, man, he fills up a piano. When I went down there to the television show, he had a bass and drums and Ellis Larkins. So when I went down to the Village Gate I expected to see drums and bass and everything. I went down there and here's Ellis Larkins sitting up at the piano by himself and I say, "Where's the bass? Where's the bass and drum?" He say, "No, this is all we have here." I say "Damn," and when I started playing with Ellis Larkins and that son of a bitch, boy, he fills up a piano and he just does it. I don't know, master accompanist, you know. And he was just grabbing a handful of notes. Ellis Larkins, he's a bad boy. I didn't know he played. I heard of Ellis Larkins in New York and I went down there and good gracious alive, I had a good time! His second show . . . we played the first show, that was alright, but boy, the next one we played . . . "Play the blues in there," I say. "Just try this, Adler done played everything else." I say, "Well, I'm going back home, just give me the blues there in this tempo." And Ellis Larkins started out . . . I had a good time, it was really one of my thrills.

RJG: *Is it as much kicks to play with a small group as with a big band?*

DG: Personally, yes. If you get a groove it doesn't matter. Big band, little band, anything. The musicians themselves inspire you. It might be a hundred, it might be one, it might be just a guitar player, it might be just a bass player, anything. Your inspiration comes actually from the musicians, not from the instruments themselves, not from a whole lot of instruments, anything, your

inspiration comes from whatever the thing does. It doesn't matter. Sometimes you be sitting in front of a big band for a whole
night, and you don't strike not one groove and you be just playing
things that you just know . . . I mean you just playing without
even thinking about it. And then again you say I'll play two choruses on this and I'm liable to play six, something like that, until
my lips just give out so much and I just can't play no more and
I say "Forgit it." And then sometimes you just hit a groove with a
small band, hit a groove and you get that groove going there, and
then you play and then sometime you don't get it, so that's what
makes jazz so fascinating, 'cause you don't get that, maybe four
times in your whole career you actually come up to your stature
that you can really play, maybe four times, maybe three. And if
you hear guys like Charlie Parker, any great, like Benny Carter,
and you hear them at their absolute best, you're lucky. You're
lucky. I think I've heard most of those guys, Charlie Parker, I
know I've heard him at his absolute best, and then you hear his
records and things like that and you don't become excited about
the records that they make because you know that you've got
that in your mind and you say, well, I heard him at his really, at
his *really* best. So that's what happens. I'm not too excited about
records anyway. Very seldom. Sometimes I sit down and listen
to some things and I hear certain things on records that I like to
hear and I put it on and I play it and when it gets to that part it
hangs me up.

RJG: *What is it that happens when you get in that particular groove?*

DG: You can't explain it. Everything is right, just everything, everything you try is right. Like baseball players, I guess. You get a guy
come up one day, he come up there . . . not ordinary, mediocre,
but I'm talking about the really great guys, guys like Willie Mays
or Mickey Mantle or when Jackie Robinson was playing, one of
these guys. Everything he does is right. Everything just gets in
there and all the chords start running and the rhythm is going

like that and it just . . . you say "Damn" . . . you wouldn't believe it, you know? Just like you're floating, you know, you're floating. But most of the great guys, they have certain levels that they never go below.

RJG: *Do you suppose other music, other kinds of music, get that feeling?*

DG: I don't know, I don't know too much about it. You know when it really happens, I guess it probably happens in these virtuosos, like the pianists Rubinstein and Horowitz. I imagine sometimes they really get it because they have that . . . they really get that . . . but sometimes they just play the notes. But I imagine it's the same thing with them, too.

RJG: *The audience gets this when it happens to you in a jazz band, doesn't it?*

DG: Yeah, I guess so. Sometimes the audience doesn't have anything to do with it. Sometimes you playing the worst audience in the world and you strike a groove and, damn, you forget the audience is there. You forget about them altogether. Just happens. But you very seldom hear that, hear guys at their best, at their absolute best.

John Lewis
MARCH 18 AND 20, 1960

∎

John Lewis never became a household name, but that's only because he rarely put that name on a marquee. He called his band the "Modern Jazz Quartet"—a remarkable demonstration of humility when you consider that the other jazz stars of the day were naming their groups after themselves. The Modern Jazz Quartet reached the top ranks of the jazz world in the early 1950s, and stayed there, with a few hiatuses, for more than 40 years. This combo proved that modern jazz could serve as the basis for a new kind of swinging chamber music suitable for highbrow concert halls. John Lewis never referred to himself as the bandleader, noting merely that he was the "musical director," but his personality and vision put an unmistakable stamp on every concert and record.

Lewis might have enjoyed a lasting impact on jazz without ever appearing onstage. He stands out as one of the greatest composers in jazz history, and during his tenure with MJQ demonstrated his mastery of an extraordinary range of forms and genres. He could write a jazz fugue or score works for a string orchestra, yet he was equally at home with the blues or traditional song forms. He played a key role in the Third Stream movement of the 1950s and 1960s, which explored ways of merging classical music and jazz. Lewis even launched a big band in 1962 to demonstrate how this synthesis could be achieved—but once again refused to put his name on the ensemble, which he called "Orchestra USA."

Others aspired to stardom, but Lewis was more interested in the next composition, or in new techniques he could apply to his craft. Within the jazz world, people listened carefully to his every utterance, and his praise carried enormous weight—for example, Lewis's advocacy of saxophonist Ornette Coleman played a key role in legitimizing the jazz avant-garde at a time when many were hostile to it. Lewis is still remembered today for his deep intellect and thoughtful commentary on all matters music (not merely jazz). That astute, clear-sighted perspective is evident throughout this 1959 interview.

■

RJG: *First thing I wanted to ask you was to tell me about the genesis of the Modern Jazz Quartet? How long this idea had been in your mind, how the idea originated?*

JL: Well, let's see. It wasn't in my mind in the first place, and actually it came about in a very natural way, I guess, from our playing together since 1946. Kenny Clarke, Ray Brown, Milt Jackson, and myself were playing in Dizzy's band.

RJG: *Aha!*

JL: And, let's see. I had known Kenny before that in the army, so we already played together and, oh, Dizzy's band was very unique, at least that band, in some ways, in that the music, you know, the trumpet players earned more money than anybody else. They did; they deserved it, though, 'cause that was some of the hardest trumpet music there is to play, so they couldn't play like that all night so therefore this meant that something had to happen when they weren't, when they couldn't play this music, so the rhythm section played. So the rhythm section consisted of Kenny Clarke, Ray Brown, and Milt Jackson playing and myself because there wasn't any music for him to play, only thing, reason he was there was to play solos or something like this and had been with Dizzy's sextet. So we had done a lot of playing up until 1948, then changed bass players, I think Ray was going with Ella then and so it was better, he was getting that organized so he wasn't any longer. Al McKibbon took his place and then after the European tour, 1948, Kenny quit and stayed in Paris. He got a job and I came back and quit also so I got a job in Paris, so then we didn't see each other maybe until 1949 again and which means, up at Minton's or any place like this. If we happened to be there we'd all play together, we'd try, and almost consciously be the ones wanted to play together or if we got any gigs, Monday night gigs, or any kind of gigs like this, why the people we'd think of to call would naturally be someone around who belonged, in other words, Dizzy's band really became the center of kind of a clique in a sense. It still is, I guess, for me to play with. I guess there's nothing to compare with them, there's no other, I really mean that too. We went and played a little while, there wasn't really any record date in the sense of a lot of people work and sweat and so forth. By this time, though, because—I don't know this must have been 1950, '51—everybody then had gained enough reputation and had, we could earn very, very good money as sidemen, doing things like this, so it wasn't the idea of, maybe at first let's say, somebody get a quartet, but Milt couldn't afford to pay us, he couldn't get paid enough money to make it, just wasn't economical for him to do this, neither could I do this, Kenny Clarke, or Ray Brown. The closest man possible maybe could have done this was Ray Brown, manage it through Ella, because she could have made, but this didn't happen so we let this go awhile. We played whenever we could. Ray was tied up with Ella and he was committed to Norman Granz, which is a lot of money, so we said anyhow the whole thing was for me to really earn a good living. That's what everybody seemed to be looking for, nobody was trying to make any great strides, only earn a living. So we decided okay then, the last bass player Dizzy had who quit was Percy [Heath] and Percy's very, very young at this time. Well, young in music, very young 'cause he started playing in 1947. In 1947 we had learned all the things that we learned about that, the rest of us, and this took a while to decide about Percy, Percy couldn't play, I didn't like to play with Percy. He played the wrong notes and the wrong time, was very difficult, it was just like murder, I really couldn't take it at all. But, okay, so I knew that something like what had happened would happen 'cause if you stay with somebody long enough you get attached to 'em, I don't care if it's the devil, it's very hard to separate apart, it's impossible. I don't care if you didn't play nothing, and when we talk to Percy and told him that this is going to be hard, you want to come and do this and so I didn't want Percy. I told him why and I say, "Well this is work, you don't even know the notes and so forth, so we're going to have to write the notes and teach you all this." Before there wasn't no need for notes or anything. It would be all by rote or because we didn't have any music or anything like that. We threw that music away that Dizzy had. We had better parts and things to do than what the arrangers were writing.

So we stayed up, I don't know, we must have stayed up one night until 8, 9 o'clock in the morning, I don't know whether it was Milt's car or Kenny's car. I think it was Kenny's car, talking, we were out there until, 'cause a better person I felt then would have been either, do it with [Charles] Mingus, we had done some things with Mingus at this time. A girl, you know, do you know a singer by the name of Honey Johnson?

RJG: *Yes, I know the name.*

JL: Well, she had been in Paris, unlike [Connie] Kay and them and when they came back to this country why we made some acetates together and I don't know whether there was a radio program or something and Mingus played on that with Kenny. Now Milt is a virtuoso vibraharp player. That's foremost, his virtuosity—that comes across to me at once. And then also with Kenny Clarke too, because Kenny would do things other drummers can't do. Either they're all too old, Sidney Catlett's gone, or 'cause there are not that many drummers can take and do these things. Buddy Rich can't. When you're playing along with somebody like that, this is what Kenny can do to an impossible degree. Buddy Rich is a great soloist. I think he's the best soloist. Max [Roach] is important I think in the way he's able to play fast, a special new way which comes after Kenny. Kenny plays fast completely where he solves and put the whole physical problem that most people learn to do and the same thing happens to the piano, you know, play the piano completely. Then what you actually do, it seems to me is you're trying to set a world record or something that has to do more with the Olympics than it has to do with music. Nobody gets this kind of sound at all. So Mingus would be this kind of thing and things that I had in mind and wanted to try and do and so forth musically. Which takes virtuoso people to make and do. That music is very hard, we have to play. That's why we don't hear people playing that music. You only hear them play the easy things. They're not going to play those hard, they're hard to play. But anyhow, Percy said okay lemme try it for a year actually. So he came and he worked hard and nobody works as hard as he, he works harder than anybody else I think in the group. He really spends time, he went to Mingus to study with Mingus to find some things out. I don't think he was the greatest innate musical ability. But anyhow, he's worked out, so there have been times when I wasn't always happy there, but other than that it's been very good with Percy all these years for all kinds of reasons 'cause this thing is not made on just the music alone, it's made on other, being malleable and all this, to be able to work with each other. And Kenny left.

RJG: *Hmmm.*

JL: Kenny had to leave the group and he left one night's notice. The next night we had a concert to play and no drummer so Connie [Kay] had been playing off-nights down at Birdland and had closed there and we were going to go to Washington to play a concert with the Australian Jazz Quartet, the Dave Brubeck Quartet, and Carmen McRae. What a spot for the drummer to leave in. So he called up Monte [Kaye, MJQ manager] to get him some Monday nights or something, but I think Lester [Young] wasn't working then, Connie had been working with him. Anyhow you listen and check this thing now. So Monte suggested his name to us. We needed somebody in a hurry. I thought maybe Jo Jones would be good. He wasn't doing anything at the time, but we took Connie and went down to Washington and played and by telling him what to do with the arrangements, 'cause we had most of the things pretty set and he came through with flying colors and mainly because Connie's got a remarkable sense of timing and also a remarkable sense of musicianship. He's very remarkable, that guy. He was intuitive, knows what's right and wrong, he, it was very good, very remarkable. I have great respect for him.

RJG: *One thing that I wanted to ask you, John, was the fact that you keep in the things that you do coming back to the Italian Commedia dell'arte. How did you get involved with this as an idea or concept?*

JL: That's probably been going on a long time. Mainly, I guess I went with a girl who was a dancer and also who is an extremely talented person. So it's through this that I became interested in this. Also I learned about Dylan Thomas through her and Edith Sitwell and a few other people who I liked very, very much. And through that it might go back farther than that.

RJG: *There are thousands of questions I would ask you, but among the things that puzzle me John, who would you credit as the major musical influences on you as a writer and as a player?*

JL: I never even really think about it. If it happens it just happens because I don't consciously try to think about anything like that. The only thing you do is, to me, you listen to a lot of music and sometimes there are things that are lacking, not really lacking in the music, but there's something else that you want to hear that can be done with that idea or something like that so you try to do that, to write music to make up for something that you don't hear someplace else, that you want to hear, that's the reason for me.

RJG: *Perhaps the way I should have phrased that: Who have been the important musicians in your life?*

JL: Fletcher Henderson, Lester Young, Coleman Hawkins and Charlie Parker, Dizzy Gillespie, Duke Ellington, Bach, Mozart, and Beethoven from time to time and I think that's, let's see, Richard Strauss and Bartók and Webern, Webern's music and Schoenberg, some of the things that Schoenberg's, because not all of those things were successful, which is good though, because it gives you the opportunity to do something with what somebody's aiming at or something, like this happens all the time.

RJG: *In traveling with the group all over this country and in Europe, have you reflected on the importance that the Modern Jazz Quartet as a unit has in the whole of jazz?*

JL: No, I haven't.

RJG: *Well, perhaps as an example, as a group, as an example to other groups, the responsibility of it.*

JL: Oh, a little bit, we hope that there are things, most of those things though would be, I hope, at least in total and not just say it's the music alone 'cause that's not enough. I think that has been a problem with jazz as I've known it, you know, professionally for a long time there is not enough responsibility among players, either musically or in trying to be professional about what you're doing. This lack went on for a long time, but it comes and goes in cycles because it was pretty good though, I think in Fletcher Henderson's time and those people who played there and a whole different attitude took place with playing. His band, Cab Calloway's band, Earl Hines and so forth, a little different way of doing things or Duke Ellington. You don't get this later on with a lot of younger musicians. But maybe that's the times. It will probably happen again too, I imagine. It probably won't stay this way. I don't say this is good for the status of it either. Maybe the only way some things can happen is if it is no responsibility for, like a revolt I guess it seems.

RJG: *Well, the reason I asked you that question, John, was that it struck me in increasing force the way in which the Quartet has tried to anticipate the problems inherent in being a traveling group and so solve those problems by planning as much as possible and not to leave things to chance. Like down to the lights and all aspects of your function.*

JL: Oh yes, I think this is necessary, because for one thing, it's only fair to an audience if they pay their money that they work hard for that they should get as much of what they're paying their money for and that's the only consideration there that I don't want to go someplace where either I can't hear what's going on or they look so bad I don't want to look at 'em so I'll just listen.

RJG: *Has that been in your mind since the beginning of the group?*

JL: You mean about this being well . . .

RJG: *Well organized, yes, planned.*

JL: Yes, before the group. This was before with Dizzy, a lot of things were wrong there that don't need to be wrong and I used to see them, all this is all the benefit of experience from other players and groups.

RJG: *Does this hold true even to the business of planning uniforms and things?*

JL: Well, when Kenny was in the group he used to go get the uniforms when we first started out. When he left then I went to pick the uniforms and 'course had to pick 'em well enough so that they liked 'em and wanted to wear 'em so I won that little battle, not battle, but anyhow they thought that I picked things well enough so, we have to go get 'em for summer and also uniforms that are, that fit the personality of four, you know, four, five personalities cause all clothes don't fit all people so it's a kind of compromise in that sense, until now, well last year we had uniforms made for the first time. Most of the time the uniforms came from Brooks or a place called Van Boven in Detroit. We don't get there too much though. Mostly now it's either Brooks or, we can get to Italy, so we had two uniforms made in Italy.

RJG: *I was really astonished when I picked up the copy of the Melody Maker that had all that business in the frock coats and what was apparently viewed by the two people that were involved in this discussion as unnecessary solemnity. Now that comes out again in the letters that I have been getting.*

JL: Yes. I remember reading something about that.

RJG: *And I'm curious to your reaction to this. It never struck me in that way, but I recognize the fact that it apparently does strike some other people that way.*

JL: Well, that may be because they are accustomed to people jumping up and down or something that most of the young players want to get away from. Say for instance Louis Armstrong's group. That's just out. I don't go in for that, which is, I think, phony and false, 'cause he doesn't even mean it. He's all happy and jumping around and all that, but he doesn't mean that at all, that's just for the benefit of those people sitting out there in the audience so it's false. We mean, I mean no more than what is here in this music. Now I'll tell you something about it if this helps you, and that's the whole purpose of that and then we go play and that's the way we play, that's the way I have to play or I can't play at all. There's no flailing of arms or anything like that. So that's the only thing I can account for in the letters that way. The other thing is they were not accustomed to this. In England for instance. However, this did not come from people. This only came from one critic, as a matter of fact. However his angle was interesting enough to draw attention. It did not come from many people who knew about it. Also, their musicians and so forth dress in kinda an old-fashioned uniform way. For one thing, the clothes we wear and so forth, they don't really look like uniforms. They're clothes that you, if we, I wear those clothes out into, we retire the uniforms every now and then, nobody ever would know they're uniforms because they're just suits. They're not red jackets or all this kinda thing which nobody in the group likes, but no, they don't like it. So there's a jacket that's being made in New York, we'll see how it works out. If it looks okay we'll wear it. If not then back to the tuxedos. And anyhow, tuxedos and all this, this is old hat. This goes back to King Oliver and all these people. I see, the pictures I see this is what they have on.

RJG: *That was the band uniform.*

JL: Yeah.

RJG: *John, there must have been many moments of concentration, of strain in getting the group up to a point of acceptability with the public, and I wondered had you ever thought sometimes it was all too much.*

JL: How do you mean, work?

RJG: *No, I'm not even speaking about musical. I'm just speaking about the fact that you had to sell the group that did not have an individual's name attached to it, you were selling a phrase that covered four people.*

JL: Right.

RJG: *You were selling quiet music in surroundings that were not used to hearing quiet music.*

JL: Yes.

RJG: *You were selling them to your own conditions of making it and presenting it.*

JL: Yes.

RJG: *Now this represented a number of problems in the context of the nightclub and jazz field. Did it ever seem to be that there were too many problems?*

JL: No, not to me.

RJG: *You always had the conviction that it, if you could stay with it, would make it.*

JL: Yes, I had that conviction. I really didn't think about it that way anyhow. I was just doing what I wanted to do; anyhow in the first place that's the kind of music I wanted to play and that's the way I wanted to play it so don't matter to me if it works or not, it's not too dependent, nobody in there is so dependent on that thing to earn a living, we still play that way whether, if we had to go earn some money some other way, we go earn the money some other way and come back and play.

RJG: *Do you have plans at any point to expand this group to any other form?*

JL: No. Expand it in what sense, add an instrument or something?

RJG: *Well, I just thought, yeah . . . This represents a complete thing to you, then.*

John Lewis

JL: Well, to make contrapuntal music, the very best thing you can do with things like this are with three pitch instruments playing at the same time. After you get four then it starts doubling. Four is the most you can get and you can't use four because the ear doesn't hear any more than that. What you hear is still possibly three individual sounds. You hear the trumpets, the trombones, usually, and the saxophones. Or in orchestra you hear the strings or you'll hear the first violins, or the viola and the cellos. The basses are just doubled with the cellos, contrabass, that's what it is. The cello's really the base of the orchestra. I notice whenever, now and then we've had a guest and tried this out and actually because of the kind of instruments we have, these are all struck instruments, so the music is really made for this. It's nice, you know, good for us. I'd like to play with something if it's possible to do, but just musically and so forth this is excellent, almost an ideal combination.

RJG: *Do you have any ideas of things that you would like to do with the Quartet that you haven't done yet?*

JL: Oh yes, there are other possibilities here I think that haven't been realized yet and which we think about and so forth, they take time to do. Particularly stimulating is the way that Milt plays in order to take and incorporate more and more of his playing into the music composition. This is, I don't know how to really put this across well. Because there's more going on there than meets, than you absorb, than you know, than the ear actually absorbs from what he's doing. But sometimes it's so busy and so forth, re-markable and all that you don't really hear everything that's going on. So I hope to be able to find something that's gonna usefully make you hear that better. Which means that the things he does have to be related to a bigger overall design in the music so that you see what this is and what it belongs to. That takes time to do, things like that. So that's all I can say.

RJG: *Do you think you have, looking back on the years of existence of the Quartet, accomplished much? How does it strike you?*

JL: Yes, we have accomplished a great deal.

RJG: *What would you say was the most important thing you had accomplished?*

JL: The most important thing we have accomplished is something that time actually has accomplished, and that's playing together. When we're able to play together very well then it's, you can't get that without years put into it and I don't know anybody that has that many years put in. Even the very best of players, I don't care how good you can play, it's not the same thing at all because it starts getting down, breaks down into seconds and split seconds, things that happen split-second-wise that you cannot tell anyone. Oh maybe this was wrong, maybe this should be a little more, you're a tiny bit late, just a hair late and it should, you don't, we've done this for years and years, talked about this and time and things like that and it's good, it's down now. It will have to get back up, but we work so, have to figure some way out so we can have a rest and all this in order to do, get this back up again. It's real nice, it was nice last night for awhile.

RJG: *Do you have plans to spend more time in one place?*

JL: Well, I have to try and figure out plans to do this if we can, which would have to be New York because Percy and Connie and Milt, they're married and children and I'm not, but at least I have, I hope, sense enough, to realize why they must stay home with these wives and these families, they just can't stay out here like this all the time. Some things they have to do, but they'll just have to be patient and we'll have to figure out some way to do it. But I know they have to stay home cause that's very hard on the wife and the children.

RJG: *Do you think that, what is your reaction when people have the reaction that there's too much discipline in this group?*

JL: What can I say about that? There's not that much discipline in here in the first place. There's probably more. Miles is just as demanding or more demanding, but you never hear about this. You only hear about this through us 'cause you see it up there on the stand. But playing piano with Miles, boy the piano player is in for trouble, all, everybody is, he's extremely hard to deal with. Oh, Mingus for instance, that's, no, no we really don't have much discipline at all. Superficial things or something like that.

RJG: *They see you . . .*

JL: Maybe so and it just looks disciplined.

RJG: *The continuity of the group, you're back again the next season and so forth . . .*

JL: Yes, that's right.

RJG: *They get to think about it.*

JL: Yes.

Milt Jackson
1959

■

J ohn Lewis may have served as "musical director" of the Modern Jazz Quartet, but vibraphonist Milt Jackson was the star soloist. His achievement was all the more notable given his choice of instrument: the vibraphone, a motor-driven tuned percussion contraption virtually unknown outside the jazz scene. The vibraphone features metal bars laid out like a piano keyboard, and each bar is attached to a resonator tube incorporating a rotating metal disk that imparts a tremulous vibrato sound to the notes. Jackson didn't introduce this instrument to the jazz world, but he did more than anyone to legitimize it as a suitable instrument for modern jazz.

Jackson first came to the attention of jazz fans as a member of Dizzy Gillespie's band in the late 1940s. Jackson also performed with Charlie Parker, Thelonious Monk, and other progressive players before settling in for a long stint with the Modern Jazz Quartet. The MJQ not only captivated listeners with its sophisticated combo jazz, but also created a different ambiance for the music. At the outset, the Quartet set out to prove that improvised music could be played in tuxedos on the stages of the world's leading concert halls without losing the effervescence and swing that has always been a calling card of the jazz idiom.

Much of that swing came from Jackson, a compelling soloist with a soulful, bluesy style that contrasted nicely with the chamber jazz complexity of John Lewis's compositions. Jackson also entered into a number of fruitful collaborations outside of the Modern Jazz Quartet, and his legacy includes seminal recordings with John Coltrane, Thelonious Monk, Wes Montgomery, Oscar Peterson, and Ray Charles, among others.

At the time of this interview, Jackson had spent almost a decade on the road with the Modern Jazz Quartet, and had recently recorded a side project with John Coltrane, released in 1961 as *Bags and Trane*.

■

RJG: *How many instruments do you play, Milt?*

MJ: Well, at one time it came to five: vibraharp, piano, bass, drums, and guitar. It's strange that I should mention guitar last because actually that's the first instrument I ever had in my hands. I played guitar from the time I was seven, vibes was last actually, and when I was about 11 I started taking private piano lessons which only lasted two years, and then all through grade school and high school I had a very strong music curriculum which led to practically everything, where I actually played most of the instruments at one time. I would play small violin also. I played that in the symphony orchestra and also played tympanies and drums in the symphonic band and drums in the marching band. I was playing guitar and marimbas in the dance band. It was just quite an active thing.

RJG: *How did you happen to decide to concentrate on the vibes?*

MJ: Well, this came about through school also. When I was in my drum class they had bought a new vibraphone for the school during this year and my teacher suggested why didn't I try this instrument to see how I liked it. And so I started fooling around with it and I liked it and became interested in it, so I switched from the xylophone and marimba to playing the vibes.

RJG: *Have you ever regretted it?*

MJ: No. Basically I had sort of an idea in the back of my mind I wanted to do something other than play trumpet or saxophone. Out of all the music students you get in school, the majority of 'em, the first thing they want to play, well especially back in those days, the swing era, everybody either wanted to be a saxophone player or a trumpet player and I had my mind set on doing something else, something different. At this particular time there were only two vibraharp players that I had even heard of. That was Lionel

Hampton and Red Norvo. I never heard of no other musicians playing vibes whatsoever. Kenny Clarke played, you know, back in 1936 and '37, along in there, but no, very few people actually do this. Plus he never built up a name as a vibraphonist or anything, it was just as a percussion man more or less. He didn't follow it up or anything.

RJG: *Would you think of either of them as having been an influence on you?*

MJ: Well, Lionel Hampton was my influence, naturally because he was the only one. But actually that was only a fascination for the instrument itself. I never had a desire to play like him at all, it never even entered my mind. But just the thought of playing that instrument was very fascinating in itself. And as I progressed along with it I adapted the idea of playing it like an instrument, like a saxophone, a trumpet, or a horn, as they say.

RJG: *Have you continued to work out problems on the instrument?*

MJ: Oh yes, there are always problems. I've always been like this. I've always had a conception about this, about life in general, that you could always learn something.

RJG: *It must have been quite an opportunity for you then to have gone to New York with Dizzy.*

MJ: Most definitely, that's one of the greatest opportunities I've ever had in my life. We used to have jam sessions at a place in Detroit. It was called the Bizerti Bar and Dizzy came through, I think he had just left Billy Eckstine. This was 1944 and he was getting ready to form a group and he came in this night when we were jamming. And I always played, even with the piano, the two-fingered style. I took up the instrument and I would more or less develop that type of style on the piano as well, and he heard this and he had never heard nothing like that before so he was fascinated by it and he mentioned why didn't I come to New York because the opportunity would be much greater in all ways and I had just about decided to leave Detroit anyway. So in the spring of '44 I had just come home from the army actually and I was working on the job with Sonny Stitt. He was also in Billy Eckstine's band, he had just left, and we both got a local gig up in a little town, Flint, Michigan, and he was getting ready to come to New York and he talked me into the idea. So I waited till the early part of '45 and I just packed my things and off to New York I went.

RJG: *It's interesting how Dizzy has figured in the lives of all of you in the group.*

MJ: Yes, it is, it is a very prominent thing. That's a fact John sometimes emphasizes in the clubs we play. One of the sets we play what we call a group of three by the most influential or prominent musicians of the progressive era, Dizzy, Bird, and Monk. And we usually play a piece of Bird's called "Confirmation" and then we'll play Monk's "Round Midnight" and end up with Dizzy's "Night in Tunisia," or "Woody 'n You," one of those tunes, and the purpose of this is to just play music of this thing and to show the relationship or the close connection because at this time in the early '40s Dizzy, Bird, and Monk and Kenny Clarke, that's where the whole progressive idea started, you know, as a mass movement.

RJG: *You were with Dizzy at several different times?*

MJ: Yes, I was with Dizzy from '45 up until '47, just before they got ready to go to Europe, then I left and I went back again in '51, latter part of '50, actually. I joined Woody Herman's band in 1949, took Terry Gibbs' place.

RJG: *Woody Herman says you know more ballads than anybody in the world.*

MJ: Well I don't know about that . . .

RJG: *How did you acquire such a reservoir of tunes?*

MJ: Well, the best way to describe it is—actually the only thing I can attribute that fact to is having perfect pitch. From the time I was in my early teens, I could just hear a song played once by anybody and I could go to the piano and just sit down and automatically play it the next time and so he always would make a big thing of this, he'd say, "You know some tunes that I played when I was a kid and I can't understand how you know them."

RJG: *What was the first band you heard listening to the radio?*

MJ: I heard bands like Duke's band and McKinney's Cotton Pickers when I go back that far. But I guess I was just always interested in music. I remember Eddie South, used to play from a place called the Chocolate Bar every night and I'll never forget it, his theme song he used to play, "Solitude." Every night there's nothing could tear me away from the radio, until he came on and went off again.

RJG: *And you always wanted to be a musician?*

MJ: Yes. From the time I was seven there was never any question about what I was going to be, it was just a question of how I was going to apply it as a writer, or as an arranger, or just a musician.

RJG: *What's the most fun for you now, writing, playing . . .*

MJ: I still get more fun out of playing, but actually that's because my writing was limited because I didn't do a lot of studying in that line. Most of the writing that I do now I've just acquired, through my own efforts, plus what I've learned from John. I've learned a tremendous amount of knowledge just being around him.

RJG: *What have been your biggest kicks in music so far?*

MJ: The first biggest kick was playing with Dizzy and Bird in 1945, which I mentioned before. I joined Dizzy in '45, around October, and in New York there's where I met Ray Brown, and three weeks later lo and behold, Ray, myself, and Charlie Rouse went down with Dizzy on a gig in Washington. And we left and in December of that year we came out here. First time I ever came to California. We went to Billy Berg's, we had eight weeks and Bird was just so fascinating I would turn around on the bandstand, I'd be completely oblivious to the people. I was just listening to Bird play and one night we played "Round Midnight" and, oh man, it was so moving I was just standing there and the tears . . . and everybody looked at me funny, what the heck is wrong with him, but then they'd know I was just so deeply moved listening to this man play there was just no other reaction I could get. That's actually definitely among the most memorable occasions that I've ever had. We were going to record "Round Midnight," by the way. Let me tell you a little story about that. We were going to make this recording for Ross Russell and Bird was out in the valley someplace, we couldn't even find him, and we tried to persuade Dizzy to put the date off for a day or something till we could find him 'cause I just couldn't conceive playing that record without Bird. And strangely enough we never did find him in time to make it so we just had to go ahead and make this side. That's the side we cut with Lucky [Thompson], myself, and Dizzy on it. I was heartbroken, man, I brooded about that for I guess the next two weeks, the fact Bird wasn't there to make . . . but it was just one of those things. This engagement lasted eight weeks and another funny thing happened, the audience didn't understand at all, they didn't know nothing about this at all, plus they didn't care. They had several acts, they had our group and Harry the Hipster [Gibson] and Slim Gaillard. Now Harry the Hipster and Dizzy's group were more or less like the feature groups, and Slim had a trio more or less like the intermission group. And do you know that it wound up Slim Gaillard became the top attraction in the place because the people went wild over that vocabulary of his and they wound up being the headline attraction. Nobody ever understood what Bird or Dizzy were doing, but I didn't care so long as I heard. It was something else.

Another, I think one of my next best memorable occasions was in the band we had in 1947. We had musicians like Cecil Payne, John Brown, Howard Johnson, Joe Gayles—this was the saxophone section—and I believe we had Dave Burns, Elmon Wright, Raymond Orr, and Matthew McKay, I think, on trumpets. You can check that, I might have one or two wrong on that, but I think that was it. And William Shepherd, he played a little trombone with Louis here a while back, and Taswell [Baird], he played with several bands, Billy Eckstine, I think, and Earl Hines. But the rhythm section, this was something else. It was John, Ray Brown, and Joe Harris. Joe Harris, he used to play with Quincy's band and we used to play an arrangement and in the last chorus, it was just a two-bar break coming out of the middle part of it, out of the channel that Joe Harris had, and I never heard nobody could play something so fascinating inside of two bars, and I used to just turn around in my seat at night and listen for this. Another occasion was in '46. He had played with us one time and left and came back again. I will never forget when he took Kenny Clarke's place in 1946. We were playing at the Riviera in Saint Louis and we were playing at this nightclub and he come in the band. He had never heard us with the band and the first tune that he played it was unbelievable. But he had heard it, we had the same arrangement that Billy Eckstine had and he had heard it, I guess. Oh, man this was really an unforgettable experience and the band was beautiful. It was the kind of band which you know doesn't even exist anymore nowadays. Everybody's too conscious about the money and the financial and the business end, which naturally is understandable, but this is one of the only groups I'd ever seen or been around in my life where the daytime was just a restless thing. They couldn't wait to get to work at night. Ten o'clock at night would be just such a happy occasion because everybody just couldn't wait to get to work at night, and from the time of the first note to the last set there were just all kinds of fascinating things going on. It was just an enjoyable thing itself—got a lot to do with things, when you're playing with a bunch of musicians you really like.

RJG: *It even comes through on those records and they're not very well recorded technically at all.*

MJ: That feeling is there, yes it is.

RJG: *Milt, do you find any restrictions inherent in working in the Quartet as opposed to working in a big band, or working with music that is less arranged or less predetermined?*

MJ: Well, no, it's about the same restriction as, say, a big band because you would be limited. But the restriction in this case, as far as the group is concerned, is due to the disciplinary form, this is a good way to put it, that the group has overall. Well, there might be a slight restriction. But actually only to a degree because what happens, it finally works out to where we have such an extensive variety until that eliminated 90 percent of the restriction that exists. Only every now and then I'll feel like I would just like to break, or get loose, say just play a relaxed tune, just play till you get tired of playing or something like that. But what happens is that in this case you learn to adjust and I guess that's the way it worked out, I just learned to adjust myself or adapt myself to whatever the situation is and you just go from there.

RJG: *Well, actually there's a great deal more variety in what you do than is apparent superficially, because the tunes change from year to year.*

MJ: Yes, there is, so that's what I'm saying. It has broken down to where now there's very little restriction actually at all. I've always had for my best asset the instrument itself. I guess that's why I have always stressed so much emphasis on playing ballads, those slow pieces. But we get a chance to play quite a number of ballads so this makes it work out very well.

RJG: *Have your travels with the Quartet around various parts of the world led you to any thoughts about the importance of jazz in the whole world?*

MJ: Yes, in traveling all throughout this country and all of the European continent, you get to learn quite a bit about the feelings of different people and their ideas. They have a very strong musical sense in Europe, which I'm sure you know. And it makes it interesting. This is only my personal conception, but jazz has become a big thing and it's becoming bigger, plus progressive jazz is here to stay. And you know, that was in doubt because they didn't know what Dizzy and Bird were doing but now a lot of people understand what it's about.

RJG: *Well, it's getting better all the time.*

MJ: It's getting better all the time, but do you know that even in a city as big as New York there's only one jazz show, actually, of any prominence and that's Symphony Sid's Show. I used to get Sid's program out here in Dallas, Texas, I was playing with Woody then and we could get the program. And that's what we need.

RJG: *There seems to be more and more interest in it and maybe it's a reflection of the interest people see in Europe in jazz. There's more*

serious interest in jazz in this country than there ever has been
before. This seems to me to be shown every day in all kinds of ways.
Your existence as a Quartet, for instance, is an example.

MJ: Yes, it has brought about many things, which is very good. First of
all the discipline of the group and the dress of the group and that
kind of thing and the form . . . well a policy, I guess you could
call it, was formed which goes on from the time we get on the
bandstand . . . it's a matter of presentation all the way which you
know, you have seen it, and it has become a very important thing
and eventually we gain reputations from it as being one of the
best-dressed groups or one of the most disciplined groups. Guido
[Banducci] at the Black Hawk, he made this remark himself. He
said this was the first group he ever had come to his nightclub
that he didn't have to worry about—like if you have a 40-minute
set and 20 off, that he didn't have to go out halfway up the block
somewhere and find the musicians, and he made this like a real
big thing because it was such a shock I guess, such a surprise to
find a group of musicians who thought this way and felt this way.
He couldn't get over it.

RJG: *Well that underlines one of the great roles that the MJQ has played*
outside of playing music, that the group has been an inspiration
and a model for other groups.

MJ: Yeah, because now most all of the small groups are trying to have
more uniformity, within the group, make everything compact
and rather than a bunch of musicians who get up and just blow.
This is only from a commercial point of view, because you have
to take into consideration the public, man, or one part of the
general public. You know they don't know anything about music
except what they hear and all they go by is what they hear and see
and if it pleases them, then they're satisfied. But if you make it too
complicated they're not. The people, if they're going someplace,
specially where they got to spend some money or something to

see or hear a group, they must feel like they're being given something, you have to make them feel that, whether you actually are or not, you have to create this impression. You see, a lot of musicians don't want to resort to commercial things because commercial to them means that you got to simplify your music so much, to such a degree until a lot of 'em feel that they don't want to do this. But you really don't.

RJG: *You have shown that with tunes of yours which have become very popular.*

MJ: We try and maintain enough variety where we can get to the audience.

RJG: *How do you go about writing a tune?*

MJ: Well, my method is much different from John. John will sit down, he's so methodical with his, he'll sit down and figure it out and plan it out and then write it. I will just sit down and as it comes to me I'll write it. What I do is maybe play it or tape it and then just sit down and write it, you know, because that's my way of making it as relaxed as possible.

RJG: *Do you find it easy to write?*

MJ: In the musical sense but not in the technical sense, because in the technical sense, I'm very limited. It would take me hours to sit down and write a simple melody but that's because my technical facility was limited because when I should have been studying harmony and theory and all that I stopped and just started making money, started making gigs. I said well, as long as I can make a gig a month, I'll forget about all of this, which I realized later on that I shouldn't have done. But you can't regret something once you've done it, you just can't go back. But I've been very fortunate like I say, because through John I've been able to make up for a lot of it that I would have to go to school and study for, and have been able to learn anyway. So that keeps it from being so much of a handicap.

RJG: *Do you have any particular plans that you look forward to?*

MJ: No, not actually, except as long as the group is going like it is, I have no definite plans except one or two things. I would like to extend my writing. What I want to do eventually is write a suite, something like that, my own type, but other than that I don't have any real definite plans. I have an album coming out that I made with strings and if we get it out on the market soon I think I'll have the distinction of being the first vibraharpist to make an album with strings. It came out very beautiful. Quincy Jones, you know Jones, wrote some fantastic arrangements for these pieces, and the album should be out within the next couple of months.

RJG: *On Atlantic?*

MJ: Yes. And I look forward to that because, for my own personal conception, I think it was one of my best efforts. Everybody was happy. One of the fellows in the string section, we were playing, I forget what tune it was, I think it was "Nuance," and he was so wrapped up in listening he forgot to come in, so we had to stop the track and do it all over again.

RJG: *Did you ever do that listening to Bird?*

MJ: Yes, at Billy Berg's, when we were out there. He was playing "Hot House" and usually I would follow Bird in playing solo spot improvisation. He played so much that night I just forgot about what I was supposed to play. In fact I didn't even want to play, 'cause he played so much that was so fantastic the way it came out, really nothing for me to play, so I just stood there like an idiot and Dizzy looked up at me, "C'mon, man, this is your turn," and I didn't even want to play, because Bird had the capacity to do that kinda thing. He could, once he got to you, he could just captivate you completely. I regret all the people, especially young musicians, that never got a chance to see or hear Bird because they missed one of the greatest things they'll have ever heard and I think I was very fortunate in being able to be in that company of people like that because you could learn so much.

RJG: *We're lucky that we have so much available of him on records.*

MJ: Yes, and there's some things that he's done, some masters, I'm going to try to collect all I possibly can, and also Lester Young, that was a very influential man also. He could do more with one note than any musician I've ever heard in my life for just getting a feeling of soul, as they say. He was fascinating, which proves that you don't have to play a whole lotta notes or whole lot of articulation and things to get a story across. You can make it as simple as possible and still get it across, which is very important because that's the object. If you don't get it across then the people don't feel that you're doing anything. Because it's of overall importance that you reach the people.

RJG: *Do you find any problem ever when it comes your turn to play?*

MJ: No, but I guess, Ralph, that's due to the outlook I've always had. I always try the best I can all the time because for instance you never know who's out there or who's listening or watching. And we have some of the younger musicians that have an idea about this which I think is wrong. Some musicians they feel they can be consistent, say tonight, tomorrow they have that don't care feeling and don't try to play and to me I feel this is wrong because I feel that you should always try. But I feel that you can overcome this to a consistency if you really work at it.

RJG: *Where you reach a professional level, where you always are at least here.*

MJ: Right. That's an exact way of putting it.

RJG: *That's the mark of a professional, isn't it?*

MJ: Well, yes, I guess you could say that because a good professional musician or a good professional anything is always striving to do better.

RJG: *But he's always competent.*

MJ: Yes. That's what you have to strive for first and once you can attain this consistent competence then you can work towards trying to elevate that and become better at it, because I'm always thinking towards improving at all times. Most of the time you can improve because there's always that possibility, nothing is actually impossible.

RJG: *You're going to scare a lot of vibraphone players to death if you improve, you're giving them enough trouble now. About the vibrato, is that a pronounced mark of your style?*

MJ: Yes.

RJG: *How did you come to the particular feeling you have towards that?*

MJ: This comes about from me having a desire one day to be a singer and in singing I found out the slower you have the vibrato, and this applies to singers and instrumentalists as well, that if you slow it down it has much more feeling to it than, say, the mechanical sound of the vibraharp or a trumpet player with one of those fast vibratos. Now for example, say in this case of Charlie

Shavers, not to take anything away from him as a musician, he's a very great trumpet player and all, but I don't particularly like the vibrato he has because it's too fast. If it were slower he'd have a much more different feeling, you know, and I found out you can create different types of feelings by doing this. And now in playing the instrument I was lucky because the first instrument I ever had, my father bought me, it was an old jinko, very small. In fact a lot of the musicians that knew me then they called me Ironing Board, "Here comes Bags with that Ironing Board Set," you know. And it had a speed control. Well, that's how I actually came upon it, you know. And then I'd be listening to Red Norvo for a long time and he doesn't use it at all. And then when George Shearing first started having vibraphone players with him they didn't use it. He don't allow it, that's one of the reasons why I didn't go with him. I had a chance to go with that first group of his and he didn't like the vibrato on the vibraharp, and to me the instrument is completely lost without it so I said, well, no, I couldn't do this because I would never have a feeling to play it, you know, because it would always be something left out and I couldn't really get into it.

RJG: *Does it make it more like a human expression for you?*

MJ: Yes, it does. In the case of playing a ballad now, like I hit a note and the feel, the pulsation of the thing going around like that and going around at this slow speed, it still creates its own feeling, whereas if it were faster or too fast it wouldn't do this at all.

Percy Heath

■

Bassist Percy Heath grew up in one of the most esteemed musical families in modern jazz. His two younger brothers—saxophonist Jimmy Heath and drummer Albert "Tootie" Heath—also became jazz stars. His nephew Mtume, a well-known percussionist, has worked with Miles Davis and written songs for R. Kelly, Mary J. Blige, and others. But Percy had the most impressive gig of them all—a stint with the Modern Jazz Quartet that began in 1952 and continued, with a few interruptions, until the combo disbanded in 1997. For the record, that invites comparisons with the 45-year tenure (1964–2009) of the Guarneri String Quartet.

"The music was so good for so long," Heath later told critic Mike Zwerin. "I remember standing there between Milt Jackson and John Lewis and wondering if I should really be getting paid for having this much fun." But life as a member of the MJQ also brought its challenges. As Heath recounted in his conversation with Ralph Gleason, the constant touring took a toll: "My wife has been sitting there waiting for me to come home for 10 or 12 years now." The intricate compositions of the MJQ's musical director, John Lewis, added to the challenges of the job. The group was constantly adding new material or preparing for the next album—more than 100 recordings testify to the range of the band's work. Finally Heath had the additional responsibility of serving as paymaster and bill collector for the Modern Jazz Quartet. This may seem like a small matter, but in the case of the MJQ, this was akin to serving as chief financial officer of a business operating in 30 different countries.

But Percy Heath's legacy went beyond his contributions to this world-famous band. During World War II he was a member of the Tuskegee Airmen. In the postwar years, he worked with all the leading lights of the bebop movement (including Dizzy Gillespie, Charlie Parker, and Thelonious Monk). Late in life, he helped launch another premier jazz combo, The Heath Brothers, which found him working alongside his talented siblings. But he didn't record his first album under his own name until the age of 79—this belated debut was released in 2003 as *A Love Song*. Heath died two years later, the last surviving original member of the Modern Jazz Quartet.

■

RJG: *One of the things that has always intrigued me about Percy Heath is the fact that you have got such a family of musicians. Are your mother and father musicians, too?*

PH: My father was a military band clarinetist. My mother, she's always been a singer in the church choir, and her mother was a choir member, and I remember way back when I was maybe 10 or 12 years old we used to have a little quartet in this little Baptist church in Philadelphia. And I think I was singing baritone part or tenor part or something, but we had a little quartet called the Family Four and we used to sing in the church there. So she's always had that musical sense and then Pop used to play with the Elks, and you speak of musical background, I guess that's about it in the family. But strangely enough the three boys in the family turned out to be professional musicians.

RJG: *That's very special.*

PH: Well, I don't know, in the way it happened it just seemed natural, in our family, 'cause we've always had music around, even, I remember, back to the old wind-up Victrola days.

RJG: *Did they encourage you at all?*

PH: Well, early in life I had to play a little fiddle—violin. I studied quite a while and finally had to give it up, being named Percy and being very thin in stature and carrying this fiddle I used to get in a little difficulty so I finally gave it up when I finished junior high school.

RJG: *Were you interested in jazz then?*

PH: I've always been interested in jazz, but not as a player. See, during this time when I didn't play anything I was singing for a kiddie hour in Philadelphia. This was, well, '38, '37, round in there. Used to sing every Sunday on this Parisian Tailor Kiddie Hour. Then my voice changed and I stopped. I got to know all the bandleaders at that time and different people in the band 'cause this thing was connected with the old Lincoln Theater in Philadelphia and if you made the program on Friday you got a pass to go to the show and you could go backstage. I must have been around 15 years old and I met Fats Waller and Louis Armstrong, all the bands, Lucky Millinder, Fletcher Henderson.

RJG: *Did you want to be a musician then?*

PH: I didn't want to play that fiddle, that was the thing. I think that was the wrong instrument to entice me to play, especially in jazz, which I really liked. But I was exposed to all the bands that ever came there in the Lincoln Theater at that time and I enjoyed it and I used to dance quite a bit. Then it got so that I would no longer dance and I would always end up in front looking at the band, and listening to the guys play.

RJG: *Then when did you take up the bass?*

PH: It was about 10, 11 years later, after I came out of the service. I don't really know how it happened, Ralph. Before going into the service I had been an automobile mechanic and a railroad roundhouse worker. I'd done several different things. And the brother next to me, Jimmy, was playing at that time professionally when I came home from the service. And I was listening to some records there at home and I heard John Simmons play with Coleman Hawkins on a record, Commodore record, big 12-inch record, and he had a way of dropping his beats. Anyway it was intriguing, and I said I think I'll play a bass. And Jimmy was working with a band called Nat Towle's at that time, out in Omaha. He was playing alto and when he heard that I had come home and I was going to buy this bass he said he was going to quit and come home and find out about Charlie Parker 'cause he had heard Charlie Parker—up until that time I think his man was Eddie Vinson and some other man out here who plays alto and trumpet as well.

RJG: *Benny Carter.*

PH: Benny Carter, Benny Carter, and he had liked Johnny Hodges, too. But then he heard Bird and he was going to come home and get his indoctrination into the modern thing and at the same time he was going to teach me what he knew musically for playing the bass. So I used some of my pay, the pay you get when you get out of the . . .

RJG: *Severance pay.*

PH: . . . yeah, separation, severance, whatever it is. I used that to buy a bass and started taking some lessons round Philly at a school, Granoff School of Music, old man there named Quintelli who could really play, very old, and I started going up there two, three times a week.

RJG: *And you were pretty serious-minded to start out with?*

PH: I used to practice, 18, 20 hours a day. As long as I was awake I'd be practicing. We bought, Jimmy and I, bought this old upright piano and he was busy learning voicings on the piano and stealing chords off of Dizzy Gillespie records, things like that. He had a big band at that time and he had taken several arrangements off the record and put 'em in the book. He's a very good musician that way, and in the meantime I was learning just chords, playing that way. Anyhow, I was studying from this book and going up there to learn the technical playing of the bass, but we had quite a time. My mother would say, "Now stop and come eat," and then about 11 o'clock at night she'd say "Alright, it's time to stop. The neighbors may call." But I remember her for the first two, three years we always had a set of drums in the middle of the living room floor, it was just a mess. She put up with it even though she didn't play.

RJG: *When you first starting playing professionally you stayed in Philadelphia?*

PH: I think I played my first gig with Red Garland, I'm not sure, one of our first anyhow, it was a non-union place in Philadelphia and let's see, it must have been about '46, late '46. I bought this bass in June of '46, something like that, and later in that summer I had this little non-union gig with Red Garland and a trumpet player. But I remember when Red Garland did come to Philadelphia he was singing and playing "Billie's Bounce" and "Now's the Time" and we hadn't heard those things, and he was sort of an authority on Charlie Parker tunes at that time. But there were an awful lot of promising musicians around Philadelphia. I really started with a trio. At that time we used to play in little cocktail bars and there was a hotel there, the Philadelphia Chesterfield Hotel, they had a lounge. We played in there quite a bit and then we'd go around to Wilmington, Delaware, and play some club down there. We had sort of a King Cole–ish trio thing going and the guitar player also sang blues-type tunes. We had a little harmony going and it was very nice and I got to learn tunes, mostly vocal tunes, but we had a few instrumentals and I was just learning anyhow, so it was good for me. Then it got so that I knew I didn't really start playing to play that sort of thing, so it got kind of boring and the guys didn't want to spend the time to advance. I think they were satisfied doing that type of thing.

Percy Heath

RJG: *When did you start moving out past local gigs in Philadelphia?*

PH: After I left this Hollis-Hopper group, Bill Hollis, Harry Clafter—I think Harry Clafter's made some records since then as a blues singer 'cause he was very good—so it happened that I had an opportunity to get a job in the old Down Beat in Philly in the house band. I used to go up there every night—Jimmy Gold and another little tenor player 'round Philly named Jimmy Oliver, Charlie Rouse, Red Rodney was working there too, and Dizzy had worked there during the war. This was about a year after I had started playing and I used to back up these stars from New York, they used to come over there, Howard McGhee and Fats [Navarro] and Eddie Davis, oh, a lot of people used to come in and just work with the rhythm section there. So among these people was McGhee, and Howard said, "Well, I'm going to get a band together and I'm gonna send for you and your little brother"—'cause Jimmy had a 16-piece band around Philadelphia, mentioned that before—and oh, it was a big thrill. Bird came over and sat in with Jimmy's band on a gig. We were doing a sort of benefit thing in a place called the Olympic or Elite Ballroom in Philly and we got pictures of it, Bird playing in front of Jimmy's band and Jimmy was leading the band and all that. Oh, it's a terrific picture—tell you who was in that band at that time, Coltrane was playing alto, Benny Golson was playing one of the tenors. There's another tenor player around Philly named Sax Young who never left Philly, he got married and started having children and he never did leave Philly, but he was a fantastic tenor player, you may never hear of him. There's a trumpet player there who went with Gene Ammons for a while, Cal Massey, think he's doing a lot of arranging now, too. Johnny Lynch, he played in the band awhile in between gigs with Dizzy. And Nelson was in that band, Nelson Boyd, 'cause I didn't know enough at that time to play the book, and Specs Wright the drummer, he was with Dizzy later, and Henry Gates, piano player, he was in Jimmy's band. And a lot of those people continued and became stars. Willie Dennis, trombone player, he was there. Can't think of 'em all.

RJG: *When did you join Dizzy?*

PH: I went with Dizzy—it was really in 1950. See, Jimmy broke up that band, Philadelphia couldn't support the band see, it really didn't get enough work at all to even think about holding the guys together, and then these guys started leaving, going to Dizzy's band, and Gates went and Nelson and finally Jimmy himself went to one of the big bands. Now, when I went with Dizzy it was after he broke up that last big band he had and he got a combo. But in the meantime this thing with Howard McGhee had materialized so that was the first name band I went out on the road with. This was in December '47, we went to Chicago and we did six weeks there and I think we got paid for two. We made a triple record there, we stayed up all night, oh, it was fantastic hours in Chicago. This was before the five-day week there and we had matinee on Sunday. We had to stay on the South Side of Chicago, they had this prejudice deal and we had to live way out south, it took about an hour, an hour and a half to ride to work on the El, the subway thing. Actually we'd leave the hotel before dark and get back at dawn, you know, and then we'd have this matinee. So anyway, we'd squeeze these record dates in and we never got paid for those, but I've heard the records since. It seems that this company we made it for filed bankruptcy or something before they paid us and somebody else bought the master and put it out and they didn't have to pay us. I don't know, it's another case of that double union business, you know, and they really couldn't do anything about it. But anyhow we never got paid for that and we got paid for two weeks of the five weeks we worked 'cause these gangsters that owned the club, why they just gave out bad checks. And one of those guys used to wave this .45 around alright. He say, "Nobody mess with Little Birdy." They used to call Jimmy "Little Birdy" at that time. He say, "Nobody mess with Little Birdy, they answer to me." And he'd wave this .45 around and it was a real scene. Anyhow it was my initial road trip in the big time. So this went on, this thing with McGhee went on for oh, until '48, '49. In the meantime Jimmy and I were still with the band, we went to Paris and played at this festival, it was just a week work and a week laying around over there having a good time in Paris. And we came back and, well, McGhee never worked too regularly and I moved to New York. We didn't work regularly enough to stay there. New York is rough, that's a rough town, and at that time I got some gigs with Fats, who was living with McGhee at that time. Milt was with that band—you know, I been working with Milt since I started just about, he was with Howard at that time and so between Howard McGhee gigs we'd have some Milt Jackson gigs and Fats Navarro gigs and this kept on until '49, or '48. Once there was this record date that How-ard McGhee had with Fats Navarro and Miles and Curly Russell made the date. I was with the band at that time and Alfred Lion, who has since become a very good friend of mine, had never heard of me so he just wouldn't give me the date, you know, it had to be Curly 'cause Curly was his man, so Howard couldn't get me on the record date. That was finally what drove me back to Philly, we had no gigs and I was depending on this date to hold us over awhile and it didn't happen. I had to go back to Philly and live and I managed to get a job in the Down Beat for the group minus McGhee, with Cal Massey playing trumpet. That's one gig I always tell Milt about, say, "Remember when I was the bandleader." Nat Segal was the owner then and I knew him from having the job there before so I got the band the gig. It was not a bad little sextet and this sorta thing kept on until '49. I was work-ing with Philly Joe Jones in a real joint in Philadelphia, place called the Ridge Point, has a bandstand in the center, the bar up against the ceiling, you know. Anyhow, I developed pneumonia there. I'd get wringing wet, you know, and then I'd go stand out-side to cool off and I finally ended up with pneumonia. As soon as I was able to come out of the hospital I moved over to New

York. This was in '49 and I started working with Miles on some things, Miles and Sonny Rollins. I moved right in the neighborhood up there, St. Nicholas Avenue where Sonny Rollins was living and Arthur Taylor and Kenny Drew and Jackie McLean, all those young promising stars were living up there at the time and all of us got jobs with Miles on different occasions. Miles had just left Billy Eckstine and he was on his own more or less. This was in between the time he went with Bird, close around that time, and we used to play dances mostly, you could always manage to pick up a couple of dances a week, a couple of gigs a week in New York, maybe a record date every other week, something like that. And with my wife working, by the way I did get married in early '50, and with her working and with a few gigs we could make it. Finally I got this job with Dizzy in that same year, '50, and I must have stayed with him about a year and a half.

RJG: *When you were in Dizzy's band that was the small group, wasn't it?*

PH: Yeah, sextet.

RJG: *Milt was in that . . .*

PH: There was Milt, doubling on piano and on vibes, Jimmy and Coltrane, and Specs and then later Al, yes, Al Jones, young drummer from Philly and . . .

RJG: *John wasn't in that band, was he?*

PH: No, I never worked with John Lewis until we got a group, we worked as the Milt Jackson Quartet. But I'd seen John, I didn't know him too well. He'd been down at our house. See we were interested in music and we had the new music in the house. June, my wife, worked in a record shop in Philadelphia and we used to get all the records first, so my mother was automatically thrown in by being around the house all day hearing it, and she really

developed a fond appreciation for modern jazz, a great appreciation. In fact we'd wake up in the morning and she'd have the
records humming, Bird's things. And Pop liked it too, he really
loved Bird and he . . . I remember him telling Bird one night he
says, "Charlie," he say, "Boy I heard many an alto player in my
life. You the best alto saxophonist I ever heard in my life." It just
gassed Bird, you know, he was so warm. As soon as a band would
come to town, some members of the band, sometimes the whole
band, would come down and my mother would cook for 'em and
try to make 'em feel comfortable, and this is how I got to know
all these people. Consequently, when I did move to New York
I didn't have any difficulty about meeting people. They knew
me and they liked me and I was developing slowly, I had something, I didn't know what I was doing at all hardly, but I had an
approach or some promise or something that they appreciated,
'cause it wasn't just all friendship. So I think I met John at my
home, he came down with one of these groups of people. I think
it was probably when Jimmy was with the band and we had some
of the guys down to the house, [Al] McKibbon, all those people.
I met Ray Brown and Milt Jackson about at the same time. They
were coming through Philadelphia with that big band.

RJG: *The first time you worked with John, then, was when the Milt
Jackson Quartet started. Now that was right after Dizzy's combo
broke up.*

PH: Yeah, Dizzy went to doing some singles—he went on a Jazz at
the Philharmonic tour or something like that. And so Kenny had
come home from Europe and I was working with Milt, he'd use
me on most of his things, we'd been playing together years and he
was teaching me things about the bass 'cause he plays bass, too.
Bass, guitar, oh man, he's fantastic, man, fantastic. We've always
respected Jackson as being the best man ever on the vibraharp,
he's fantastic. Just think the way he plays now, it's a little different
and more developed, I guess, naturally over all these years, but I

could still hear this same thing, he warmed those milk bottles he had up. He didn't always use this set.

RJG: *You can hear it back in those records of Dizzy.*

PH: Yeah, and he still had this thing. He's definitely a stylist as far as that instrument is concerned and, well, we loved it way back. We started making some jobs with Milt Jackson Quartet. Then at this time John Lewis decided that he no longer wanted to build anybody else's name, he wanted to have this non . . . what you call it . . .

RJG: *Non-personal . . .*

PH: . . . non-personal-type organization and he would write the music and we would go as the Modern Jazz Quartet. But even the first Prestige record, if you'll note, it says Milt Jackson and the Modern Jazz Quartet 'cause Milt had the strongest name and they really didn't want to do anything without that strong name. We had a hard time convincing club owners, it was a big deal at first. Meantime I had to do a lot more studying and whatnot to kinda catch up, I been catching up ever since, man, it's been really hard for me that way, especially in the early part, I didn't even read very well, and here comes all this notation!

RJG: *Did you go take lessons?*

PH: Well, I studied a little while with Mingus, a few lessons with Mingus. He gave me some exercises which I've been able to use and they are good forever, as far as getting intonation and finger strength and whatnot, and fingerboard, too. I'd have to spend two or three weeks on a part and learn it. It's been hard, though, 'cause John is very sensitive. What I play is probably one grand conglomeration of just little things that struck me as being the way a bass should sound 'cause I really never had this deep musical knowledge. Only thing I play is probably something I heard or something I just feel like it should be this way. It's really not from something I know should be, so I've been handicapped that way. But now since I have been working with John I've learned why about a lot of things and changed a lot of things that were wrong and really learned a lot.

RJG: *It's always struck me as interesting that the group had such a common bond having worked for Dizzy Gillespie. Has Dizzy been an influence musically?*

PH: I can't say. We do a lot of things that we did with Dizzy and different little arrangements we still have in the repertoire, but you see at that time John was even writing some for Dizzy and I wouldn't say that Dizzy had a direct influence on the music because I'm sure that the music is all John's own music, some of which he had even written for Dizzy in that time. So I guess the only common thing is that we were associated with him and we all admire his ability.

RJG: *When you started out, after you transformed the Milt Jackson Quartet into this non-individual name, did you envision the ultimate success of the group?*

PH: From what John said, and the confidence he had in the type of music he could use this instrumentation to present, it was a pretty nice dream, it was a nice goal and I believed in it from the beginning. Well, I don't know, the success bit, I think I'm really a sorta beatnik type, I like money but I never really thought of this get rich aspect of the music business. My whole aim has been to play, and learn how to play well, and naturally I knew that with this would come some sort of financial security, the right break or whatever you call it.

RJG: *Not so much in terms of financial reward, but did you have any idea how good it could get musically?*

PH: Well, I never did have any doubts about music, I always did like John Lewis' music. It was difficult for me to play, but it was, I don't know, it was like each piece was like a lesson in music, and to make this come off the way he pictured it or intended it to when he wrote it, that was my aim, to try to get it so he'd say, "Yeah, that's what I mean there." At first people just wouldn't be quiet to listen and it was too soft, and that's where the difficulty with Kenny came up, he didn't want to play like that 'cause he could see people out there getting bored with this quiet thing and he'd want to drive it on like they wanted to, like he had been accustomed to. But this group sound that we were working for didn't include all that extra embellishment by drums and driving the band—how you gonna drive the band, you got four people up there? It's not necessary and since Connie's been with us I think it's developed more toward the sound of one thing happening up there and at the same time you can hear everything that's going on.

RJG: *I notice the number of times that you have any disturbance in the club, even to somebody laughing or carrying on a conversation, is much less frequent now than it used to be.*

PH: I don't think those people even come in. In fact, if the real whipper-snappers come to the door and we're on the stand they don't usually come in or they don't stay because it's too quiet when they step in. They look, say, "Oh, oh, we're in the wrong place."

RJG: *Percy, do you think that the whole presentation of the group, not just the music that you make, but the whole way you look on the stand, with the clothes that you wear and the way you are positioned, all contribute to discouraging the non-listening audience?*

PH: Probably does, Ralph, because it's quite different from the décor of other groups on the bandstand. You know how it used to be, they used to do a lot of things on the bandstand that we just don't do anymore, and other groups have tried to get away from drinks on the piano and send the boys a drink and all that business. I think that's a little outmoded now.

RJG: *Is all the discipline of the group restricting? Do you feel the need, for instance, to go someplace else to play music?*

PH: It might seem more restricted than it actually is. Of course, it's different, say, for instance, when Jackson, Connie, and I go out sometimes and play together. But there are a lot of things that you just can't do in order to get this group sound. More or less out jamming you get a jam sound, but then the Modern Jazz Quartet wouldn't be the Modern Jazz Quartet if we just got up there and jammed all night. So I don't think it's restricted in any way. It's just that when you say "the Modern Jazz Quartet will now play" it plays like that, that's how it sounds, and not that each person would play differently, but the fact that the whole thing is the end result is the important thing. That influence is not a restriction, I don't feel, it's just a different scene. It was more of a problem in the beginning than it is now. There's a lotta things that I still don't like and that's when I'm not on the bandstand to be shirt-ing and tie-ing it. That rubs me the wrong way, but it seems that it's necessary to be that way on and off. This is one of the things that's distasteful to me about being popular and in the public eye and all that business, it robs a person of his own individual desires, and likes and dislikes. You have to more or less do what's expected of you where if you were just nobody in particular you could do what you wanted to and it wouldn't be news if you didn't.

RJG: *Do you ever go out and sit in anyplace?*

PH: Yeah, especially in Europe, not so much in America. Well, I do it in America, too, but it's illegal. But in almost all little towns in Europe there's a jazz club or a jazz cellar or something and somebody will always come around and ask. I probably do it more than the rest of 'em 'cause I really like to go around and meet other musicians in other places and they usually have such great admiration for you as an individual, they really get such a kick out of walking down the street with you let alone go to a place to play with you, and some of these guys are very good. I have a friend in Milano who's a fantastic guitar player, he's playing bass now, it's just ridiculous, man, he can really play, Franco Cher is his name. I know people like him throughout Europe — Horst Jankowski, pianist, German boy, he's a very energetic little Horace Silver–influenced pianist, and these guys have all these records and they've heard you for years and when you do come to the little town if you don't get around with 'em, it's sort of a disheartening thing. I just like people, I guess. Almost everywhere I go I know somebody and, you know, I have some communication with people.

RJG: *Do you find that the whole role of jazz music is becoming more important throughout the world?*

PH: It's always been pretty important over there, it's just recently been realized by people here, government people, they finally have realized the tremendous affect and appreciation these people have over there for this. In fact, a lot of people say that's the only thing they like about America or Americans is their music, the rest of their policies and things are kind of accepted 'cause they have to, because they depend on these people for support.

RJG: *What is it about jazz that makes it so acceptable, so attractive to those people?*

PH: I think it's the very personal expression that's given, and it's different. You know them when you hear them, which wouldn't be true of other music. It could be such and such an orchestra playing so and so, or another orchestra playing so and so, the same thing, you couldn't sit down and say who's on cello. When I was just listening to jazz it would be a very thrilling thing to hear a good orchestra, Basie and Pres [Lester Young] and all those people would come to Philadelphia, and Erskine Hawkins had a hell of a band there, and it would just be an enjoyable evening to go stand in front of that band for two and a half hours and watch these different people perform and listen to them play. It must be very exciting to people to hear this difference, these different sounds and the different personalities expressed. It must be quite a thrilling thing and it evidently is because, for instance, in London, for three consecutive weekends we do two concerts a day completely sold out weeks ahead, three straight weekends playing to about 8,000 people a weekend. I don't know of any other place in the world we could do that, though.

RJG: *How does it come about that things that have been in your repertoire over the years have altered?*

PH: Everybody changes. Comes about in many ways, we're not machines up there. You may feel one way one night or one way another night and this is all reflected, projected in the music. And then, too, this thing going on between John and Milt is so flexible and spontaneous. Even though a lotta times I may play the same part, I may add one note, stick one in and leave one out. It keeps changing every night. Never gets dull up there, never. It just keeps changing around. The improvised parts are never the same identically, if you could tape the Modern Jazz Quartet any two or three nights of the same program and compare it, you would very readily hear that different things happen throughout the whole performance of each piece. It's never identical. It has never been and we've played 'em now five, six years nightly and it's never the same thing happening.

RJG: *I would also think that over the course of the years it would have become not only easier for everyone individually to take this music and work with it, but also easier for John to write this music in terms of the four of you.*

PH: He's gotten so that he knows exactly what we can do and what we can't do. In the beginning it was hard 'cause I was playing catch-up. The simplest thing he could write for me I'd have trouble with it, with intonation and a lot of other things and really bug him. When they decided they wanted to have this type of group, I knew John always did really dig Ray Brown, I think that's really who he probably had in mind at the time, but then I was there with Milt and Kenny and here he comes from outside and in school still and whatnot and at that time Ray Brown was with Oscar Peterson. I knew he wasn't available for any experimental group, so he just more or less settled for me, I guess, in the hope that I would eventually grow into what he liked. I guess he's gotten used to me by now. He can get real touchy sometimes but he's not so bad, not so sensitive. Sometimes things go wrong, okay, it's not enough to shake him up all evening. But then sometimes, man, I don't know, he may feel that what's done right now will mean so much and usually that's the time when things go wrong 'cause he's so bent on doing tricks and things and it's difficult, it creates too much tension and it really blows up.

RJG: *The Quartet right now seems to be in a sort of warm and relaxed period.*

PH: Last night was nice, alright. It was a pretty good night last night.

RJG: *You handle the business?*

PH: Yes, as far as getting the money and paying the bills. But Connie has the department of transportation and whatnot and finally we gonna use this corporation that we've had all these years. It's been operated on a partnership basis and I'm gonna be relieved of some of the duties. That is a pain in the neck.

RJG: *Have you ever thought much about the role that the Modern Jazz Quartet has in jazz itself?*

PH: Well, it's been a very influential group, I'm sure, in the whole scene, but I don't know, Ralph, we reach one thing and then there's always this plan for something else and then with that sorta going along there's always a plan for another thing and I'm just at this point, I'm just wondering when the pioneering will end, if ever, 'cause I would really like to relax a while, and spend more time at home and a lotta other things. The success in that respect has been greater than the financial success, 'cause we make good money and it's really nothing like people might think and I just don't see the end of the pioneering. After seven, eight years it seems that a man should be able to say, "Well, okay, I've done it. Let somebody else do it," but I don't think John will ever stop reaching for things. But I'm not that way.

RJG: *Of course it must be rewarding to go to Europe and see the position that the group enjoys.*

PH: Yes, it is, it is that way, but my wife has been sitting there waiting for me to come home for 10 or 12 years now. She's raising the boys, I'm not doing it. They got a father a third of the time and the rest of the time it's all the responsibility on her. Not that I'm not enjoying myself going these places but she's always stuck there, man, one day she may just blow up and it will be my fault. Like this trip that's coming up now, first it started off as being 6 weeks, now it sounds like it's going to be 3 months. It's too long, I've been out here a month now, I got 5 days home and then I'm gone for 3 months. What is that? It's no good. So all this is on my mind, too. So in spite of the good it's doing to go to these places and present this American thing to people, development of music and whatnot, and its cultural value and all, it's still a tremendous sacrifice on my family status, and especially on my wife, and it's just getting to be too much, too long, it should have been over by now, or either it should have been lucrative enough financially to say, "C'mon. I'll hire someone here to stay with the kids" if she wants to run to Europe and stay with me a couple of weeks or a month. Then I don't care, I'd stay over there 3 months. It's not that I don't have a good time, I meet people and go places, see Europe, everything like that, this is my life, this is what I've chosen to do. But that's a big personal problem so maybe I'll just say, "Well, get another bass player, I'm through with it," 'cause I could really stay in New York and make records and make appearances and do as well financially. I don't need a big pile of money as long as I can continue to function.

RJG: *Percy, what has been the best for you in jazz music?*

PH: I really don't know, Ralph. Every time something really happens on the bandstand, that's reward enough. I don't guess you can say what it does or anything. I think one of the most thrilling things for me was, well, of course, I was very green then and it was all new, but I still remember a band we had in Birdland for a couple of weeks in I guess it was '49—what year did Fats die?—it was '50 or so, yeah, early '50, anyhow we had a band down there, it was the last job he played on. It was Miles and Fats and Sonny Rollins, J. J. [Johnson], Art Blakey, and Bud Powell and I . . . I'll never forget that as long as I live, never will forget that. Oh, man I was getting to work hours ahead of time, getting ready. Whew, and that was something there! I remember that.

Connie Kay

MARCH 18, 1960

■

Drummer Connie Kay was a late arrival to the Modern Jazz Quartet. He didn't join the band until 1955, when he replaced departing member Kenny Clarke. Kay continued with the combo until shortly before his death in November 1994, and appears on the group's last commercial recording, *MJQ & Friends*, from 1993.

In an era of flashy, extroverted drummers, Kay took a different path. He ranks among the most musical percussionists in the history of jazz. He could mesmerize an audience with the softest of sounds: scratching his cymbals with his fingertips, or playing the side of the drums, or making music from chimes and triangles. When he used his whole drum kit to drive the band, Kay created a sweet, clean swing that was a delight to hear.

Many jazz fans would have been shocked to learn that this same understated drummer, who could play the most delicate jazz chamber music, had propelled R & B bands on various early hits for the Atlantic label. You can hear him shaking, rattling, and rolling on Big Joe Turner's "Shake Rattle and Roll," which helped pave the way for the later rock and roll revolution. He flourished as accompanist for Ray Charles, Ruth Brown, and LaVern Baker, and would be remembered today even if he had never played jazz. But even earlier Kay had served as house drummer at Minton's, the Harlem nightspot which served as incubator of the bebop movement, a place where the phrase "chamber jazz" was never uttered.

Kay famously observed that he never heard a drum solo that didn't go on too long. But he proved the exception to his own rule, making his name as the drummer that always left audiences asking for more.

■

RJG: *When did you start playing drums?*

CK: I don't know really. When I was a kid. Cab Calloway used to broadcast from the Cotton Club which was in Harlem, old Cotton Club, and my mother could never get me to go to sleep at night until I heard Cab Calloway or Duke Ellington, and my mother had a hassock in the living room and I used to get the bar out of the hangers and make drumsticks, I'd get a knife and make drumsticks, and I used to stay up at night and play along with Cab Calloway. I think he used to come on about 11:30 at night, it was late, and then if I was in bed I wouldn't sleep until Cab Calloway came on. Then when he went off that's when I would sleep, and it was just something I liked to do. Although my mother, she was a piano teacher, she taught piano, but I always wanted to play the drums. So when I got old enough to work after school my mother went to Wurlitzer and bought a set of drums for me on time, and with the money that I made working after school I paid for these drums. That's actually when I started playing the drums themselves. A neighbor of mine, his uncle I think was a drummer or something like that. Oh I must have been about 10, 11, and his uncle left his snare drum there and we used to sneak and get his snare drum out, we'd bring it over to our apartment, but I never actually played on a set of drums until I was in my teens.

RJG: *Was this in Tuckahoe?*

CK: No, this was in New York. I was born in Tuckahoe, but I never lived there except in the summer. My aunt and uncle owned a home in Tuckahoe and every summer I'd go up there and spend the summer, but I was more or less raised in New York.

I just liked that type of music and at that time that was the only chance I had to listen to it, was on the radio, was Cab Calloway. He used to come on "hi-de-hi-de-ho" and all that sort of attracted me. But I never picked out the drums to listen to the drums. I just wanted to hear this music so I could play along with him, that's all.

RJG: *Then when did you start professionally?*

CK: I'll tell you a funny thing about that. I started playing profession-ally about four days after I got my first drum set.

RJG: *You were ready.*

CK: I got these drums, it must have been a Monday or Tuesday, and I was living on the street level. I used to play and there was a night-club around the corner from my house and I knew three or four of the fellows that played in this band, and the drummer they had playing there he didn't show up to work so somebody told him, "There's a guy around the corner there that plays drums," he says, somebody told him, "Go by there and hear him practice. There's a drummer around the corner. Go around and git him." So they came around and knocked on the door and the guy says, "You want to work tonight?," and I say, "Ya," so he say, "Well I got a job for you. So-and-so didn't show up. C'mon around." So I went around there. I didn't even have to have my drums because the guy's drums were there and everything. And I just made the job. It was good experience for me 'cause it wasn't actually playing jazz, it was a show. The chorus girls and comedians, tap dancers and things like that, and funny part about it, my high hat I couldn't play two and four, I was so nervous I couldn't control the high hat. I, every time we started playing I'd played two and three on the high hat, and so finally I just gave it up and then at that time they weren't using the high hat too much anyway. Everybody was playing more or less on the ride cymbals and back-beating with the left hand and I could do that so I kept the job 'cause the guy said, "Well you keep good time and that's the most important thing." He said, "You'll get the rest of it." I was still going to high school, too. I guess I must have been around 16 or 17.

RJG: *When was that?*

CK: Oh, 1940 or something, '40, the war was on, '42, I think. But after that I started going to Minton's and jamming in Minton's with Dizzy, Bird, Bud Powell, Monk, Ray Brown, Don Byas, Duke . . .

RJG: *Did you think when your mother got you that set of drums that you were going to be a musician?*

CK: Well that's what I wanted to be. One of the reasons I wanted to be a musician was I didn't dig getting up in the daytime with the lunch pail, I didn't like that at all. I didn't like to get up in the day even to go to a school, but I had to do that. So that's one of the reasons I wanted to be a musician 'cause I was just a nightlifer, I guess.

RJG: *Did you study drums?*

CK: Not really. When I started playing by being able to play the piano a little—that's one of the reasons I didn't like the piano, getting back to that: I couldn't sight-read good on the piano. I knew all the notes. I knew where they were on the piano. But I'd always have to look at the sheet music, then look down at the piano to make sure I was playing the right note. But once I got the tune I could close the book and I could play it. I couldn't sight-read very good and that's one of the reasons why I lost interest in playing the piano. And my mother used to whack me on the finger when I played the wrong note, she whack me with the pencil or something and I didn't like it. She used to give recitals every year. I said, "Well Ma, I want to play drums. I don't want to play the piano." She says, "Well, you play on the recital this year and I'll get you a set of drums." She says, "What would it look like, the piano teacher's son not playing the piano?" So she got me. Every year I'd go for it and I never got those drums. So it took me until I was old enough to get 'em myself to get them, because my mother really, although she likes music she didn't think that a musician's life was the best life for a man. She wanted me to be, I guess like most parents, a doctor or lawyer or something.

RJG: *Do you have any brothers or sisters?*

CK: No, I'm the only child. So she always wanted a doctor or lawyer. But the funny part about it, the first job I had she was the one that let me go. My father, he was kinda skeptical about it and she was the one who said, "Alright, go ahead." I had to ask 'em. I said, "Well, this guy came around and he wants me to go round here and play. Can I make it?" And she says, "Well, see what your father says." Between the two of them, my father was the hippest, he'd been around and I guess that's one of the reasons he didn't want me to go. He said, "I don't know 'bout that." She says, "Oh, let him go make it." But I think in the long run my parents helped me quite a bit, because a lotta guys struggle in the business and my parents, once in a while they'd heckle me about getting a job, but I never had to worry about eating and sleeping. In a way, it was a good thing 'cause if I didn't have a gig I didn't have one. A few times it was a long time between jobs and they never bothered me too much about getting a job. Every now and then my mother would say, "You better go round to the post office for the Christmas rush, get you a job 'cause we're tired of feeding you."

RJG: *You were lucky.*

CK: That's right. A lot of guys didn't have it as easy as I did. I appreciate my parents for that.

RJG: *The piano helped you with the drums, though, didn't it?*

CK: My being able to know the piano, the value of notes—see, the drums all you have to know is the value of notes. Lines on the scale don't mean too much. It's the value and I know that. So that enabled me to read drum music pretty good plus I didn't have to look back to see if I was hitting the drum right. Like on the piano I had to see if I was hitting the right note, but on the drum I just had to hear the rhythm. So I bought a drum book, lessee, the first drum book I bought was Gene Krupa because he was the thing then. Boy, this Krupa drum book, how to hold the sticks and the press roll and one beat, quarter note in one beat, half a note you hit it once and count two, that sort of thing and I more or less taught myself and then there was a drum shop in New York, Bill Maters' drum shop and I went, I used to go down there and he had a fella there name Drew Scott. I think he was from Scotland, either Scotland or Ireland, and he was one of those original drumming, what is it, bagpipe men.

RJG: *Military?*

CK: I heard a few drummers say he was a good teacher. So I took some lessons from him. But I had been working for quite a while then at playing.

RJG: *Did any of the drummers that were working then, and were already established, help you?*

CK: Sid Catlett. Now here's a funny thing about him. We never actually sat down with the drumsticks and the drum pad or the drum book, but I got more out of him by sitting, just talking to him, not talking about drums, but about anything in general, but by his conversation and his feel for things in life I could see why he played the drums the way he did and I learned more from him that way about the drums than if I, I think if I just sat up and said, "Sid, show me how you do this and show me how you do that, how you do this and how you do that." We hung out together, sorta just pals. And I really got a lot out of it.

RJG: *He was a wonderful guy.*

CK: Very beautiful man. It really hurt me when he died, and the thing about it, I had two favorite musicians die and I wasn't around, Lester Young and Sid Catlett. I was out here when Lester died. I got kinda fed up with New York. Things weren't going too good and I got this job with Frank Tully, Rock and Roll, to go down South for some one-nighters for about six weeks to about two months and in that space of time that's when Pres [Lester Young] died. I think we were just coming back when I heard about it. We were in a restaurant, I heard about it on a newsreel.

RJG: *It's a funny thing, what you say about Sid is what so many drummers say about him today. He was apparently sort of a father to all the drummers who came along after him. He had a remarkable effect on everything.*

CK: I think I was pretty lucky because I don't know any other drummers he was as friendly with as he was with me and it was on a sheer chance because I had a raggedy '53 Studebaker and one night I went down to Fifty-Second Street. I used to go down there all the time and I didn't know him at all really. And places were closing up and everything and I, in fact I still had a learner's permit, I wasn't even allowed to drive the car. I had to have an adult with me to drive and there was a fella lives in the same house with me who played alto saxophone a long time ago had a band and whatnot, but he had given it up. He was really a truck driver, but he used to like to hang out and anytime I felt like taking the car somewhere I used to go to his apartment and say, "C'mon, c'mon let's go down to Fifty-Second Street, something" and he use'ta say, "Well, ok, c'mon," so that was the only way I could drive around legally. So this night we were getting ready to, the place was closing out so I said maybe Sid would like a ride. So I asked him, I said, "You going uptown, Sid? I give you a lift?" So he, his favorite word was buck, he says "Ya, buck, I'm going uptown," he said. "You gimme a lift," so at that time he was living on 138th Street right opposite across the street from the Renaissance Casino, and so on the way up we started talking so I told him I played a little drum, just like the kids tell me now, and he said, "You see that house over there?" He said, "That's where I live." He said, "Anytime, c'mon up." So from then on he couldn't get rid of me. He used to call me up sometimes, we got to be such good friends, he'd call me up and say, "Look, I got to go so and so." He said, "Would you mind taking me so and so?" And I used to come with the car and drive him to gigs and I took him, one time they made a short, they used to make these shorts with John Kirby. And I took him to make that and I even loaned him my drums one time too, when he went to Billy Rose's Diamond Horseshoe. He needed a drum so he could see how the drums would place in the show, and his drum was somewhere else. So he says, "Just lend me the drums," he says, "I just have to set 'em up on the stage so they can see what's what," and I even had his drums in my house. I thought that was the biggest thing in the world for me, to have Sid Catlett's drums in my house, and I kept his drums for him a couple of times. And we just got to be buddies, that's all.

RJG: *Did you ever see that short that Norman made,* Jammin' the Blues? *Boy, I'd like to see a print of that just to go look at it, boy that was wonderful.*

CK: Yes, it was.

RJG: *Absolutely.*

CK: I haven't seen anything like that since . . .

RJG: *Oh no, that was the only one that's been made. After you got a regular driver's license, did you go out on the road with bands then, 'cause the first time I saw you was when you were out here with Pres.*

CK: Well, the first band I ever went on the road, if you call it the road, was to Philadelphia. I went to Philadelphia. I was playing, what was it, Skippy Williams, Skippy or Pinky, Pinky Williams. We had a sort of entertaining group and I used to be singer, four-part harmony, cocktail bar things and we went to Philly to play the club they call the 421 Club. And that was the first time I actually left home to play, go anywhere for a week. I think we stayed two weeks there. Then after that I struck up a friendship with Cat Anderson 'cause he lived in the Bronx and he was playing with Duke at the time and I used to go see Duke and he used to ride home with me in my car. Duke was playing at, what was the name of that place, where the Metropole is? Oh, I can't remember it. Well, anyway, then he left Duke and he started this big band and a very good friend of mine played saxophone with him, fella named Fats Noel. He was a good tenor player. Sorta like Coleman Hawkins, Ben Webster style, great big fat guy, but he had a wonderful tone. And incidentally, he and Sonny Payne went to school at the same time. Sonny Payne lived right around the corner from me in the Bronx, and he was playing drums in high school, same thing he's doing now, did that in high school.

RJG: *That was the Bronx school of drummers as opposed to the . . .*

CK: When he went to Benjamin Franklin High School, they were in the school band together, Fats Noel was playing tenor with Cat Anderson's band and Cat Anderson broke the big band up and he started a five-piece group and there was myself, Fats Noel, Earl May, and a very good piano player named Albert Wallace. He started this group and we did a few one-nighters with Wynonie Harris and we went into the Baby Grand and he stayed there for months and all this was still in the '40s. We stayed in there for months and then Cat started up the big band again and I played with the big band. Then I left Cat and went back with Pinky for a little while, and then I left Pinky again and went back with Cat, and then after I left Cat I went with Lester.

RJG: *How long were you with . . .*

CK: With Lester? Well the first job I had with Lester was in '49, when Roy Haynes left. I took his place and then they broke the band, they had a six-piece band and they broke the band up. All the musicians weren't from New York and it was hard to get a job in New York 'cause they didn't want to pay over scale so they broke the band up. Then the agents were telling them that the guys didn't have names and whatnot so then he started working with Jo Jones and Emmett Berry and Joe Shulman and a few other people. They worked in Bop City and then after that he got the band back again and instead he got all New York local musicians and I think that was when I went back, it was in '50. I stayed from '49 to '50 and I went back in '51. I don't think it was six months in between the time. But I'll never forget when I was playing with Pres he had this manager Charles Carpenter and he's always yelling, "Whyn't you play like Jo Jones? Don't you know Jo Jones, have you ever heard Jo Jones play? Can't you play like him?" I used to get that all the time.

RJG: *You didn't get that from Pres, did you?*

CK: No. That's the funny part about Pres: Pres never had nothing to say. In fact I think he could have had better bands if he put his foot down and say what he wanted. Because he never was happy. Guess he and I got to be like that and he used to tell me, "Lady Kay," he said, "you know I can write music and things like that," he said, "but why should I?" he said. "It's a waste of time. Today I have five pieces, tomorrow I got two, next week I have three, then a guy cuts out and another guy comes in" and he never was happy with the band. People he wanted to hire their manager told them, "No, he's no good. Keep this guy, he's reliable," and so eventually he'd just come to work and play and go home. Another thing about Pres was, it was very hard to get Pres to play a ballad. We used to beg him every night. We'd say, "Pres, why don't you play so and so?" "That's too slow, Lady Kay," he says, "these people will go to sleep on you. You got to keep them awake 'cause if you play the ballads they'll go to sleep," and it was very hard to get him to play a ballad. And that's one of his greatest things that I used to love to hear him play, a ballad.

RJG: *It must have been a great experience playing for him?*

CK: I think so because I learned a lot about rhythm. He's great with rhythm. His rhythm is tremendous, he could play back so far and catch up, you think he's behind. He could do a lot of things. The guys don't know anything about that now.

RJG: *Phrasing was fantastic.*

CK: Another thing about him was he could hold one note down and get about three or four.

RJG: *Mmmm.*

CK: Where another guy have to move his fingers to get those three, from one note he could get three or four different notes. The same notes that another would have to use the keys for. He was fantastic and another thing about him he used to tell me people used to ask him, "Pres, why don't you play like you used to play?" And he say, "Well," he used to tell me, he'd say, "Lady Kay, I don't want to play the way I used to. I used to play down here, at the bottom," he'd say, "but I know how to do that now." He said, "Now I'm experimenting on the top." He'd say, "I can play like Ben Webster and Coleman Hawkins and those fellas, if I want to," and, he used to tell me, they'd say, "Why didn't I play like I was playing with Count Basie?" He said, "But that's fifteen years ago. Time marches on, you know."

RJG: *Did he ever make suggestions to you about things to do at all?*

CK: Not a thing.

RJG: *You just worked out your own way of . . .*

CK: Never told me how to play, Pres. Never did. The funny part about it is, I had met Pres before, through a friend of his who was in the army with him and he didn't know I played drums. So Jesse Drakes, who was playing trumpet with him, was a friend of mine, he went to the same school with Sonny Payne, and they, all three of 'em, went to the same high school incidentally, and Junior Mance was playing piano and a fella named Leroy Jackson and I was working this job in the Bronx with Pinky Williams and Junior and Leroy knew Pinky and they weren't working that weekend and Pinky got them to make the job. So they came up and played, and they liked the way I played. And they said, "Well, Pres is looking for a drummer 'cause Roy left the band. Whyn't you make the gig?" So I said, "Okay." So they told Pres about me, I think Carpenter, anyway he told him that they had a drummer, so Carpenter says, "Alright," so I was supposed to meet them in Penn Station to go to Philly, and Pres was standing up with his hat on, waiting, so I walked up and I said, "Hi, Pres, how you doing?" "Well," he says, "Hi, Lady Kay, what are you doing out here?" I said, "Well, what are you doing?" He said, "Well we waiting for a drummer to make the gig in Philly." So I said, "I'm the drummer," and he says, "Oh, no."

RJG: *Were you with him when you got on this job with the Quartet?*

CK: More or less 'cause he had left to go over and tour with Jazz at the Philharmonic and usually when he does those things we just laid around, waited for him to come back so while he was away, Monte [Kaye] called me up to make this job with the Quartet and I just stayed.

RJG: *Had you had any previous contact with the Quartet?*

CK: No, except on records, and I knew each one individually and I'd heard them in person and whatnot, but not a close thing.

RJG: *And you never played with them?*

CK: Never played with them before. I played with John, jamming, and Percy, Percy and I worked for a few jobs together. I remember when Milt first came to New York, we used to jam in Minton's. But I never worked on a job with them before.

RJG: *Were you surprised?*

CK: In a way, because you know why, the night before I had just seen the Quartet. They were in Birdland with Basie and they closed that night and when I got home, it must have been about five or six in the morning, the phone rings and Monte says, "I got a job for you to play with the Quartet," because I had spoken to Monte 'cause I think he was booking Sonny Stitt, I had spoken to him. I said, "Look, if you need a drummer to make that week with Sonny Stitt in Birdland, I'm available." So when he called I thought that's what he was calling me about, to make the week with Sonny Stitt. So when he tells me he has a week with the Quartet, I was very surprised, you know, to hear that because I was wondering what happened to Kenny. They said Kenny quit, but I didn't know that they wanted me to make it a permanent thing. I figured I'd just make those few one-nighters and then Kenny probably got over what was bothering him and he'd be back, or something.

RJG: *It must have been an interesting contrast to go from a group like Pres into the Modern Jazz Quartet?*

CK: Well, the only thing that was different to me was the vibraharp. I knew the vibraharp wasn't as strong an instrument as a saxophone in the sense, but the rhythm was the same so I just had to worry about that vibraharp, playing, overshadowing the vibraharp. But, and I don't feel any sort of strain or nothing, and then, too, at that time we weren't playing any educated numbers. It was "Vendome" and "Concorde" . . .

RJG: *They weren't rehearsing as much then; were you?*

CK: Well, when I first joined the Quartet I had to rehearse quite a bit so I could get all the arrangements together and whatnot, I had to be running around buying triangles, different things. I enjoy it because it's a challenge, in an ordinary band you know what you're gonna do when you get there, but with the Quartet you didn't know what they expect because it's so many different things you have to do. They sort of open, made you more like a percussionist. More than just a drummer.

RJG: *Does the disciplines of a group like the Quartet interfere with your instincts on things at all or is it an asset?*

CK: Now, it doesn't. But when I first joined I had to be kind of listen to see what was going on. I just couldn't go in there and play the way I felt because it was a different circumstance. But now it doesn't because I know exactly what each person is doing. I know more about John and what he wants. So now it doesn't bother me at all because actually what he wants is same thing I want. I want music, and it doesn't stop me at all. The thing I feel about it is that you don't have to play loud to express yourself on a drum and I don't think that playing soft stops you from expressing your feelings. You can still get the same message across. There are times when you have to play loud for effect, but just to be loud because it's a set of drums, I don't think that's necessary.

RJG: *Do you ever go somewhere and sit in just to work off steam?*

CK: I work off quite a bit of steam every night down there. There's quite a bit of steam going down there. I like to go sit in, but now for some reason, the guys that's playing now, they just don't inspire me. It was just something out of this world to sit down and play with Charlie Parker, or Dizzy or Ray Brown or Bud, but I just don't get that feeling now when I sit in with guys. Once in a while, you run into somebody that does that to you, but most of the musicians I hear just don't give me incentive to even want to play with them. I don't know whether that's bad or good or what.

RJG: *Maybe it's changes in you too.*

CK: Well, I'm getting older. You know, like Monk, Bud, and I just want to play with them. That's not a good example down at Bop City there.

RJG: *Oh no, that's lost.*

CK: You don't feel like actually playing.

RJG: *I've always been curious to know the way you have worked with the group when you come up with some surprising little touch, those curious tom-toms or any little thing that you may do here or there and stand out sharp in the course of something. Do you contribute these things, do you think of these things, are these things that John might suggest to you or is it a combination of circumstances, how does it work?*

CK: Well, John might write a tune and say, "This is supposed to sound like this." Like we have this new tune "Cylinder." He says, "Now I want this to sound like a cylinder." "Well," I said, "how does a cylinder sound?" You know he has to try and make something sound like a cylinder. So between what he thinks a cylinder sounds like and what I think a cylinder sounds like, we got something.

RJG: *As you were saying.*

CK: My first real good jazz professional job, I think, was in Minton's. I worked with Sir Charles Thompson and Miles. Now before Miles it was Leo Parker. We had a trio—piano, saxophone, and drums—and Leo Parker quit and Miles took his place. It was just a trio and at that time Miles was playing like Dizzy and I was around when Miles started getting this other deal going from a very good trumpet player named Freddie Webster. Freddie Webster used to come in all the time and Miles used to bend over on the stand and Freddie used to show him how to do these things, those kind of sounds, and that was the first real jazz job I had and I don't know what the year must have been, '44, but I was pretty lucky because I wasn't what you might call a technical genius. But what the guys liked about me was I had good rhythm and I kept good time and I never got in anybody's way, so everybody always wanted to play with me. So that's what kinda helped me.

RJG: *It was good experience for precisely the kind of spot you're in now. Has it been useful to you to have studied the piano and to think of playing drums in terms of various tonal values?*

CK: I think so, although I didn't get that far. I took piano from ages six maybe to thirteen and I really didn't get into the theory and harmony part of it. I really just took the basic piano lesson and my mother didn't teach theory, harmony, or anything. She just really taught basic piano, how to hit the notes, scales, and how to read and things like that.

Connie Kay

RJG: *How do you see the role of the drums in a Quartet such as this?*

CK: Well, in this quartet actually each person is supposed to be an in-
dividualist and he's supposed to make something happen on your
instrument individually, and it's all supposed to blend together.
So that's what I tried to do, I don't know if I do it or not but that's
what I try to do. You're supposed to be able to take, say, Milt will
stop playing, Percy stop, and John will stop, and if I still play you're
still supposed to get something out of it and if I stop and Percy plays
you're supposed to get something out of that, and if John plays and
the three of us are out, something's supposed to be there, and if
Milt plays by himself something's supposed to be there.

RJG: *It's all part of the same thing.*

CK: Yes. And with the three together, with the four together, it's one
big thing. At first it was kinda hard to get to think like that.

RJG: *I imagine it must have been.*

CK: But after a while I sorta got to it. Plus it was something that I really wanted to do anyway. You know, make music out of the drum
instead of being just a drummer so . . .

RJG: *Had you ever talked about that with any of them before?*

CK: Well, when I was playing with Lester I used to try to do it. But
it was harder then because the other guys weren't thinking like
that. But I always thought that the drums should be something,
and Percy had the same idea. He's another one, he never said
anything about it, but just like Sid Catlett, you hold conversations with him and you could see why his conversation, about
anything, what made him play the way he played and I think,
you play with somebody you have to be sympathetic with him.
You can't go up on the bandstand and say, "Well I'm so and so

· 146 ·

and this is what I want to do," a straight line and forget about everybody else that's up there. I always figured that a drummer was supposed to support the horns I think. After you get them in their happy groove, then if you have them in a happy groove then you definitely have to be in a happy groove because then the whole thing is swinging. But if you're swinging and they're not swinging, then it's sometimes not swinging, or if they're swinging and you're not swinging, it's still the same thing.

RJG: *It cancels out.*

CK: It cancels out the other thing. So I had a ball 'cause I used to love to go to work with them, very happy. Only drag about it was the state of mind he was in really. He was a very self-conscious, timid type of person and very sheltered in a shell more or less. He didn't like crowds of people. You could never get Pres to go in a restaurant. That was the hardest thing, to get him to eat in a restaurant. He didn't like people staring at him.

RJG: *Did you find any things you learned with him that was useful now?*

CK: John Lewis in a way plays a lot of Lester Young–type piano, to me, anyway, and it all helps in that way plus John played with Lester too, so I guess he understands exactly, we have sort of an understanding about that.

RJG: *Is it a difficult process for you to work out a new number that's one of the more complicated things?*

CK: No, because we've played for so long nothing seems complicated really 'cause it just, I can't explain it. But by playing together for such a long time, the hardest thing to me was "Fontessa," because that was a new type thing for me. When I first joined the Quartet they was just working on that. And that was entirely different to me to have these different interludes and go into this, but after that it's just as easy, to me anyway.

RJG: *Now I notice that some of the numbers alter from season to season in various ways. How does this come about?*

CK: Well, in one way I know that when I first joined the Quartet, I played more brushes than I do now. Now I play a lot more with the sticks and that helps to change the sound and the feel of a lot of our pieces. Like, "Vendome" we play now and I play sticks on it. When I first joined the Quartet it was all brushes, and I think the reason for that is it was recorded that way, and it's changed, the tempo is changed and everything and John says that now it's really the way that he intended it to be, but at that time it was a new thing and John knows what he wants but sometimes it's hard for him to explain to you what he wants.

RJG: *How does it come about that you changed from sticks to brushes — or brushes to sticks, rather — on a thing like this?*

CK: Well, the Quartet was at one time supposed to be such a delicate-type thing and now that that's established it doesn't matter any-more so now you can go ahead and just play.

RJG: *Once when you're playing the tunes, you just played it with sticks instead of brushes?*

CK: Yeah. I feel freer now to do what I want to do because I have a basic idea of what the thing is all about so now I can experiment a little on my own, too, whereas before I took a little time, now I feel within myself, I can still make this happen and play it some other way.

RJG: *Hmmm.*

CK: Like tonight we might play something and I'll play a different rhythm or tomorrow I'll play it some other way. Sometimes I play sticks where I never did that before. It was just a feel . . .

RJG: *So there's actually a lot more variations in what goes on in this group than the casual club patron or record buyer has any idea.*

CK: Yeah, 'cause lot of things that we have on records don't even sound like that now. This is changed. And just all of a sudden we might go back to a quiet groove. Say, "Well, we'll go back to this other groove." You get tired of that groove, you change. You get stale if you play the same way every night. So you have to change it around, tempos, the way you play has to, if you play the same thing every night and, playing with four cats for five years, that gets to be a drag too, so in order to make everybody happy you have to change things around.

RJG: *Do you spend much time talking about playing music without playing it?*

CK: Not really. Like when I'm home I don't even think about music. I'm just a family man, play some records and most of the records, I love singers, good singers, I put a lot of vocal records on. I like pretty ballads and things.

RJG: *Do you do much recording outside the group?*

CK: Well, I'll tell you I was a great rock and roller. But now I don't do too much. I make some dates with Milt and I make some dates with John and once in a while Nesuhi [Ertegun; jazz producer at Atlantic Records] call me up to make a date with somebody. But I haven't made too many, I think the only other record date I made outside of making it with the Quartet I made some records with Chet Baker. I think it was year before last. Philly Joe disappeared or something and the guy asked me to make the date with Chet. But a lot of people don't know that I'm available. A lot of guys are surprised to know that, they ask me, "Can you make record dates with somebody else beside the Quartet?" I tell 'em "Yes." And then, too, I'm not home that much really to do it and when I'm not home no one sees me to even know I'm there so that's one of the reasons why I don't.

RJG: *How do you see in your own mind, Connie, the role of the Modern Jazz Quartet in the whole of jazz music today? Do you ever think about that?*

CK: I never thought about that really. I never thought about what role, what the Quartet's playing. Everyone says we play good and it's the best Quartet and whatnot.

RJG: *Well, that stems from something I was thinking about because all of you in the group, in the last five or six years, have done so much traveling in Europe I was also going to ask you, what the reactions you have had to the role of jazz music in the whole of the world, which is something that comes up to you guys that go to Europe a great deal more strongly than just coming around here.*

CK: Well, I know one thing: the Quartet is very popular. Everyplace we've gone, except I'd say in Switzerland. I don't know the reason for that. Switzerland is not a jazz country or something, I don't know, but in Germany it's tremendous, England it's fantastic. I can't believe it myself, to think there are that many people really appreciate the Modern Jazz Quartet. I can't believe it.

Festival Hall we did 2,000, both of 'em sellouts and we played in two theaters that were bigger than that. And they both sellouts. I just can't believe that. In London. It's really fantastic. Italy is very good, Milano, Rome, places like that. Sweden and Denmark I can't say too much about that because we've only played up there once and that was the Birdland show and that was a package with Miles and Lester, but we've gone, we wanted to go back this time.

RJG: *Do you think the Europeans, for instance, regard jazz more highly than the public does here?*

CK: I really don't think so. It's just that it's newer to them and it's something that they don't have, whereas over here it's not, it's new in a sense 'cause a lot of people don't know what it's all about but it's like a television set, everybody has one so it's nothing really, I wouldn't say they don't appreciate it, they just take it for granted, it's something we have and we'll always have it. But the audiences here are just as attentive as audiences in Europe.

RJG: *It struck me that it would be hard to get an audience any more attentive than you get them in the Blackhawk for all of its being a joint.*

CK: That's right.

RJG: *They sure shut up and listen.*

CK: That's right.

RJG: *When you work out your more complicated things, is this the result of a lot of rehearsal?*

CK: When we rehearse we really rehearse, most of our rehearsals when we rehearse are at least three hours a day. Sometimes we rehearse every day if it's something that we have to get in a hurry or if it's something that's very intricate, like the tunes we do with the symphony and things like that. We might rehearse three hours, sometimes four, it all depends . . .

RJG: *Will there be drum music for those?*

CK: Ya. Gunther Schuller writes some very fine drum parts.

RJG: *Does John write drum parts for you?*

CK: Some of them he writes drum parts and some of 'em he just leaves it up to me, or when we get to a certain spot he'll say, "Well, I'd like for you to see if you could do this there or something."

RJG: *Do you all discuss these things that come in with a new piece to lead a group's experience to it?*

CK: Well, John, he picks me out, as someone with a good ear, 'cause he'll ask me, "How does that sound to you?," or sometimes I'll say, "Well, I think it would sound better if so and so did that," and he'll try it and say, "Yeah, that's good, leave that in," or sometimes he'll ask Milt or Percy.

RJG: *But it functions as a group thing?*

CK: Yeah.

RJG: *And if you didn't want to do something, would you still have to do it if it were in the arrangement?*

CK: Well, I've never run into that yet if it's something that I don't want to do. I've never had a part that, John writes very beautiful drum parts. He's got a very good feel for rhythm, he writes good drum parts, very good drum parts. and he leaves a lot of room for imagination, you can play the drum part and still get enough room in there for something you want to do.

RJG: *Has it continued to be kicks with the Quartet?*

CK: I think the kicks is over as far as the traveling. I've lost all enthusiasm for the traveling part of it, but it's part of the game so you have to go along with it.

RJG: *What has been the biggest moment for kicks for you in music?*

CK: I guess playing with the Quartet 'cause I had never thought that I would reach the point where I am now, 'cause I've always said to myself I didn't want to be a great drummer, I just wanted to play jazz and be comfortable. I didn't care where it was, I just wanted to play drums, make a good living so that I could eat and sleep and keep clean and take care of my family. But I never started out drums with the thought of being in the greatest combo or being the best, world's greatest drummer or anything like that. I didn't have that in mind. My object was just to be able to play music and be in that environment, just make a living, that's all. So here I am.

RJG: *It's been very fascinating to watch the impact of the group in different moods at different times and alter from year to year, and I was struck both this year and last year at the way in which more and more of the things in the group seem to be pointed towards the drums or to stem from the drums, maybe they always did and I just never noticed it, which is another thing,*

CK: Maybe I wasn't playing it.

RJG: *Depends on what's in your stomach and everything else when you go listen to something, too. Do you have any particular plans that you want to work on?*

CK: No. In future years? You know what I'd really like to do, Ralph? Be my own boss.

RJG: *Everybody would.*

CK: That's really the only thing I would really like to be able to work when I felt like it, you know. If I could do that I mightn't be happy either. But that's the way I feel now. I'd like to be able to go on the road when I felt like going and be able to stay home when I feel like it, with no strains in my pocketbook. I would do that now, but it would be a strain on my pocketbook. Say, if I left the Quartet and I'm gonna stay home. As I stay home awhile and then after awhile the bank account would.

RJG: *Do you have anything that you would like to say about the Quartet other than what you've said, anything on your own mind?*

CK: Not really, I don't know. I know it's a great experience for me to play with the Quartet because musically I've learned quite a lot by playing 'cause John is a very great musician and he's taught me a lot about music and Milt is a genius and that's about all, I guess.

RJG: *I have the feeling that John is a great teacher as well as a great musician.*

CK: Yeah.

RJG: *Because I know I've learned things from him that don't have anything at all to do with music.*

CK: Yeah. He's something, he's a fantastic person. It took me about three years to know him though.

RJG: *I'll bet it did.*

CK: Took me quite awhile. I don't think I still know him, but it takes a little while to know John Lewis. He's not the type person you can meet once or twice and say, "I know this guy's game"; takes a little while and you can imagine what it is with a guy that's on the outside and I'm on the inside and it took me this long.

RJG: *He used to scare the life out of me . . . terrify me . . .*

CK: He's a nice man. I know the first day that I met John, first job with the Quartet was in Washington, and he waited for me in the train station to go down to Washington to make this job and what was in my mind I said, "Oh, these guys get all this music. How will I ever get all this music together?" And so John Lewis, he's got all these degrees, I know he's going to come up with all this difficult music and what have you, but that's what was more or less on my mind. But after, we sat on the train and he said we going to play tonight so he says, "There are only two tunes you have to worry about, you have to learn, one is 'Django,'" he said. "'Django,' this part you don't play and this part you play and so and so and it's a little interlude in here," and I think it was "Vendome." Those were the only two. But the rest of them were just plain swinging ballads. I made that. It was a concert with Carmen McRae and Brubeck, or was it Brubeck and the Australian Jazz Quartet? Then we went to Boston for two weeks in Storyville and that's when we had the rehearsals and got all the music together. Then he threw this "Fontessa" on us. He said, "Now this is one, two, three, five parts," five different sections. And Percy kept telling me, "When we go to Philadelphia everybody knows 'Fontessa,' they're going to ask for 'Fontessa.' Get this 'Fontessa' down." So Jesus, because if he played that there that was one of our big tunes, but it came easy. Took a little. Then, too, if you play, like, with Lester, you know the music is all how you feel, it takes you a little while to get back into the practice of reading and playing music, but if you do it constantly like when I used to make record dates, reading music was easy because I'd gotten used to reading the music and playing and you get away from that for about three or four months and then go back to it, it's like starting all over again so that's in a way it's like that.

RJG: *You just settled into it, the whole thing became comfortable.*

CK: Yeah.

RJG: *What a feeling it must have been the first night you played without any rehearsals.*

CK: Well, it never struck me like that. I don't know whether it's arrogance or not, but I just figured, here's a gig, and I'm gonna make it and I just went and made it.

RJG: *Calmness and that's to be desired.*

CK: I wasn't nervous about it or anything cause I figured that the guys know this is my first night here, you can't expect the world, so I'm gonna do the best I can and if you don't dig it, later. So I did the best I could under the circumstances and it must have been alright. I'm still here!

Sonny Rollins

APRIL 15, 1959

■

As the 1960s dawned, jazz fans debated who was the greatest saxophonist on the scene. And the disputants invariably fell into two camps: one group picked John Coltrane, and the other opted for Sonny Rollins. Coltrane was the visionary whose music sought a quasi-spiritual transcendence, while Rollins fought it out in the trenches, presenting a muscular tone and trusting the inspiration of the moment as he worked endless variations on every kind of melody, whether populist or sophisticated. Like planetary giants, these two tenorists tended to stay in their own orbits, but when they met head-to-head—as on the 1956 recording "Tenor Madness"—who dared judge that either of these masters deserved second place?

But Coltrane passed away in 1967, leaving Rollins to reign unchallenged for decades to come. And even when jazz styles changed and rivals came and went, he stayed at the very top, inspiring each succeeding generation of players with his sound and style, both widely imitated although never surpassed.

Even at the peak of his fame, Rollins never took much notice of the praise and remained his own fiercest critic. The most famous moment in his career occurred away from the bandstands and recording studios, when he temporarily retired to focus on practice and self-improvement. At the end of the 1950s, jazz fans who wanted to hear the inimitable Mr. Rollins were advised to hang out on New York's Williamsburg Bridge, where this master of the horn would play for hours at a stretch, lost in the reveries of his own private music making.

Sonny Rollins spoke to Ralph Gleason just a few months before he embarked on this period of reclusion—an interlude that would last more than two years. "I want to reach people," Rollins explains here, then quickly adds: "Only if I can satisfy my own level." Although Rollins has given many interviews over the years, this frank conversation captures his outlook at what, in retrospect, must be seen as the most important juncture of his long career.

■

RJG: *When did you first become interested in jazz?*

SR: I always liked to play music. My brother was a concert violinist so I always heard that around the house all the time, classics and so forth, which I think is a very good beginning for anybody.

RJG: *Did your family encourage you in music?*

SR: No, not at first. Jazz-wise they thought just like most people do, that it's something kind of debased or something. But after I began to make a little bit of headway they began to be more receptive to my endeavors.

RJG: *You played the piano before you played the sax?*

SR: Yeah, I did.

RJG: *Did you study it?*

SR: Yeah, I studied the piano, but I was about eight years old then and they had to make me study. I wanted to play ball and so forth. What a drag! I wish I had known, I would have stayed with it. But of course I was too young to understand.

RJG: *Did they have to make you study the sax?*

SR: No, that they didn't. By the time I started to play the saxophone, that was completely my own wish and I used to practice all the time. In fact, I used to drive everybody batty practicing around the house all the time.

RJG: *Who was your first inspiration on the horn?*

SR: Let me see . . . actually I would say Louis Jordan was the first influence that I had on the horn. I used to enjoy his records immensely. And then Coleman Hawkins because he was playing much more music. And then, of course, Bird, and then the others . . . Lester [Young] and so forth. But Louis was the first one.

RJG: *Did you know him at that time?*

SR: Jordan? No, I was pretty young. Of course, I used to go to see him at the theater where I used to go after school as much as I could, play hooky from school or something and go some way. And I used to be there every week for every band that came in. Louis was my favorite band at that time.

RJG: *Did you get to know Hawk when you were young?*

SR: Yes, I did. In fact he lives right near where I used to live so I used to get autographs from him and so forth. I still look at him really with awe, he's still so great to me and it kind of makes me feel funny to know that I am in the same field and that I am regarded in that class, because I still think that he's really out of sight. It's a hard thing for me to understand that I am in this . . . I don't think I am but I'm sure other people do.

RJG: *Did he help you, show you things, talk to you?*

SR: Not to any great extent.

RJG: *Did he encourage you?*

SR: Yes, I would say he encouraged me. Lester Young, Pres, showed me a great deal and Ben Webster showed me more than anyone . . . gave me hints and so forth. Ben did a great deal for me. I guess

I got to know him earlier and he always, in fact he still does . . . every time we see each other we just discuss the horn and music. He's always been a very great inspiration to me.

RJG: *And of course there was Bird.*

SR: Oh, yeah! And Bird was also very great and he also helped me quite a bit, in many ways. He wouldn't actually tell me much, not in so many words, but it's a thing with these guys that if they see you do want to play, they make it so that you can learn things, but they don't come right out and say, "Well, play it this way and do it this and do it that." But Miles did that to me. He used to tell me exactly how to do a lot of things, how to play behind people and so forth. I learned quite a bit from Miles, just in a straight teacher-to-student-relation style. He helped me a great deal when I first met with him, I learned quite a bit from Miles.

RJG: *When did you first decide that you were going to be a jazz musician?*

SR: I guess I decided it when I first began to play. I was very intrigued with the horn and the way it looked, the picture . . . the horn looked very glamorous to me. So I guess I would say about the time I first began to play. When I got my first horn, I would say that was when I thought that it would be fine to be a jazz musician.

RJG: *When you were coming up in music, what was your greatest thrill?*

SR: I would say with Miles. We played a concert at Princeton University, that was with the small band, and this particular night I played . . . I think I was playing over my head at the time, but I just sounded very good to myself and to Miles, too. In fact, well, he always did give me a great deal of encouragement. But on this particular job I think I got a little bit more confidence in myself and I always look at it as a high point in my career. 'Course there's been other times.

RJG: *How does it make you feel, a moment like that?*

SR: Just completely exhilarated, light as a feather, wonderful, just great. There's no kind of whiskey or anything can give that effect, you just feel wonderful, you're just above everything.

RJG: *Do those moments come often?*

SR: Unfortunately, not too often. Not often enough. But when they come they give me enough steam to go through the rest of the times, but they don't happen as much as I would like them to.

RJG: *Do you think they happen more regularly as you mature?*

SR: Yes, I would say that I reach a level—as you were saying the other day, I guess I do have a level on which I remain more or less higher than at one time, so I get closer to my highs and further away from my lows.

RJG: *Is it kicks to find yourself in new situations with new guys, new ideas? Does it stimulate you?*

SR: Yes, it always does, especially saxophone players. When I play with other guys, it always gives me a great deal in incentive. And, of course, now when I'm thrown in with a new group of guys, the rhythm section, for instance, it can be hard because there are a lot of little, small, intricate aspects of playing, which, if you're not used to playing together, can be most disconcerting. Even though they're all great in their own right and in their own particular styles, I sometimes have trouble with guys that I haven't played with before.

RJG: *Do you find it easy to adapt them to your way of thinking?*

SR: Yeah, I think so. If I get a chance to work with them for a while, I can adapt them because I don't think that anything that I do is anything out of the way. I mean I think the things I'm trying to do are the basic things in jazz. I don't try to do anything that I think is inconsistent with the idea of jazz itself. So after we work a while together, they usually see exactly what I'm doing, which is the usual thing. I guess I just have my own way of playing it, but it's mostly the basic stuff that I try to do.

RJG: *How would you express what you're trying to do in jazz?*

SR: I'm trying to do so many things. I'm trying to sound fresh all the time, and rhythmically I'm always trying to invent. I try to do a lot of different things. I'm trying to play my horn to a greater technical degree. Actually, there's many things that remain to be done, which I'm very glad about, too, because you have to save something else to go on to. I am the first one to realize that I have a lot of work to do and there's a lot of things I'm not doing which I hear a lot of times, which is very good because it keeps me sincere and interested and trying.

RJG: *Do you find expression for humor in jazz?*

SR: Oh, definitely, very much so. A lot of time I do . . . I laugh at myself and it's good, it's wonderful. I think there always should be a sense of humor in jazz. Monk is another one that made me cognizant of how important it is to always have a sense of humor in playing. I've been told that I do at times play with a sense of humor, at times more subtle than other times, which is the best way. I would prefer to play with a subtle sense of humor although at times I do play with a more direct slapstick style, but the subtle sense of humor is more to be desired.

RJG: *When you're playing a solo, are you aware when you're quoting from something?*

SR: I don't understand.

RJG: *Well, the other night you began a solo with something that sounded to me like an echo of "The Champ." And then, in the next eight or ten bars, there were two other references to what sounded like nursery rhymes. They were just the beginnings, a hint at it and then you were into something else. Are you conscious of this or does this just happen?*

SR: It depends on the degree of ease that I'm playing with. There are times when I play more forced and there are times when I play more at ease, and at times when I play with ease these things just happen. Then there are times when I do them more deliberately, which of course are times when I'm not as flexible, I would say, as at other times. Actually, it's a little bit of both, anyway, but I'd rather just have it come without too much . . . predetermination, I guess would be the word.

RJG: *Free association?*

SR: Yeah, come more freely. But there are times when I force ideas and I play these things because I know them.

RJG: *Do you work out approaches to specific tunes? Points of view, so to speak?*

SR: Yeah, and this is something which is a little bit difficult without a piano, to capture the idea of a song and so forth. It seems that I've got to be very familiar with all of the chords in the song and everyone in the band has to be. But I try to approach each song with its own flavor, if I can use that word.

RJG: *Do you think of the words?*

SR: Yes, I do. I used to employ that quite a bit. I find it's very helpful in getting across the idea of the song.

RJG: *A lot of guys don't seem to do that too much.*

SR: Well, some guys might not have to. If you can bring something to the music itself, it's good. But the way I play, I have to resort to everything to really help me, you see, so I really need the words. In other words, I need as much help as I can get, so the words help me a lot. I know guys, Miles, for instance, I don't know if Miles is too aware of the lyrics, but yet he can play . . . get a good feel from the song. But it helps me a great deal if I know a few of the words of the song.

RJG: *You spoke before of how you had a difficult problem because you didn't use a piano player. This is, of course, your choice not to use a piano player. Why do you do that?*

SR: This is a question I've been asked a million times and my answers are beginning to vary a little bit. At times I would say it was because after I began to use just the rhythm without the piano, it got to be sort of a gimmick, which was good. I was trying to prove a point, that I could do it without a piano, so I kept it up. Of course I do like to play with pianos, and there's a couple of piano players who are my two favorites in jazz: Art Tatum and Bud Powell. I like the piano very much but, as I said, it's hard to find someone that can play very good accompaniment and still play a solo in his own right. It's not easy to accompany and it's becoming a lost art among the younger kids, I think. And so I have found it very hard to find a piano player that would enhance what I was doing rather than lead me into some other thing. Because the piano is a very dominant instrument and everyone has to go along with it if there is a piano in the group. I think in Miles' group you can see Miles thinks the same way that I do because of course he does use a piano, but you will see the piano always plays just a little. Especially now, the guy plays very seldom, just a few chords here and there, unobtrusive, but just the right chords, which is not easy to do, and there are very few piano players around that are doing it. Wynton Kelly, who's with Miles now, has almost changed his style completely to be with Miles because he used to be a very dominant-style piano player but now he's playing very subdued even in his solos. When he is playing by himself he's using that same touch and approach, which is not necessary in solos as much as it is when you're accompanying someone else.

RJG: *Well, it can't help but affect him, of course.*

SR: Yeah, it does.

RJG: *Is it more of an inspiration to you to carry the whole weight as the solo voice in the group, or is it easier for you when you're able to share it with someone like a trumpet player?*

SR: Well, it has its good points and its bad points. There are times when I feel it's easier for me to do it by myself because I know exactly what I want to bring to the particular tune that we play. Sometimes someone else's conception can be different, except of course if you have someone who is in complete sympathy with the way you play and sort of hears the same things, and then it becomes good, a pleasure. But of course I like to have a rapport going, it's always nice. So I can play with or without someone, about equally, depending on who it is.

RJG: *Do you find that your playing is affected by the audience reaction?*

SR: Sometimes I find I might try harder if I don't get any good re-action, I might try a little bit harder. But as a rule I try not to be affected by it because you find yourself playing for the people instead of for yourself, and you're supposed to always play for yourself. My standards are supposed to be good enough for the masses, you see. If you try to garner the public reaction too much, it can disconcert you, I think.

RJG: *You have to adapt to listening to audience reaction and reading reviews.*

SR: It is a thing I've had to adapt to. It used to be very disconcerting and you've got to sort of brace yourself. You can get a certain attitude that the applause wouldn't mean anything to you, it does, but still you've got to sort of act like it doesn't.

RJG: *Does an audience that reacts very favorably push you on?*

SR: I think so, yes. In fact there was a time when I used to play better when there wasn't anyone in the house. Now this is changed, now I find I try more and I do better when people come in. I guess this is because I have to make a living from this now.

RJG: *Do you want to reach people?*

SR: Yes, I want to reach people. But as I said, only if I can satisfy my own level. In other words, I don't want to reach people at the expense of the music itself. If I can do this and still reach them, fine, I'd love to, I'd like everybody to like what I'm doing.

RJG: *Do you find that the more you work, the better you play?*

SR: Definitely. And then, of course, it's a psychological thing because if I don't practice, it puts a bug in my mind and I just don't do as well, whether or not the practicing itself has any effect. Of course, I think it does, I know I should play and practice a lot and so if I don't, I feel that I just don't play as well because I know that I'm doing something I shouldn't do.

RJG: *What do you practice when you practice?*

SR: I practice everything. I practice out of books, exercises, millions of things, academic, technical things to practice. I find that anything I play is always helpful. Anything that I practice helps in playing, everything helps.

RJG: *Did you ever do things like play Bird solos?*

SR: Yeah. Not in later years, but when I first began to dig Bird and everybody, all the guys, I used to copy the records and that was a wonderful thing to do, but of course it shouldn't be done too much. I think it helped me a great deal, it helped a lot.

RJG: *Like a whole education.*

SR: It certainly is, because I learned so much from copying Bird's records note for note. And Fats Navarro also used to do that. He used to be able to play a solo by Dizzy note for note perfect. I remember hearing Fats do that a couple of times and then I knew that it wasn't a wrong thing to do.

RJG: *Do you ever find now that something you play will throw your mind into some phrase from one of those?*

SR: Yes, I do. You see now I have to try and be original. I have that thing going and I don't like to borrow too much now, but actually I think it's okay to use something that's been said and said in a nice way. I mean there's nothing wrong with playing that if it's good. It's all music, you know. I don't think there's anything wrong with it. But of course people look to me to be original all the time, so I shy away from trying to play anything too much note for note. I hear a lot of things that I would like to re-create.

RJG: *Did you at some point consciously decide to not sound like other people?*

SR: No, I don't think so.

RJG: *It just kind of happened?*

SR: It just happened. In fact, my style, whatever it is, whatever it may be, just happens. I didn't make any effort to play in any particular way. That just came out.

RJG: *Do you think that the whole business of listening to other guys and copying things becomes a trap for some people?*

SR: Yes, it does, and that's why I'm not prone to endorse it. But, as I said, it also has its good side and if a guy is sincere and is interested in playing, he won't stop there, and assuming that he has got some ideas of his own, then it can only help you, I believe.

RJG: *Where do you get ideas from?*

SR: I tell you, I like to listen to all kinds of music, everything kills me, any kind. I would say that I get ideas from music that I hear . . . in fact I think that I'm the kind of a guy that gets a great deal from other people. I might not play note for note, but it inspires me to think of other things. I wouldn't call myself completely original at all, I have to hear someone else do something and then it inspires me to perhaps do something else, but I still got the idea from someone.

RJG: *Is it an interesting thing to you to play one of your own records for the first time?*

SR: Yes, it is. Of course, now I'm able to listen objectively to myself. A year or so ago it was very painful for me to listen to a record of my own, but now I can listen to them a little bit better.

RJG: *Does it surprise you to hear them?*

SR: Yeah, it does in a way. I did a lot of things that I am not doing now, that I forgot about, so it's good in a way to listen to your own stuff. And now, as I said, I can do it much better. At one time I hated to listen to my own records.

RJG: *Do you ever then go back to something you have done?*

SR: Yes, definitely. It reminds me a lot.

RJG: *A notebook almost?*

SR: Uh-huh. Music is a thing that you've got to do constantly to keep up because you can forget so easily. You've got to practice all the time or work all the time to keep up with everything that you learned because it's so easy to forget things that you have played. Once you forget them you might find them again sometime after if you keep your standard of playing up.

RJG: *Do you think this is true for all musicians or just true for the ones who have decided that music is the most important thing to them?*

SR: No, I think that this is true for everybody because everyone I'm sure plays things which sound good at the time and which they forget. If they don't play for a couple of days, or get in a different groove the next day, they might just pass up an idea which is good. I'm sure that if they knew about this particular riff or idea, they would do it all the time.

RJG: *Do you find that the way you play any given night affects the way you feel?*

SR: Oh, very definitely, the two are so close. If I don't sound too good, there are times when it has a very adverse effect on me, a very bad effect on me. And if I sound okay, I feel good. But the other night, for instance, I sounded bad to myself and I felt very depressed all night. After I left the job, I felt very depressed. This happens quite a bit, the two are very close.

RJG: *Do you ever go a day without practicing?*

SR: Oh, yes, I do. Too many days without practicing. And at times the conditions are responsible, it's not just me. At times I can't practice. I have to take care of some kind of business or whatever the case may be. Many days I go without practicing and it always hurts me, I always think about it in a bad way. It always bugs me.

RJG: *Does it affect your playing that night if you haven't practiced that day?*

SR: I think it does. Usually if I practice in the day I have a good night as a rule, because, for one thing, my chops are in shape. It just gives me more of a confident outlook and I have a good night.

RJG: *Have you ever gone a long period, like a couple of weeks, without playing?*

SR: Not in the past few years. Years ago, I'd say about three or four years ago, I used to go long times without playing, I don't play for weeks and months at a time. But of course I try not to do this now. Fortunately, I have been employed quite a bit here of late so I just have to play anyway. In fact, I never go a week without playing my horn now. That would be completely out of the question. I couldn't do it. Now if I can just boil that down to every day being completely out, that'd be good. I just have to get to the point where I think that much of it.

RJG: *Your approach to the discipline of music is similar to that of John Lewis. Have you talked of this with him?*

SR: He has always been a great inspiration to me insofar as discipline is concerned, and he's made me aware that you have to practice and be very serious about it and rehearse. We are very much alike in that respect. And his music also influences me, he's a very great musician.

RJG: *I was wondering if you had any students. Do you have guys that come to you to learn?*

SR: I've been approached by quite a few guys, but I don't have the time, actually, to teach. That's a big step in itself and it's a thing all in itself. You've got to actually devote a lot of time to it and I don't have the time to have a student. Plus I don't think that I have so much that I'm learning all the time myself, I don't exactly feel secure as a teacher so I haven't thought about that too much.

RJG: *Do you think that guys continue to learn? For instance, a guy like Hawk, does he continue to learn or has he reached a point where he knows all that he's going to find out?*

SR: No, I think he continues to learn. A lot of things that he used to play that were great he doesn't play now. You have to keep on playing. A lot of times he might have forgotten things that he's learned. Then, of course, Hawk gets a lot of inspiration from young guys. Actually, I think that a person should always advance, I don't see any reason why you should ever get to the point where you don't advance in style and in conception of playing. I think there's enough to be done that you should always have new things to do.

RJG: *Have you ever thought about doing an album all by yourself?*

SR: Oh, very much so, yeah, I'd love to do that sometime. I don't think I'm equipped to do it right now, but the idea has always been in my mind, to be able to play unaccompanied.

RJG: *I was always gassed by that solo thing that Hawk did.*

SR: Yeah, "Picasso." It was wonderful. But, you've got to have a lot of equipment to make it sound good and not monotonous. I don't think I can do it effectively right now. I might be able to do it for one song, perhaps; in fact I've tried that a couple of times and it just barely gets over like that. An album would be a lot of work—or to play a concert by myself would be a lot of work.

RJG: *Do you like to play concerts?*

SR: I do, I like to play concerts.

RJG: *Would you like to do things like those tours that the MJQ does to colleges?*

SR: Yes, I'd love that, because there's always a feeling of accomplishment connected with a concert, more so than with a nightclub. Plus the audiences seem to be more intent on what's happening, although you do get good nightclub audiences also. It's different, it's not the same. I mean I feel more important and more . . . at a concert I feel more dedicated, and I think I try to rise to this. There's a little more incentive, perhaps.

RJG: *Why do you think it is that great musicians like Hawk and Ben Webster and even Pres have in a sense lost their audiences? At least their audience has diminished, let me put it that way.*

SR: Well, I think I read an article somewhere, I can't recall where, which spoke about this and said that in recent years jazz has begun to get an audience which can appreciate everybody. But it's just beginning to happen now. Years ago there weren't that many people that liked jazz. There were just a few for every era. But now I think there are beginning to be more people that like jazz itself and can appreciate all styles and eras. So now I think it's getting to where people can appreciate everybody that is a good jazz artist, regardless of period.

RJG: *For instance, a lot of young guys who are coming along won't even pay attention to Dizzy. Why do you think this is?*

SR: I don't know, but it's completely wrong, because jazz is a thing which is built upon what has happened before, it doesn't begin with any one guy today. The greatest that anybody can be is just as great as what has come before and to be great you have to be steeped in what has happened. Anybody that is great in jazz has the background, at least has a great appreciation for a lot of the older people.

RJG: *Audiences today don't seem to exist for Hawk, for instance.*

SR: That's unfortunate, but I think things are getting better. I think that when I get to be Hawk's age that things will be at a point where even though there'll be new styles and ideas, they might still appreciate me and I might still have a large audience. I hope so. I hope that things are going in this direction.

RJG: *Do you find yourself interested at all in the attempts by various guys such as Gunther Schuller and Mingus and Teddy Charles and those people, to write compositions in jazz?*

SR: Yes, to a certain extent. As I said, there are so many things which can be done and which haven't been done, so I'm sympathetic to any new ideas like that as long as they have good jazz roots. I'm for experimentation.

RJG: *Was it fun to come up with a waltz?*

SR: Yeah, that was a big kick, that was crazy. I got a big bang out of that and the people liked a few of the things we did. Although it wasn't anything new; Fats [Waller] had done it, Fats had done it many times before. But it was nice because it hadn't been done recently, not since around the bebop era.

RJG: *Sonny, for some young guys coming along today, there's practically no place he can work in a big band. Do you think that this is a lack, a gap in his education?*

SR: Yes, I think it is. Playing in an orchestra does offer you a great experience. It's wonderful to be able to play with other guys. You just can't beat that experience. The guys today don't have that much of a chance to do it. I'm very interested in a lot of groups that just get together to rehearse. Like Kenny Dorham has a band now that he rehearses all the time. They don't work, but it gives the kids a chance to read and the feel of playing with each other, which is good. Freddie Hubbard, my trumpet player, was with this band, in fact. It's invaluable experience. I'm all for it.

RJG: *Does the discipline of that help them conceive of form in their solos?*

SR: Sure it does. Because if a guy is a great soloist or has great ability in that line, he will eventually come out of this environment himself. It can't hurt anybody, even the greatest. Pres, for instance, spent so much time with Basie. It's a wonderful thing and it's a drag that there are not enough opportunities for big bands today. As I said, if guys would just get together and rehearse, it's nice.

RJG: *Was it interesting for you to do that album with brass?*

SR: Yes, it was. It was the first time that I had recorded with a big band and although it didn't come out like I had hoped, it was pretty well done at the last minute. Everybody came into the studio with the music for the first time and four hours to do it, so of course it didn't . . . I would have liked to have worked on it more, plus I would have liked to have written some of the arrangements myself, which I didn't have a chance to do. But I do like to work within a large group.

RJG: *One of the things that has always intrigued me about your albums is that you always come up with tunes that are real ballads, real, almost schmaltzy, ballads. Do you select these yourself?*

SR: Well, as I said, I like to listen to all kinds of music. I find kicks . . . like listening to Lawrence Welk a lot of times, you dig? I mean they play some pretty tunes and I enjoy it a lot. I always hear a thing that I like and then I play it, I guess, in my way, but the basic song is there. I like a lot of these things, pop tunes, even, come out that way.

RJG: *Do other guys ever put you down for those?*

SR: No, because I guess what I bring to it changes it from what it is, so I've never been . . . in fact, everybody seems to enjoy the fact that I use this type of material.

RJG: *Jazz is a very direct form of communication. Do you find that you can get your mood to the audience?*

SR: Sometimes I do, of course, but then other times, I don't. The mood that I try to project is wrong at times, because it is something that I can't necessarily feel. I might not be at ease so that sometimes the mood that I project is not a good one and at these times it doesn't reach me, either.

RJG: *What do you think about when you're taking a solo?*

SR: I try not to think about anything. This is a thing also that can be a bug because it's easy for my mind to wander. I've had to make a concerted effort towards not thinking about anything else, just keep a free mind and play. I think I'm beginning to do it more and more now. At one time I had a great deal of trouble within a solo to not begin thinking about the people or something completely unrelated to something I was doing. And as soon as my mind goes away, I would lose the essence of whatever I was starting to build. These things still happen to me, but it's a thing where you've got to discipline your mind and just concentrate on what you're playing, then it comes out by itself. It's a thing I've had to work at a bit because my mind wandered often when I played.

RJG: *How about when you're practicing?*

SR: Usually I can concentrate, but sometimes I go off then, too. When I read music I have to concentrate and it's a little easier. The main thing is not so much how long you practice but if you can bring a great amount of concentration to a little bit of practicing, you've accomplished a great deal. There are times when I play for a long time and actually I'm not concentrating on what I'm playing and it isn't any good. I practice for an hour and I'm not retaining anything. But I can practice for 10 minutes and concentrate and that 10 minutes is like a whole day. It's a tricky area, that concentration thing.

RJG: *Do you find that you will subconsciously retain some of those things you didn't think you retained and they will come back later on?*

SR: Yes, they do, they come back. In fact, you never know just what you learned, it just comes to you. You can't pinpoint what you've done, but if you do it and concentrate at the time you do it, then it will come back to you at other times. It's interesting.

RJG: *Do you play different kinds of music—I don't mean on the phono-graph—for yourself, on the horn, other than jazz?*

SR: Yeah, I play a lot of classics. In fact, I wanted to do an album of excerpts of the classics. I've been fooling around with that idea for about a year now and I haven't actually gotten all of it together yet. The horn I play isn't accepted really in classical orchestras, so I would like to make a step in that direction, towards bringing the tenor into a better light within the classical framework.

RJG: *Do you think of music when you're doing other things, like when you're driving a car?*

SR: Yeah. Some of my best ideas come to me when I'm doing other things. You know, music is always going around someplace and sometimes when I talk to my wife, we might say things, titles of songs or something, and we sing the song. I think of things, of different ways to play things and everything, and I usually carry around a pad that I wrote down ideas on because a lot of good ideas come to me when I'm doing other things. If I don't put them down, I lose out and I have to wait for them to come back again.

RJG: *What are the best moments in music for you now?*

SR: Within my playing? Listening to others? What?

RJG: *No, within your playing.*

SR: I guess when I make a good solo and I satisfy myself. Of course, now, when the band sounds good, because it's not just me now, it's the group, so when we get the right thing going, which is not always so easy to do, but when things happen right, it makes us all very happy. Everybody. And it's a thing that everyone can feel when it happens right.

RJG: *When you do have one of those good nights, is it easier physically?*

SR: I'm not tired, I can work indefinitely. That's the thing they used to ask about when we played with the trio. "How can you play so long without being tired?" But if the things begin to sound good, there is no physical awareness at all, it's just as if it's not even playing, I don't feel tired or anything. You can just play on and on and never have any awareness of anything.

RJG: *The length of the solo has no effect at all?*

SR: No, not at all. And if it's good, the people don't even realize that it's so long because they're all engrossed. I used to do that quite a bit with the trio. I remember one time we played a song, one song, for a whole set at Birdland. In fact we were still playing and Pee Wee [Marquette, the emcee] had to come up and tell me, "That's it, the set is over."

RJG: *Do you lose consciousness of the length of time, then, yourself?*

SR: Oh, yeah, definitely. If things go right it's just like time isn't even . . . it's wonderful, you just forget everything.

RJG: *Then it would almost be impossible when it was going right to do something wrong.*

SR: Yeah, it would be. You just can't do it. It's a force that's so moving. It's wonderful when those times occur.

RJG: *Have you ever had this thing occur on record?*

SR: Well, there are some cases that I think we got a kind of a good groove on. There was one side I did like "At the Vanguard," I think we got a good groove with just three pieces playing. And there was one particular side we got a groove on and it lasted a long time, it kept on building. It's hard to get these things going on record. Recording is a different area and it's very difficult.

RJG: *Do you think somebody like Bird, that they achieve these highs more often?*

SR: I think so. But of course, knowing Bird like I do, I don't think *he* does, he probably feels exactly the same way I do about it. But listening to him I wish that I could achieve the grooves that he achieves all the time, because practically all the time that I hear him, he seems to be playing with a great deal of imagination. Him in particular, I would say. He's really the epitome.

RJG: *Do you find that European musicians are beginning to have more of a feel for jazz?*

SR: Yeah, I think as a rule they are, especially in the country I went to, Sweden. I found they had some very good musicians sensitive to these little inroads in jazz. More so I would say than any country in Europe. And the standards of the music are beginning to rise and there is much more distribution of records. This is good because the more people who come into it with the sincere desire to play and create, the better, the higher we will climb with it.

RJG: *Maybe music is going to be the salvation.*

SR: I think it is a very important force in the world today. People just don't understand enough about it, not just the music itself, but as a force for relations between folks.

RJG: *A force for peace . . .*

SR: Peace, of course. It just makes me feel very good to be able to serve in any capacity. I mean I feel very good to be associated with jazz.

RJG: *You spoke of the fact that when you started to be interested in jazz your family, like other families, didn't regard jazz as worthy of that respect. How did you come to the conclusion that it was?*

SR: That jazz was worthy? Well, it was always a great thing to me, the music itself. I just knew it had to be good. Of course there's many bad things that have been connected with jazz, this I'm very well aware of, just like other people are. These are things which haven't got anything to do with the music itself, external things. The music was so strong and so great to me that I realized that it must be good and that these other things did not necessarily have to be connected with jazz. That's what I'm trying to prove now, that you don't have to be a bad guy or a degenerate or something to be a jazz musician.

RJG: *Louis Armstrong said a great thing on a television program when they asked him about being an ambassador. "Well, there's one thing I know," he said, "this ain't no cannon!"*

SR: Oh, boy, he comes out with some great things, doesn't he? He's the most eloquent . . . "this ain't no cannon!"

RJG: *"Music is the ambassador," he said, "I'm just the courier."*

SR: He is a great man. He's one of my gods. I know him personally and he's just wonderful . . . it's hard to assess everything that he's done, he is so great. I like everything he does, I don't think he does anything in bad taste. He sings a lot and makes a lot of jokes and everything, but I think that this is good for jazz. Although it is a serious art form, there's plenty of room in it for laughs.

"Philly" Joe Jones

DECEMBER 6, 1959

∎

Over the course of four decades, the leading stars in jazz sought out Philly Joe Jones for their bands. For many, he was the dream drummer, the hard-swinging master who set the example for all others. Miles Davis, who played with almost every great drummer of his day, put Philly Joe Jones at the top of the list. "Philly Joe was the fire," Davis later wrote in his autobiography. "See, he knew *everything* I was going to do, everything I was going to play. . . . Even after he left I would listen for a little of Philly Joe in all the drummers I had later."

And he probably heard echoes of Jones in these later players. Countless percussionists tried to imitate the "Philly Joe sound." His rim shots even got called the "Philly lick." And if a drummer didn't play it, the bandleader might ask him to learn it.

Ralph Gleason talked to Philly Joe Jones a little over a year after he left the Davis band. In the months leading up to this interview, Jones had made records with Thelonious Monk, Bill Evans, Cannonball Adderley, Chet Baker, Jackie McLean, Abbey Lincoln, Benny Golson, and other jazz stars, and was leading his own big band and small combo. At the time of this conversation he was in the midst of the most fruitful period of his long career, and he would remain one of the most in-demand drummers for another three decades.

∎

PJJ: In 1945 I came home, I was just out of the service and I wanted to play and I knew about the drums, I actually knew about the drums in 1939, an old fellow in Philadelphia who's still there playin', he's playin' every night, named Coatsville [James "Coatsville" Harris], and he used to help me, he used to teach me how to play the drums. I used to sit underneath the bandstand in the club because I was too young to be there. I wasn't supposed to be there but he'd sneak me in and I'd be underneath the bandstand. It was an ex-bank and they made a nightclub out of it and they had a floor show and I used to watch the dancers and the chorus and the three, four girls in the line and this drummer. I just idolized him and he's still one of the swingingest older cats I've met, and I wanted to play so that he used to help me.

RJG: *You were playing drums before this, though?*

PJJ: I went into the army in 1940. But in '38 and '39, I used to watch this guy and another old man, he used to play drums, used to sit up with a pipe in his mouth and play every night. I lived across the street from a place called the Lennox Grill in Philadelphia and I used to peek through the windows in the back of the club, they had bars on the windows, so I used to always stand there and peek and look at this drummer. This man used to kill me, he had a pipe in his mouth and a regular old setup of drums, you know, no high hat, nothing like that, just a bass drum and a little cymbal. Cymbals were small then, but he was swinging like I don't know what and I used to like to go there. My brother used to come around the corner and look up and see me peeking in the window and say, "Come on now!" and I'd go home—I only lived across the street. I used to sneak out of the house sometimes at night because they'd be playin' after my bedtime, I had to go to school, but I used to sneak out, run across the street, 10:30 and 11 o'clock at night I used to sneak out of the house and run across the street and peek in that window and listen to him playin' drums. And when I met Coatsville who was considered the greatest drummer in the city at the time and he started teaching me and helping me—he wasn't teaching me because he never was reading at that time, but he was showing me how to play. Then I went away with the army and I used to listen to drummers playing in the USO and whatnot, and I never got a chance to really play. During my stay in the army I took about nine guys out of a company and had them all playing drums, the snare drums, big fat snare drums. In the company we had drum and bugle corps. The buglers could play, the chaplain taught them to play bugle, but I taught all the drummers. In Shenandoah, Pennsylvania, we paraded in the streets and the drummers were all together and I had made the format of what we should play and I never will forget that it was a beautiful thing, the people in Shenandoah . . . It's a funny thing, in Shenandoah, Pennsylvania, at this time, in 1940, the middle of '40, '41, the people of Shenandoah, Pennsylvania, it's a strange city, there are no colored people in that city. There were none at that time, and to see us, it was strange to them, they looked at us, it was a very funny thing. We went to, they call it, Indiantown Gap, the train station, Linkdale they call it, and went on the train and went there and paraded through the streets. We had a big parade, nevertheless the people were very fascinated with the things the drum and bugle corps were playing. And so the drums just fascinated me too much then and I wanted to play drums.

After I was discharged I went home and I didn't get too much chance to play drums because I had just gotten married and I wanted to work, I had to work to take care of my family, and whatnot, that is, just my wife I had to take care of. Anyway, I went and bought a set of drums and was in the cellar practicing, myself, teaching myself how to play, I didn't have nobody to teach me. At the time I was driving a trolley car while I was learning the drums in the house. Our neighbors would come and say, "Ah, you're not playin,' stop that noise!" and my mother-in-law would say, "Stop that noise! . . . Get out! . . . Stop that noise in the cellar!" But nevertheless at that time I was thinking differently about drums. I wanted to play drums and I went on into '46, '45 I went to work for my first time in Café Society with a guy in Philadelphia named Bass Ashford, who was a very popular, competent bass player in town and he used to love me and he used to help me with the drums, and he used to tell me certain things that were good for drummers. It was good and he was a seasoned bassist, and so I changed my mind about drums then, like I was saying to you earlier, when I met O'Neil Spencer and O'Neil used to come into Café Society in Philadelphia at this time, during these years, because John Kirby was working in the city. I hadn't heard much of him, but listening to him, he was a beautiful bassist at that time and I used to listen to him. O'Neil was the first "name" drummer that I met, and as I often say to myself, thank God I met him at the time I did. John Kirby was working in town, but he wasn't working the club I was, and he happened to come by one of our sessions and he liked what we was playing, and I was playing with this bass player and his brother is an excellent altoist who has an identical sound to Benny Carter. So I used to love to listen to him and I wanted to play with him and he had a girl piano player named Margie Wood, who played excellently, and so John Kirby used to come over with us every matinee, he was in town for quite a few weeks, and play with us. Then one day he brought his drummer up to hear us—John liked me and he brought his drummer, who was O'Neil Spencer, who I had heard, and when I met O'Neil, I don't know, something just dawned on me. This man was such a beautiful drummer, did so many things, that I dreamt of.

RJG: *He made you think about drums differently?*

PJJ: He most certainly did, because at that time, the sock cymbal had been converted from the low floor, tiny stand about 12, 15 inches off the floor, and I think O'Neil, if I'm not mistaken, I'm pretty sure of this, O'Neil was very instrumental in making the long pole sock cymbal, bringing it up to the snare drum where you could play the sock cymbal after beat instead of having it just sit there and make accents with it. And O'Neil used to say to me, "Why don't you do this and do that," and he said, "Why don't you play an afterbeat on the two and four with it," and that used to fascinate me and I'd never heard anybody do this and John Kirby used to say, "That's it! That's the way it's supposed to be!" and

O'Neil was the first person I ever heard do this with the two-four thing.

RJG: *Had you heard the Basie band before this?*

PJJ: I had heard Jo Jones years ago, with the Basie band, way back, way back, with Pres [Lester Young], and I been listening to Basie years ago and I always admired Jo's drumming and I loved him and loved the things that he played, I used to listen to the drum and my mother used to really holler at me 'cause I kept the radio on all night, I'd be listenin' to those broadcasts, but Jo Jones was really a heck of an influence on me when I was a kid, but my mind used to go past Jo Jones because at the same time the Savoy was hollering and Chick Webb was playin.' And Chick is the drummer I used to listen to, because he used to have, I could never forget it, it stayed in my mind so long, Chick Webb used to have a theme song called "Liza," that was his theme at the time, at the Savoy, and I memorized that theme. It's in my mind right now! I could hum the tune the way he played it. I used to listen to the drum solos that he played, in between . . . that's the reason why I fashioned the theme I'm using, of course I'm using "Blue 'n' Boogie," but I'm inserting drum things in between, here and there, let them play a few and then I play some drums and then go out with a big splash. Chick used to do that with "Liza." It always impressed me, it was a beautiful thing, in fact people applaud for it so they must enjoy it.

RJG: *Do you think of using the drums in your group, as in Miles' group, sort of in duets with other instruments?*

PJJ: He used to have a firm hand on me with different things. Well, with Miles I'm a sideman, and there's so much I can do and so much I can't do. Miles used to get angry about something I would do and limit me and have me play certain things and tie me down and I couldn't progress. I feel that if a drummer can experiment on the bandstand without upsetting the rhythm and disturbing people, it's good for you and only betters you and makes you progress more. But Miles wouldn't let me experiment too much, because he'd say I'd be getting in the way. So with my own group I can experiment the way I feel, because it's my group! Yet still I don't want to get in the way of the soloists. I want them to be heard because by them being heard, if they're great, makes me. I don't want to overshadow them. With my own group I feel at more liberty if I feel something to go into it. I used to feel things with Miles that might have been some spectacular things, but I wouldn't do them because I was afraid he would reprimand me.

Drums are changing constantly, because you have so many young drummers that are coming up and the young drummers hear drummers that they will idolize just like I idolized drummers—like Chick and Jo Jones. But the things I used to hear them play, I wanted to play some different things, and the younger drummers that are coming up, they listen to me and Art [Blakey] and Max [Roach] and different cats that are playing, and *they* want to be different. They're constantly trying to surpass. That's the way I feel about the older drummers, I want to surpass what they did, so that I can be doing something progressive and get recognition, and the younger drummers that are younger than I, are doing the same thing. Youth just comes on. Youth comes through and it's a different flavor, they're constantly searching and there's no end to drums, what you can do with the drums, there's no end.

RJG: *Did you ever study formally at all?*

PJJ: There's been several different things in books about my studying, about what I did and what I didn't do. I left Philadelphia in 1947 and came to New York to live because during and before those years Max and Art used to come to Philly and I'd be working in the clubs when they came in town and I idolized them. Max

Roach and Art Blakey, I idolized them. They used to say, "Why don't you come to New York and live, man, you'd get work, you play good, you should come." And I said, "I'm going to do that one day." In fact Art or Max would confirm they've ridden with me when I was driving on the streetcar and then Max came back a few years later when I was driving a grocery truck and used to ride with me in the afternoon! We were very close friends and I used to commute, maybe twice a week, from Philadelphia to New York with Kenny Dennis, who wanted to play drums at the time. He used to hang around me all the time because he loved me and I loved Max Roach and Art and I wanted to talk to them and be with them and I couldn't because I was in Philly. So I used to buy myself a train ticket and come to Max's house over on Monroe Street in Brooklyn and stay maybe seven, eight hours, six hours, and we'd play. We'd go in his bedroom and play and Max would be showing Kenny and myself different things and we'd be, so to speak, swapping notes. But at that time Max had so much more technique, he had been up during the Charlie Parker era and Max was pretty well seasoned and he'd be always laughing at Kenny and I. We were so enthusiastic about playing. For a couple of years I was going to Max and then I met Kenny Clarke and had heard him, Max introduced me to Kenny, he tells me this is Kenny Clarke, forerunner of all of us, Kenny was the drummer that started doing all the stranger things that other drummers didn't do . . . they talking about bebop and re-bop drums and Kenny was breakin' the rhythm and playing the way that we're playing today, which is very beautiful as far as I'm concerned in drums. So Max introduced me to Kenny. Shortly after that I went to work at the Three Deuces with a rhythm and blues band that had a modern book and a rhythm and blues band book. Joe Morris. Johnny Griffin was in that band and Matthew Gee was in that band and Elmo Hope was in the band, and we had a young boy named Wally Williams from the Bronx, he played so much then, he was really good. And we had a good little band and we worked opposite George Shearing's first trio, the first time

George had come to New York. If you look back through the years and check up on George Shearing, you'll see that George Shearing had Shelly Manne and Oscar Pettiford in his first trio, they were the first two members because that was the first job he had. I used to kid Oscar, I'd call Oscar "Seeing Eye Dog" because Oscar used to take George home every night, and George used to kid with me when they were off but George used to finish his set and sit down by the piano and listen to Elmo Hope at the time because Elmo was really in shape during those years. That was when I met Kenny Clarke. While I was in that group, in that trio with Slim, I had been to New York and had been studying with Cozy Cole and been learning to read, but Cozy hadn't gotten me into the back of his books where he has all those maracas and things, so I went back home in '50 and worked with Slim, and Slim Gaillard used to teach me all the cowbell tricks. The things that he plays on cowbells was authentic. Other guys, other drummers might not dig it, might not get close to Slim and listen. I *had* to listen to him. I was playing with him every night and he plays authentic, actual rhythms on that cowbell. He plays huaraches and different things and of course that throwing up the cowbell in the air, that bit is something different, but believe me Slim Gaillard can play the cowbell authentically with different rhythm and he taught those to me and he taught me the things to play on the top of the bell of the cymbal. All those things come to season in you and get you to learn different things and, then after you learn all those things, you take 'em and turn 'em around your own way, but to know the right way, the basic way, what's the correct way, then you can improvise your solos and get your own originality. But Slim was responsible for all of the Latin things that I've learned probably, other than the later Latin things that I learned in later life with Miles, because Miles had this uncanny sense of time and rhythm, real different from anybody I've ever met. And he often said that my sense of time is strange and so between the two of us having the strange senses of time, we just seem to get together with the sense of time and I could never lose him and he could never lose me. I always knew where he was and no matter how much—I say this, I'll say it this way—as much as I like to play the *melody* in things, on the drums I could get with Miles and go into *anything* just like he does with me. He never stays with the drummer, he goes way out, but I know where he's at, I know what he's doin' and what he's doin' is impressin' the people, and with Miles I could play some drum clichés without having to stick close to the melody with the drums to let him know where I was at 'cause he had such an uncanny sense of time, he would know the amount of time that I had, I had to be playin,' and I'd come out right and it would bring him right back and he'd come right back where *one* was. It was always beautiful. The greatest experience of my life was with Miles—of course, I could never deny that, the greatest of friends, I can't deny that, the greatest experience in my life *other* than the few times I worked with Charlie, meaning Charlie Parker, they were the greatest experiences of my life. To work with Miles later gassed me because I knew that he got all of his seasoning from Charlie.

RJG: *Ever get tired of playing?*

PJJ: I never get tired of playing. Sometimes the house rules so far as time is concerned, cuts things short. You can't always do that because sometimes you play, to play them in their entirety goes into maybe a minute more and if you cut the tone off, then the audience they don't get the fullness of the tune, they don't get the full arrangement and hear the ending, and it's the ending and the introduction that to me—that affects the audience. Of course, the solos, naturally the solos, if they're swinging cats, but if you start an arrangement off with a beautiful introduction and end it out precisely, the applause has to come, because it's done with so much perfection.

"Philly" Joe Jones

RJG: *Is it more kicks to play with a small group or a big band?*

PJJ: My first love is a big band because I am comparatively a heavy drummer. I like to play heavy and I play forceful and sometimes I tend to get loud and it might be overbearing because I've seen some customers who sit close to the drums get up and move so I understand. You see, a lot of drummers play for themselves and don't think about the audience. I do. I think about the audience at all times when I'm playing and I have a feeling for their ears as far as volume is concerned. But some tunes, you just cannot come down and make the tune effective, so I have to play loud, which might not appeal to them but some other people there will get the feeling of what I'm trying to project to them, and if I would play it much softer it wouldn't be any good, it would kill the brilliance of the tune.

RJG: *Do you try to work out the acoustics of the room?*

PJJ: That's the first night in every club. The first night in a club I play just the way I feel, I don't try to do anything so far as the house is concerned, I just play and see what I get. Some clubs offer you different things, acoustically, and then you can judge yourself accordingly. Like today at our session, it wasn't capacity like tonight so I was still playing as full as I would play with capacity and it was not really so good because it was heavy. But at night when all those people are there, the warmth gets into the drums and you don't have to hit the drums so hard to play 'em and it'll come out. But even though a drummer can play loud, drums can be loud and musical, I notice the public will accept it, he'll be accepted. If you're loud and *not* musical they won't accept it.

I believe in everybody in the band, lettin' them play their own arrangements. That makes a happy group rather than just say, "No, you're going to play all MY arrangements." I don't like that. When I was in Miles' band that was the thing I didn't like in the band. Miles would never play anything that I would write or that anybody else in the band would write. 'Course we could suggest, which I did, I suggested on numerous occasions how the format of an arrangement should be—"I'll play brushes here," like on "All of You," different things like that, at the beginning, that concept was me. I said, "Miles, I want to play brushes in the front of that" when he started the opening of "All of You," that's my idea, we dreamt that up on a plane flying to Detroit or somewhere. But I think you should have a good band and let everybody express themselves with their own arrangements. Not only that but I like to play *all* excellent composer's arrangements, they're beautiful, like that thing of Benny Golson's.

Young drummers are coming up in a different era, coming up in an era where all of us, where everybody today, are playing modern drums so therefore young drummers don't have the thought in the back of their mind of the older drummers like we spoke of earlier, Chick and them, where the drums came from. You were speaking about Baby Dodds. Young drummers haven't never seen Baby or sat and watched him play like I did. Or Sid Catlett. These are the drummers that if any drummer from now, for the next 30 years, can tell me can't play, I don't care how the drums move, if they can tell me 20 years from now they can't go back and listen to Chick, David Tough, Sid, and Baby Dodds and tell me that that's not drums, I'll break the drums up and forget it!

I'm very funny about drums. When you try to be self-taught and you can't, you don't study right away because of different problems, you learn the best way you can. Sid was very close with me, he liked me and I *loved* him and I used to just want to be around him as much as I could. Everywhere he was, I was there. And Dave, well, I used to visit his family in Newark, and I used to hang around and try to learn. I went across the street when I was working with Joe Morris opposite George Shearing in the Three Deuces on Fifty-Second Street, I went across the street one night to the Onyx, just casually, you know, went across the street and I happened to look at the placard outside that said "Baby Dodds."

Well I had always been reading books and things and I seen that Gene Krupa had been influenced by Baby and Baby had been hanging out with Gene and they had some things going on together, so wanting to play the drums as bad as I wanted to, I said I'm goin' to listen to this drummer. So what I did, I went in the Onyx and Baby was playing in there with a bass drum and a snare drum and *one* cymbal, a ride cymbal. It wasn't a sock cymbal. He was swingin' so much, I was late a whole entire set! Joe fined me, I think it was, a 30-dollar fine for missing the entire set. But I couldn't leave. I had to. I sat down and just stayed. And then whenever I would run into Sid, and of course a lot of drums would get in my head and this was the right way, the best way, and the right way, and I think it's the best way *and* the right way. All the brush work that I dream up, of course the thing I dream up, now I try to dream up original things, but of course the direction I got earlier, the foundation, the right way to go, Sid Catlett used to sit down and show me the things I wanted to know, and Sid had taught Teddy Stewart of Kansas City, had taught Teddy brushes. Teddy showed them to me, told me Sid showed them to him, and, a funny thing, he and I were doing the same brush things when we used to practice together and he said, "Where'd you learn that?," and I said, "Aw shuck," and it came out that Sid showed it to Teddy. Teddy's very adept with brushes. I got most of my brush work from him, from Sid Catlett. We used to talk about how Sid used to play the brushes with so much finesse, so much finesse, that it was just fabulous.

It looks good, it's flash, it looks very good with those sticks bein' twirled in your hands, but you should be kept on the drums, you're supposed to be playing the drums. A lot of guys will say, "Ah, man, I left my tom-toms home, and my other cymbal is gone." Drums can be played with the bass drum, snare drum, and *one* cymbal, or if you don't have the cymbal you can use the snare drum. I know a lot of guys can sit down and play the snare drum. In the past few years all of that twirling, I don't like tricks, I don't like to resort to tricks. Now I try to do some kind of trick things with the cymbals but I want to do them in the rhythm. It's not just a trick, and you don't hear it, it's a trick and you *hear* it. Twirl the sticks and that's a trick and you don't hear it and nobody hears it, it's alright, it looks flashy, but what looks flashy is one thing, but what you hear it still rhythm that keeps it swinging. It looks good but it stops the beat. You don't feel it. Nevertheless I think you can do anything that has showmanship to it, and let the people hear it, and don't do pantomime drums, 'cause pantomime drums can't be heard on a record. But in the past few years, about seven, on different occasions I been fortunate enough to play with Buddy Rich and I been in his band in his group with him, and Buddy, he's phenomenal, he is phenomenal. He and I get down and discuss different things, different ways of gaining power in the hands, and I have a ball with him all the time and Buddy does things that are unbelievable for any drummer and if a drummer tells me that he can look at Buddy and say, "Ahhh," something's wrong, because it's unbelievable! I used to sit and play congas. I'd play the conga drum onstage. While he was playing drums in his solo, I'd be playing rhythm, just keep the cha cha going, and I used to look over at him to see when he was going to come out of his solo and I couldn't see his hands. I couldn't see them, they were a blur, the sticks were blurs, he's always been very modest . . . the greatest drummer I've listened to.

When you start saying go in there and play those drums, he plays the drums and I said all that to say this: I've seen him play all kinds of solos, in every way you can think of, and I have never seen him do any tricks. He plays drums and cymbals, all the time, both the hands and feet. But that doesn't mean that I'm against twirling of the sticks and whatnot because the old drummers used to do that, 'cause that was the thing in those days and when a drummer could do that he was of course flashy, but like we were just speaking earlier, the era has changed and it's getting so the people are getting more modern-minded. We're talking about the moon, the drums have got to go to the moon, you can't be playin' the drums in 1923, the drums have got to move along and progress too. The only thing I can say is for all drummers, including myself—and I'm *really* scuffling just to stay this way—I want to keep time behind me and don't let it catch up with you. I always say this. I'm used to making statements sometimes may sound a little catty, when I'd hear somebody I didn't approve of the way they were playing, I'd say, "Emit" had caught them— e-m-i-t—I used to say Emit has got him. Emit is time backwards: T-i-m-e. In other words, when time catches up with you, you become passé, so I'm striving to keep time behind me, I don't want time to pass me and go ahead and drums wake up someday and go in front of me, then I'm going to be old-fashioned and I fight to stay with it and I always say, "Don't let Emit catch you!"

Bill Evans

■

Just 11 months before his conversation with Ralph Gleason, Bill Evans had made music history as part of the famous Miles Davis band that recorded *Kind of Blue*—often lauded as the greatest album in the history of jazz. Evans played a key role in shaping the aesthetic vision behind this seminal album, and one could hardly imagine Davis achieving its distinctive sound without this pianist's presence in the band. Yet even before the *Kind of Blue* session, Evans had left the Davis combo to strike out on his own.

At this stage in his career, Evans had gained recognition among jazz insiders as one of the most provocative pianists on the scene, but his name recognition among the general public was almost nil. Yet he was about to embark upon a period of extraordinary creativity. His trio with bassist Scott LaFaro and drummer Paul Motian redefined the role of the rhythm section in jazz. LaFaro's death in a car accident on July 6, 1961, put an end to this remarkable band, but the albums the trio made before his passing rank among Evans's finest works. His subsequent 1960s albums include *Undercurrent*, a collaboration with guitarist Jim Hall, *Conversations with Myself*, a Grammy-winning project that was one of the first jazz albums to experiment with overdubbing, and *Alone*, a solo piano project that would earn another Grammy for Evans.

In the liner notes for the latter project, Evans remarked on the irony that he made his living as a public performer, but his most cherished moments of music making came when he was simply playing without an audience. Gleason shows in this interview his skill in penetrating through Evans's shy demeanor and getting the artist to open up about his music and aspirations.

■

RJG: *Have you ever explored the reasons why you're in jazz?*

BE: I don't know. I never thought about it that much. In fact, like I said to someone the other night, Lord knows why we're doing this because there's so many rough spots on the road. It was not like an ambition where you sit down and say, "Well, I'm going to be a jazz musician and then I'll buy a book of hot licks." I can remember when I was in college, my theory teacher said, "Why in the world are you going into jazz? I can't understand it." I said, "I don't know," but I just knew I was going to and I could have gone the other way.

RJG: *What attracted you first?*

BE: Well, there was a stock [arrangement] of "The Lambeth Walk" that I picked up when I was about nine. And "The Big Apple." And then, some records started knocking me out when I was 12 or 13, typical things like "Well Git It." I didn't hear too much jazz then, but fortunately there were a couple of very hip people, young guys in my hometown (one very tragically met an early death) and they turned me on to a lot of things like Fatha Hines and stuff like that. Also, what Bird and Diz were doing then, that was kind of a revelation when I finally got with that. It was a funny thing, but the first couple of things I heard, I don't know whether it affected you the same way, but I didn't really know what was happening, it was really a flash.

RJG: *After Hines, did any other piano player strike you with any particular force?*

BE: I just listened to more or less what you might call the jazz mind wherever I could hear it, in any horns or in arrangements of music . . . musical thinking, let's say. After that I liked Nat Cole very much, and when I finally heard Bud Powell on Dexter Gordon's sides he knocked me out because he had much more of a feeling of form in his soul. He would really bring it to a conclusion and go into the next thing and he had a feeling . . . I don't know, but I really liked him more than anybody, I guess. Then just everybody I heard I would listen to. A whole mess of musicians, local musicians, just anybody, wherever you go, because by that time I was going to all the clubs and sessions in different cities. I was near New Orleans when I went to college so I spent a lot of time around the French Quarter and there was a real mixture of all kinds of odd influences there. There's modern musicians and then going all the way back.

RJG: *When you were still in school, was there any indication that you might not go into jazz?*

BE: I don't think so. I started to realize that I was going strong in that direction I think maybe when I was about 15. I started to get interested in learning about how it's built, the theory of music and so on, so that I could begin to make my own lines. I don't think there was any doubt in my mind when I graduated from college. I was 20 then and I really knew that I wanted to go out there. But that doesn't mean that I didn't have a real strong interest, participating interest, in some other kinds of music like classical music, or whatever you want to call it, 'cause I have and I've spent a lot of time with it since then. In fact, I learnt an awful lot from that kind of music.

RJG: *You used a very interesting expression a moment ago, Bill, the jazz mind. How would you describe the jazz mind?*

BE: I don't know, lemme think a minute. There's a particular attitude, I think, sort of an instantaneous response or something like that. It's just sort of a direct thing, and this immediately imposes, I think, a closed area within which you have to work, an area in which you develop the facility, you know. It's just like if you pick up a ball and you know how to throw, you don't have to think about throwing it. In jazz it would all have a certain similarity because it has to be within a certain area of facility and knowledge, and that's the difference because your feeling sends out sort of a motivation and that has to be answered without so much figuring and tearing apart. There has to be a real facility to answer that motivation.

RJG: *Would this indicate, then, that the more you were to apply deliberate thinking to writing something in jazz, deliberate planned thinking and rewriting and so forth, the more you would dilute the thing that you were producing?*

BE: I wouldn't say dilute, because that would be a qualitative thing. I don't think it affects the quality, but it affects the character, and when you write, I think the character of the work is different. It can't be the same. So the jazz mind, to me, would be the player, it would have to be the player, it could never be the writer. The writer could write jazz by learning from the players and then composing. Then the form and the texture and so on would have a different character and would be maybe much more perfect in its structure because the guy would have time to . . . I think George Russell does wonderful work like that because he really absorbs, I think, the feeling of what everybody is doing and yet he's strictly a composer and he composes things that sound as if they could be improvised almost. It always has to depend on the jazz player, though, because I think if the jazz player vanished and then the composer started to go off on his own, he would end up again with a cerebral kind of thing. The only thing that gives the thing roots is the essential thing that he hears in the jazz players.

RJG: *What about the things, for instance, that Gunther [Schuller] and John [Lewis] and André Hodeir have been doing?*

BE: I don't know anything about André Hodeir. I've heard some of the things that John Lewis did and I've played some of the things that Gunther's done. I hardly know what to say about that. I just performed a piece of Gunther's that he wrote for the Modern Jazz Quartet. I performed it with the Baltimore Symphony not long ago and I really didn't get a great deal of musical satisfaction out of playing the thing. I didn't really feel that I was playing something that I believed in that much and yet there's maybe nobody I respect more than Gunther Schuller as a musician. But as a participant it wasn't that satisfying to me. I could listen to it and know there's so much there I don't know about and I know that Gunther hears everything he writes because it all sounds musical to me, but I don't know how it relates to jazz playing that much. I think I might if I studied his pieces more. I really haven't studied them. As far as contributing to the language or something like that, he may have a way of developing ideas which could be of use in jazz or something like that, I don't know.

RJG: *Has it ever struck you that there's a possibility of exclusion or a possibility of a barrier between the sort of thing that John and Gunther are working towards, and the sort of music that Miles [Davis] represents?*

BE: Yeah, there's some kind of a big difference there. Miles seems to be always moving towards more simplicity. Now I don't know whether that will be the way he goes, 'cause he's always changing and he may just start changing and go the other way. But it seems the opposite so far with Gunther, at least. I mean he's dealing with real complex, compositional techniques and instrumentation and sounds and form and everything. There's quite a difference there because no jazz group could simulate a composition of Gunther Schuller's in any way.

I think Charles Edward Smith hates to bring this into any jazz discussion, but there are sociological implications, I think, in jazz playing and the philosophy that's in back of it. I think any group effort takes on a different significance from an individual effort because there's a lot of different factors involved and that might be one big difference. I mean there's nothing more degrading to me than to think of 70 or 80 musicians who have become almost machines serving this one thing. It's a respectful thing, it's a wonderful testimony to people that they'll go this far to serve somebody's mind, but somehow it bothers me. I think if they're going to do that they should also be making music on their own. Like myself. Maybe that's why I went into jazz, because I love both and I love to play both, but somehow you have got to have your own identity as well, in an expressive way, even if it's on a much lower level, or inferior level. It's you. That may be the big difference and maybe that's the change that's happening.

RJG: *Is it a problem to perform in both of those frameworks, one after another?*

BE: Not if you're trained for it, it's just like anything else. If you have ability or facility to do it, you can do it. It's just the difference between talking to one person and then turning your head and talking to another person. It's the same thing; you just change your attitude or your feeling. Maybe not too many people have the time or the opportunity to develop a fair degree of ability in both.

RJG: *How did it come about that you worked with Miles?*

BE: It was just another one of those things that all fits together, you know. He said he heard me a few times in the last couple of years before I worked with him. I guess Red [Garland] had wanted to leave or something; anyhow, I was around, worked a weekend in Philadelphia with him and then he asked me to stay.

RJG: *Had you any inkling that something like that might be in the wind or did it come as a surprise to you?*

BE: It came as a complete surprise. In fact, things were going very slow up till then. I'd been in New York about five years and different little things would happen, but actually not too much. I'd wanted to get a trio going for about three years and I just couldn't. I didn't try too hard because I don't believe in pushing too much, but I talked to a few people and presented it to a couple of booking offices and everything and nothing happened at all. Then I went with Miles and I think that's helped tremendously to get this thing going.

RJG: *When you work a weekend with a group and then the leader says stay with the group, what is it like? Do you rehearse? How do you fit in?*

BE: Well, in this case I was a fan of Miles' band so I was familiar with a lot of the things that they did and as it turned out we never did have a rehearsal, ever. But I knew most of the things they were doing. I learned the rest on the job and Miles would show me little things that I didn't know, and so on. Actually, I was pretty frightened, you know. This was the band that I idolized and I had them way up out here someplace.

RJG: *How long were you with the group altogether?*

BE: About eight months.

RJG: *Does Miles, as a leader or as a fellow player, structure the thought of the people that are with him? Does he discuss the music at all?*

BE: No, we very seldom talked . . . in fact, I don't think we ever talked in this way about music. We got together on some tunes a couple of times just before a date, or on a date or something, but not, . . . he was never in any way analytical or philosophical and anything. I never thought about things this way 'til I was about 21.

RJG: *Is it more emotionally rewarding when you're in a club with people close to you or on a stage at a concert?*

BE: I think it was most rewarding to me when we recorded, maybe, because the piano was that much better. We had some terrifically bad pianos in clubs. It was, I think, one of the reasons I left, even. We had some ridiculous pianos. The thing about working in a club is you're playing so much that it takes that nervous edge off. You just can't be on edge that much so pretty soon you forget about that and you just do your work and it begins to have a more solid kind of performance feeling. It might not always be at such a high level, but at least it has a sort of solid thing and then the highs come every once in a while.

RJG: *What are they like?*

BE: It just happens, I think. You're playing and then all of a sudden you know that something special is happening. You never know. I remember one night Miles was playing the blues and he sounded like he was a little distant or something and it played all the way through. I thought to myself while he was playing, "I hope you don't stop playing with this feeling," and he finished up with about four bars of the most beautiful, just about the most beautiful idea I think I've ever heard. That was it. You know, the whole solo was nothing, and I was afraid he was going to go out with it, but he didn't, he capped it with this one thing, and that was it.

Coltrane is just impossible, he's always got a million things going, you never know what he's going to do.

RJG: *It's curious how he alternately excites an audience to a great pitch or leaves them absolutely cold. There seems to be no middle ground for him.*

BE: I don't know what his personal playing problems are in that respect, but I'm sure that when it's happening for the audience, it's probably happening for him, too. It's really hard to get up there and do it all the time, it's a killing schedule. No concert artist in history would even . . . they'd have a nightmare about a schedule like jazz players have. It's something.

RJG: *Does the audience reaction to your performance, either emotional or vocal, have any effect on what you do?*

BE: Sure, you can't help it, really. It's a two-way thing. I would hate to think that if there was no response that I wouldn't feel like playing or something like that, because that's not true. But response is a great thing, the audience can definitely inspire you. Some concerts I've played have been surprising that way because sometimes you think nothing is happening and then you get this tremendous response. It's as if the people are giving a lot more than you, it makes you feel ashamed sometimes, you know, but that's the way it is. Sure, an audience has a lot to do with it, at least the consciousness of an audience, because you're communicating with somebody. When I'm playing I like to feel that I'm enjoying what I'm doing, and the trouble with me lately is that I'm not enjoying it too much. I still have to be the foremost authority about my own playing, but I hope that if I relate to people, then my music, what I'm doing, will relate to people and they'll respond, or like it or be moved in some way. There's another thing, too; there are certain kinds of music which do not move people to express themselves out loud. There are certain kinds of, say, religious music, where people are moved inside and they may never express it outwardly, so you can't always depend on just noise as meaning a response.

RJG: *A number of fans and some musicians that I know seem to have a definite spiritual feeling about jazz music.*

BE: I think it's there, without a doubt, just because it represents a person, and that's part of a person.

Bill Evans

RJG: *Would you say that there are certain types of jazz music that are in a sense religious?*

BE: I think so, sure, definitely. Maybe the difference is that jazz doesn't single out any particular part of our character that much, or make so much of any particular part, but just sort of speaks in everyday language and represents the whole person. Naturally there's going to be a spiritual side and practical side and maybe some humor.

RJG: *Do you think it's possible for a musician to play jazz part-time or does it require a total commitment artistically?*

BE: Well, no, I don't think so. It just depends. I mean, if you get satisfaction from something, why shouldn't you do it even if you only do it a little bit? The only thing is, if you are really going to try to make your living at it, or you want to be in some way meaningful in the profession, it just requires a great amount of time because there is no shortcut to the tremendous amount of experience necessary in just learning your instrument and learning music. Because it's a skill, it's not an intellectual thing at all. It's intellectual only in the sense that you use your mind to learn the skill, but it's not intellectual in conception. That's why it takes practice. You can think about a golf swing, but eventually you have to swing that club without thinking about it. That's just the way it is. But I'd say, no, everybody ought to enjoy it as much as they can. If they want to be part-time, why not? I think a lot of people could have that fun.

RJG: *Yet in order to really make a contribution, it requires at least the investment of the time.*

BE: It requires an awful lot of things and it ends up the most important thing is the intangible, which is your whole person, and that's the hard part. I don't know, maybe I do everything for music. I live my life for music, in a way. It's almost as if it's made me want to be a good person just for the sake of music.

RJG: *Has it been a source of satisfaction to play jazz on your own, with your own group and your own scene?*

BE: I think it will be, more and more. It has been, except that I'm so dissatisfied so far with what I've been doing. But it takes time, I'm sure it's what I want to do. I'd much rather be in this situation. I figure if I weren't playing with my own group or something like that, I would certainly have rather stayed with Miles, because that was a great experience.

RJG: *Is the piano your main instrument? Do you play other instruments?*

BE: I play the flute, but I haven't played it much lately. I played it pretty good by the time I got out of the army. And I tried violin when I was a kid, but I couldn't make it, I couldn't stand the sound I got. I tried it for about five years, just couldn't stand it. But I wouldn't say I play anything besides piano.

RJG: *Do you practice much?*

BE: Well, I guess . . . let's say till I was 28 I did an awful lot of practicing —I call it practicing, somebody else wouldn't. At least I spent a lot of time at the keyboard and thought about different things and played a lot of music, read through a lot of literature and so on. But this last year or so I haven't done nearly as much, I don't know why, maybe I'm getting old. I haven't done as much . . .

RJG: *Who would you say has been the most important musician in your life?*

BE: Oh, probably Bach. I don't know, because he was kind of a late comer in my life, but I suppose . . .

RJG: *What about the most important influence in your playing?*

BE: I suppose Bud Powell, but, like I say, there's really so many. It's more a process of developing, a thinking process that you feel strongly, and being able to do it. But I think probably Bud Powell.

RJG: *What pianists today interest you?*

BE: Well, there are some guys that I really love to listen to. I might not approach them as a student, but just as a listener, you know. For instance, I like to listen to Sonny Clark, I like to listen to Tommy Flanagan or Red Garland, and I don't know how many others I could mention. Probably anybody that can play I enjoy listening to. There may not be that much in what they're doing that I could learn from. I might learn from Lennie Tristano, who I wouldn't enjoy listening to that much, so there's a difference there. I love to listen to John Lewis play. He's one of my very favorite pianists.

RJG: *How about Ahmad Jamal?*

BE: Yeah, I enjoy listening to him very much. I've heard some criticism of Ahmad Jamal, that he's a cocktail pianist and everything. The environment that has given Ahmad his background is a real world and his music is just as real as anybody's as far as I'm concerned, much more real than some who feel that they're really arty because I think they're just pretending and he's not. It's a real thing he's doing.

RJG: *The only pianist you mentioned you might learn from was Lennie. Are there any others?*

BE: I'm sure I could learn from Monk, but his personality is so strong that it seems to me he is the only person that can do what he does. I wouldn't want to imitate his idiosyncrasies 'cause I couldn't, he's lived his unique life. Still, I think there's quite a few musical things I could learn from him. I've played quite a few of his songs or tunes or whatever you want to call them, and I have an idea of the way his mind runs. What he does with them is so much him that it's even getting to the point where there are some songs I don't want to play anything but the melody on because I feel that it's, you know, that's it . . . some ballads I hardly want to mess with. I might put a couple of things in, but basically I just like to play the melody.

RJG: *Do you find it interesting or surprising or curious that you yourself are now an influence on other pianists?*

BE: If that's true I'd be surprised and I guess I'd be flattered, but I don't know how true it is. Just a couple of times some people have mentioned to me that they've heard some people trying to do some things that I might have done, but I don't know if that's true. I never really felt that original, to tell you the truth. At least if there's any originality, it's only maybe in the fact that I've worked with the materials in my own way, but I don't think the materials are that different.

RJG: *Do kids come up to you and talk to you about taking up jazz music?*

BE: Yeah, sure, every once in a while.

RJG: *What do you tell them?*

BE: Well, I usually just tell 'em that I don't teach, but I would be happy to get together with them if they want to talk sometime. So we usually get together once and I tell 'em the way I believe, which is that if you're going to do it, you're going to do it. And maybe if they want to, if they really lack some theoretical knowledge, I'll suggest that they go to a conservatory because it's very well organized there. I think you get a much broader and better and thorough musical training in a conservatory than you would get from any so-called jazz teacher. I'm talking about a good school. Then how you apply musical principles to jazz, depending on your experience and how much you participate, is up to you and how your life goes and everything. There's no way to teach, so that's the way it usually ends up.

That was the question up at Lenox last year. I finally tried to teach. I've been avoiding teaching all my life. There's a lot of participation. The students play nine hours a week in small ensembles and, I think, almost nine hours a week in large ensembles, and there's all kinds of discussions constantly, sessions, everybody's talking about jazz. They get private lessons, but it's more sort of just being with somebody who's a professional and you can work out some things. It's more like that. It's a very intensive jazz experience, and I think they will feel the fruits of it for years. I will, too, because it was very stimulating for me, too. I don't know whether I'm going to teach again because I felt if I teach a specific thing, then I'm teaching style and if I don't teach a specific thing, all I can say is, you got it, and then what am I there for?

So I tried somehow to get in the crack there. I really don't know how well I did. What's left is to teach musical principles. Either I would teach the mechanics of the piano, which I tried to give a little to everybody because most people lack that, or I'd teach musical principles, which takes a much longer time and then I would say, go to the conservatory. Or else I'd teach specifics, which are style, and I don't want to teach that, and then most people resisted that up there. But you can't circumvent everything, which is what some people want to do. There was really a great amount of talent. It was scary almost. There was so much talk about originality—too much, you know, it was fear almost, it was a fear of doing anything that was the same as anything else. I never really strive for that kind of originality—avoiding anything anybody's done—because that's the only way I've learned, in a way.

RJG: *This striving for originality at all costs, which goes all through jazz, particularly at the moment for the younger guys, do you think this leads to a certain unnaturalness?*

BE: It could, yeah, I think so, I don't know. The thing that I look for as the most essential ingredient in my music, to quote a composition teacher I once had, is "melodic impulse." This melodic impulse I think is the most essential ingredient, and that comes from a mass experience, an experience of—there is where it gets social again—all music, all players, everybody, all of your experiences and all of your relationships with people and things. Now if you're striving for originality by cutting yourself off from all these things, I don't see how it can have a real strength or have a real quality of communication or meaning for other people. Take someone like Coltrane, as opposed to Cecil Taylor. Coltrane has set his mind to the task of progressing with allegiance to the tradition, and whatever he does will fit over what is heard by the greatest amount of good musicians. I don't know whether this is true, but it seems as if Cecil Taylor would ignore that allegiance, you know, and just go off. Well, there's a difference in philosophies there, but one is, in a way, a much more socially responsible philosophy, to me. To relate to other people as much as possible. I guess there's my attitude about it. To sort of find this melodic impulse by working in tradition or working within a language that I've learned, to hear through experience or something like that.

RJG: *Has it been rewarding to you, then, to go back to men from the '30s?*

BE: I haven't really done that consciously. I don't seem to have a real impulse to do that because I really played with a lot of those musicians. I've been working professionally with good musicians since I was 14. I was lucky when I started. I played with musicians much better than myself. Good musicians in my hometown have been an influence, men very capable of having made the so-called big time, or maybe developed into much greater musicians than they are. Anyhow, they helped me a lot.

RJG: *How about guys who are still playing today successfully, like Ben Webster and Harry Edison?*

BE: Well, I've worked with Ben Webster and worked with Harry Edison and they're great, I love 'em, but they were more of an influence on me about 15 years ago . . . 10 to 15 years ago. Ten years ago I worked with Harry Edison. I worked with Budd Johnson and a whole mess of good musicians like that . . . around New Orleans, a lot of good musicians. I've really had personal contact with influences like that. I feel like if I wanted to be a Dixieland pianist I could be one. I've had a little experience there. I know that I'm far from being a good Dixieland pianist because there are such subtleties in every style that you don't realize until you get into it. I'm not that interested in developing those subtleties.

RJG: *Have you ever gone back and played old records?*

BE: Not too much. I've played a lot of older styles because we had to play a lot of Dixieland around New Orleans and I played a lot of Dixieland in New Jersey on jobs, for that matter. In a way I guess I've played almost everything that you could play as a professional musician. I've played with polka bands and the whole works, bar mitzvahs, society bands in New York, I've played with some of the best society jobs in New York and worked with some of the best men and learned all that repertoire, played all the mambos, cha-chas, peabodies . . . but that music isn't too much of a challenge. It's a challenge for a certain type of feeling, but there's not too much of a musical challenge there.

RJG: *You were at Lenox the summer Ornette [Coleman] was there. What is your reaction to him?*

BE: I enjoy him. I tried to play with Ornette one day at Lenox and it wasn't really successful for a number of reasons. I enjoy listening to it, but I don't know how much I could fit in or anything like that. I don't hear anything wrong in his conception, I think he's very natural. I don't think he's trying to be far-out. I think maybe Don Cherry might be reaching farther away from himself than Ornette is, but it's alright because he's got a steadying influence there in Ornette. The rest of the group now is perfect. Billy Higgins and Charlie Haden, I don't think any one of those guys could be replaced or changed without really hurting the group. But I don't hear anything unnatural in Ornette's playing.

RJG: *The tendency to always be looking for something new in jazz is one of the criticisms that Ornette has inadvertently acquired.*

BE: I don't understand that business. There are so many motivations, there's jealousy, and there's fear. I know there's a lot of musicians that are probably just afraid. They are saying, well, if this is it, I know I'm far from it, so they may be afraid. Anyhow, no one person is that much of an influence. I mean Dizzy and Bird and so on played a composite of people. It wasn't just like one person came along and then everybody copied them or something, not at all. Ornette plays some old-time licks, you listen to him. In fact, I was sitting with Percy Heath the other night down there listening to him. He played something that sounded like about 1910, but maybe in a different place and with a different key. He's definitely right out of everything, only he's moved to put these things in different places. Somebody was telling me Ornette was playing with somebody and every time this guy would hit a change Ornette would play something and it would scare this guy so he said to Ornette, "What are you playing that for? Can't you hear what I'm playing?" And Ornette said, "I was surprised because it was what he was playing that was making me hear what I was hearing." But he hears that way. He probably has terrifically sensitive ears and hears all these separate things and it just fits in there.

RJG: *Do you have an active interest in other arts?*

BE: I've never really been able to appreciate visual art very much. I probably would like a calendar picture as well as a Rembrandt. Especially, in modern art, I really don't know what's happening. I sort of see something but, I don't know, I don't respond too much. I don't really get a strong feeling. There's nothing that even begins to approach music as far as my own responses are concerned. I used to do a lot of reading, just fun reading, when I was younger and then when I went through certain growing-up problems I read a lot of philosophy, psychology, and religion because I was going through those problems. I was looking for an answer which was not there and when I realized it wasn't there I sort of lost interest.

RJG: *You mean the answer is in music, not in books of philosophies?*

BE: Well, it is for me. But even before I did it, I responded to music much more than anything else. I don't know what it is.

RJG: *Do you think some people are just made that way?*

BE: Well, I would say it's more my own limitation. I'm limited to music. I think almost everybody responds to music very strongly at some level, which you can see easily enough, but maybe I just closed my mind to other things or something. I think lately it's opening up a little more because I actually begin to appreciate painting a little more. I just sort of walked with my eyes in one direction for quite a while.

RJG: *I'm sure you've had the experience of people liking something that you did that you weren't satisfied with or that their response was out of proportion to your own . . .*

BE: Yeah, it makes you wonder a little bit, but like I said before, you have to be your own authority. I don't think the people are wrong either. As a professional musician and as a practitioner in the art, you're going to produce even when you're not satisfied with what you're producing, but you're still producing at a certain level. There might be this much difference to the listener and to you it's a tremendous amount of difference because you're always hoping to take another step. I used to sometimes feel like I should put people down or something because I'd say I know it's no good, but I don't think that's true anymore.

RJG: *How about the reverse of it, when you do something with which you are almost thoroughly satisfied. Does that always get through?*

BE: It doesn't seem to all the time, but I think one of the reasons is that sometimes the feeling that I enjoy most is a quiet feeling and it might just evoke a quiet response, like I was talking about before. But I think when things are really happening, it will communicate.

RJG: *Dizzy said one time that there were only four or five times in his entire life that he had been thoroughly satisfied with what he played.*

BE: I don't think that's unusual, though, among musicians because I know Coltrane said he hardly likes anything he's ever recorded. I think he might like one thing. I know I have a hard time mentioning maybe three. I guess that's what you have to be satisfied with. I've heard artists, musicians, people in general talk about this a lot. I was tremendously unhappy with my first record. I don't know how I can explain how unhappy I was, but after about a year I began to tolerate it and now I think it was pretty good. It was as good as I could do at that time, in fact, maybe better. The same way with my second one. I was pretty unhappy with that at first, but I grew out of that quicker than the first and now I've just made another one which I'm almost happy with, and I think this is a bad sign.

RJG: *You think you're weakening?*

BE: Yeah, I really do, getting much more tolerant about myself.

RJG: *What do you want to do with your music now? Do you have a definite concept of what you want to accomplish?*

BE: No, I don't. That bothers me a little bit sometimes and then sometimes I'm glad because I feel, well, then I can go in any direction. Lately I've been more satisfied I think, and more sure that what I'm doing is exactly what I want to do. I don't know where the heck I want to go and sometimes I feel I almost could be a disappointment to people.

RJG: *Do you feel a responsibility to them, then?*

BE: I do, yeah. I feel a responsibility. I don't know how. Somehow to be . . . to do good work, I suppose that's it. It's pretty hard because I'm really a lazy person. If I hadn't been interested in music I couldn't have forced myself to do it all, I just couldn't. I've never been able to force myself to do things. It's hard for me to teach because I can't tell a person to be interested, or you have to go out and play jobs for 10 years and live fully for music. How are you going to do that? Because I wanted to do it, that's the only reason I ever did it.

Horace Silver

APRIL 16, 1961

■

ianist Horace Silver did more than anyone to create the hard
bop sound that came to the forefront of the jazz world in
the late 1950s and early 1960s. This music attracted audiences with its more soulful variant on modern jazz. Listeners
could hear elements of gospel, funk, R & B, and Latin music in
the work of Silver and the other leaders of the hard bop idiom. These
artists never completely abandoned the experimentalism that had char-
acterized jazz during the bebop era, but Silver & company also wanted
fans to tap their toes and snap their fingers to the beat. Even as jazz lost
much of its mainstream audience during the Cold War years, Silver
could still attract a sizable following and generate radio airplay with his
hard-grooving melodies.

Silver first came to prominence in 1950 as a member of Stan Getz's
band, but a short while later he left to launch the Jazz Messengers, one
of the defining hard bop bands of the period. While with this group,
Silver enjoyed his first hit, "The Preacher." Alfred Lion, owner of Blue
Note Records, had argued against releasing the track, but Silver in-
sisted. "He may not have liked it," Silver later recounted in his autobiography, "but he made a lot of money from it." Silver never had another
disagreement with the label over song choices, and soon other artists
recording for Blue Note were imitating the Silver sound.

In 1956, Silver left the Jazz Messengers—which continued to thrive
under the leadership of drummer Art Blakey—and began recording
with a new quintet under his own name. Even as jazz styles evolved,
with avant-garde and rock-oriented approaches capturing the attention
of cutting-edge fans and critics, Silver enjoyed a string of successes,
perhaps most notably his *Song for My Father* album (1964), which incorporated aspects of Cape Verdean music that the pianist had learned
from his father. During this same period, Silver's band proved to be a

training ground for future star jazz bandleaders, including Joe Henderson, Woody Shaw, and Michael Brecker.

Silver was 32 years old at the time of his conversation with Ralph Gleason. He still had many of his best-known works ahead of him—now classic albums such as *Song for My Father* (1964), *The Cape Verdean Blues* (1965), and *The Jody Grind* (1966). This interview is one of the best sources of information about Silver's priorities as a composer and bandleader during the heyday of the hard bop movement.

■

RJG: *What are your own favorites of the tunes you have written?*

HS: I don't know, to tell you the truth, Ralph. It's kind of a hard question to answer—I try to write a varied type of thing. I know that I'm noted by the public for writing these bluesy-type tunes I guess are the most popular, most accepted out of the things I do. "Soulville," "Home Cooking," "Juicy Lucy," "Señor Blues," "Doodlin,'" "Sister Sadie," those things, but I don't limit myself to these things, this is a part of me, a very large part of me, but there's another part of me, too, which probably the real strict Horace Silver fan would dig, but the average person that might buy my records goes for the other part of me. I'm very strongly influenced by Latin rhythms as you probably know, I dig Latin rhythms, I think they swing. The Latin music itself doesn't carry a whole lot of depth to it, harmonically and everything like that, but the rhythms are something else, you can get into all kinds of stuff with Latin rhythms. And I like to write in that vein and ballad-wise I strive to do something a little different. My ballads so far haven't seemed to have caught on too much, but I'm not giving up because I think that I'm doing something a little different as far as ballads are concerned. I'm not speaking of radically different, but I'm just speaking of originality as far as ballads are concerned. I've always thought of it in this way. As far as writing is concerned I admire Monk, and the few things, of course Bud

[Powell] hasn't written as much as Monk but I mean I admire these two guys pianistically as well as their writing, but the things that Bud wrote I like very much and Monk also—naturally Duke, that goes without saying—and John Lewis also. But outside of these guys I hear so many jazz ballads that seem trite to me—and have no particular style to them and I've strived to get a different style in my ballad writing than the regular run-of-the-mill stuff, jazz ballads, and I think I've done this. Hasn't seemed to get across too much to the people, as the bluesy things I do.

RJG: *Of the ballads, which one do you dig the most?*

HS: I can't say.

RJG: *There was no thing that you had a particular soft spot for?*

HS: Well I like "Cheryl." Of course, I wrote that for somebody that I was very fond of, and it has a sentimental thing with me. I like "Melancholy Mood." "You Happened My Way," I like that one, I like "Peace." Incidentally Blue Mitchell just recorded "Peace" with strings. Benny Golson wrote the arrangement of it.

RJG: *How did you happen to write that song. How did that come about?*

HS: "Peace"? I don't know, I just sat down and tried to write a ballad and it came about—when I say I sat down, I don't have no particular idea in mind, I just tried to search for something pretty. In a ballad, it should be beautiful but also I try to search for a pretty chord pattern in most of my writing, I mean aside from the blues things I do and maybe up-tempo blues, slow blues, medium blues, or "I Got Rhythm"–type tunes, the easy blowing–type things, but I mean getting away from those things with the ballads or with maybe some of the Latin things or some other type of things that I write I try to find a different chord sequence, and interesting chord sequences. The only way I can sort of explain it is like, say you're walking down a road from one point to another like from where are we now, in Oakland?

RJG: *Berkeley.*

HS: We are going from Berkeley to San Francisco—well you can take the main route and this way, straight, right over the bridge, into S.F. and then you can deviate this way and twist around that way and still come out at the same point, and that's what I try to do.

RJG: *When you're writing a ballad, do you start with any phrase or idea or little run or chord changes that you happen to be thinking about at the moment, or do you just sort of start it and—?*

HS: Just start from scratch. I don't have anything in mind usually— well, this is true of mostly everything I write, when I sit down to do something I have nothing in mind. The only thing I might have in mind is that I'd like to try to write a new ballad and I'll try to do this, but I have no melody in mind to start off with or no chords in mind to start off with. That's true of mostly everything I write, with a few exceptions, like, say, "Juicy Lucy," that was based on the chord changes to "Confirmation," which I like to play on those chord changes, so I just thought I'd try to write a line on those changes. I've done that on a few things, but most of the things that I write have some original set of chord changes and original melody. I don't have anything in mind when I sit down. I just stumble around until I luck up on something. Sometimes it comes all at one sitting, but most times it comes a little at a time.

RJG: *I should think that the tunes that you write should then be fun for you to play too, because they would fall into your natural conception, wouldn't they?*

HS: Yeah, they are. They're most easy to me to play.

RJG: *Well, they're an extension of you in a very real sense, aren't they?*

HS: Yeah, I get a big kick out of writing, because all of those tunes that any composer, the tunes they write are sort of like having children, sort of like your kids and you listen to other people. It gives you a big thrill when somebody else records or even plays one of your tunes, the fact that they play it means that they like it, and that pleases you. Plus you get a kick out of their conception of the tune, and I'm always anxious to hear some of my tunes done by somebody else to dig what kind of conception they put to it.

RJG: *Has any particular version of one of your tunes by someone else knocked you out more than another?*

HS: I like George Shearing's "Señor Blues." He's doing "The Outlaw," now too, incidentally.

RJG: *Oh, he is?*

HS: He recorded it, too, he told me, should be out pretty soon. I'm very anxious to hear something that J.J. [Johnson] wrote. This is not my composition, but J.J. wrote a tune and recorded it with his last group before they broke up; it had Clifford Jordan, Freddie Hubbard, and he calls the tune "In Walked Horace," and I'm dying to hear that thing. I wish Columbia would hurry up and release it.

RJG: *I wonder what he did. That's going to be you.*

HS: Well J.J., I love everything he does, he's long been one of my, rather, I've been one of his admirers. I admired his playing and his writing for a long time.

RJG: *This is going to be "In Walked Horace" as J.J. sees it. I notice more and more musicians today perform an increasing percentage of* *their repertoire from their own works. Now, is this just a natural thing or is this on purpose? Does this fall logically out of what you're doing? Is it more fun to do these than to take songs and do them?*

HS: Well, with me, I can only speak for myself, it really, it comes easier to me to be frank. I like standards, we do a few standards, but we do "Round About Midnight," which is Monk's thing, that's a jazz standard. We do "I'll Remember April," and "Darn That Dream," we do a few standards, but with the standards I would like to be able to do something very, very different with them—I mean we could just blow 'em like a lot of people do, I mean, a good solo is a good solo, a good feeling is a good feeling. But I would like to arrange it in a manner that had something different about it, and lot of times it's much easier for me to write something myself than to do this. It comes easier to me than to write an arrangement on a standard because I feel that sometimes I write an arrangement, although it might be a good arrangement, it's not that much different. So I've done a few arrangements on the standards like "My One and Only Love," I thought that came off pretty well but on the whole I find that the originals flow better with me, they come easier to me. And I feel that they have much more originality to them.

RJG: *What is the thing about your own playing in the group and the whole music scene that's the most kicks to you?*

HS: On the nights that we're really popping, when we really get together as a unit, really swinging, that's the most kicks. I mean this group I have now is a pretty good group, musically. On the stand and off the stand we get along well together and we have a lot of fun playing and we've been together long enough to maintain some sort of a level every night, but there are special nights when we really hit that stride, get that peak thing going where you just swing all night long and you get the dynamics right, and the level is right, the acoustics in the club are right, and the audience is with you, and that's a heck of a feeling when you get that happening.

RJG: *Easier to play then?*

HS: Yeah, much easier. The ideas just flow out, everything flows. It's like you're sailing in space, floating.

RJG: *That's an interesting sort of free form thing that happens then, isn't it?*

HS: Yeah, the tighter a rhythm section is and the tighter a whole group is, when you, 'course a group can be tight but when you really hit that stride, on those certain nights when everything is cooking, the rhythm section is cohesive, everything is smooth, the horns are really wailing and I don't know, it's hard to put into words but everything seems to flow, it's like you're sailing, floating around in space, there's not no real effort to anything. It's when the rhythm is flowing your ideas seem to flow too, just everything comes out so much easier than ordinarily.

RJG: *It's almost as if you couldn't do anything wrong?*

HS: Yeah.

RJG: *Be hard to go against it?*

HS: That's right.

RJG: *That's fascinating. Those are the real kicks?*

HS: Yeah, really.

RJG: *How often does that happen?*

HS: Well that's hard to say. Doesn't happen every night, though, I'll tell you that.

RJG: *Be a groove if it did.*

HS: But when you do, when that happens and everything comes off like that, it gives you a heck of a sensation, it's almost like being high. It's a natural high!

RJG: *Better than being high?*

HS: Yeah, really—because you're elated.

RJG: *Is it hard to stop then?*

HS: Stop playing or stop the groove?

RJG: *Stop playing.*

HS: No, everything just seems to come natural, everything just flows.

RJG: *What I mean is, like all of a sudden it's 2 o'clock—?*

HS: Oh yeah, well I know what you mean, sometimes you don't want to stop.

RJG: *Do you guys rehearse much?*

HS: Yeah, we do quite a bit of rehearsing. We do all our rehearsing out of town, because in New York one fellow lives in Brooklyn, one lives in the Bronx, and they're all spread out, and it's hard to get together. So, whenever we go out on the road we usually stay at the same hotel and we go down to the club during the day and rehearse. We had couple of rehearsals while we were in Los Angeles and we're going to have another one this week. Because I've written some new material which, we're playing some of it now and I've got some more of it to write out this week, and we're going to rehearse it and do some of it because we're planning on a new album.

RJG: *Well, now when you write out new things for the group how much is actually written?*

HS: There's usually an introduction that's written out and the melody, and if there's any interludes or an out chorus and an ending, that's it. I never write down drum parts. I don't think I've ever written a drum part for any of the drummers I've had. Because, I'd rather have them just cop it from listening, comes more natural, I think writing out drum parts kind of makes things a little stiff.

RJG: *For instance, if you work out a, you take this intro and the melody and your interludes and your chorus, which is a skeleton for your final performance, and you do it in rehearsal several times, do things fall into place that you hadn't written out that are worked out in your rehearsal that you're then going to keep?*

HS: Sometimes, it depends. I usually have everything in my mind, what I want to do. I know when I write it out what I want to be happening with the tune. But sometimes when we get to the rehearsal and rehearse it, I change things around or something might happen spontaneously that I say, yeah, keep that in or throw that out or something.

RJG: *Do you try to think in terms of the guys that are working with you?*

HS: Yeah, I do. I try to write in terms of the guys I have with me. On the whole I do, I'll say that. To be completely honest, most times when I sit down I think of the guys that are with me and I try to write something easy for them to play, but that has depth. This is a twofold thing because it's good for them, it's easy for them to play. The chord changes are easy, but they're saying something, that's the hard part. Simplicity is very hard, you know, being simple without being corny. To write a simple melody, easy for them to play, easy chord changes for them to play, and yet have it be saying something and have some depth to it, something that's going to be a good piece of music, that's very hard and this is what I have in mind I'll say 90 percent of the time, but sometimes I get tired of that, I don't know, sometimes I just say to myself, what the heck, this one is for me, I'm just going to do whatever I feel like doing here. If it's hard to play it's just hard to play, that's all. I'm going to write it anyway.

RJG: *Who are your favorite composers?*

HS: Monk is one, Duke Ellington of course, John Lewis. Bud, he hasn't written as much as these other fellows have, but I like the things Bud wrote. Let's see, J.J., I like his stuff, Miles, of course, I like Sonny Rollins tunes—well I'm sure there's some more but I can't think of them right now, those are the things that come to my mind first of all.

RJG: *How about classical composers?*

HS: Well, I haven't had that much classical training, to be honest, Ralph. I like classics, but I only studied it for a very short time. I had a good classical teacher. 'Course I've went through a series of bad teachers back home in Connecticut on piano as I did on tenor. I was taught the wrong way on both instruments and I had to undo all that wrong training and start all over again on both instruments, but when I finally got a hold of a good classical teacher I did study with him for about a year, maybe a little more than a year, and then he died and I stopped taking lessons for awhile. This teacher I had was a very excellent teacher and he did more for me than the rest of the teachers, he undid all the wrong that was taught me and he had me doing the right things. He taught me the correct fingering, the correct way to hold my hands and all that. He had me doing the Hanon exercises and the Czerny exercises which the other teachers didn't even give me, scales, minor, major, and all these different scales, he really was a good teacher, but at that time I was playing a little jazz at that time, my first jazz influence on the piano was boogie-woogie and then from there I went on into Teddy Wilson and started to listen to Tatum and then Bud and Monk and different things like that, but I was interested in harmony at that time and I could play a few little standard tunes on the piano and I knew a few chords but I didn't know too much and what used to bug me about these classical lessons is I'd practice these things like mad and I'd get them down and, I'd have a few pages per week and finally I'd get the whole thing down well and then he'd tell me I'd have to go over it again and do the whole thing for my next lesson, and what would happen, I didn't know no harmony, and I'd get in the middle of one of these things and I'd get hung up, get lost, and I'd have to stop and go back to the beginning and start all over again whereas I realize now, if this guy had taught me harmony and I'd really known what I was playing harmonically, maybe I'd have been able to fake where I goofed off at and continue, but I didn't know any harmony. It used to bug me because I played boogie-woogie at that time, and if I messed up playing boogie-woogie I could fake my way out and keep going but when I'd get into this classical things and I'd get lost I'd have to stop and start all over again and it used to bug me and sort of took my interest away from it for a while, because I wanted to know what I was doing. I don't believe in being overanalytical but I was kind of analytical, specially in those days because I learned more from phonograph records, I think, than anything else because back in Connecticut, I'm from Norwalk, very few jazz musicians around there and maybe one or two good ones at that, and the record shops hardly carried any good jazz records, I had to go into New York to pick up some records and when I'd go into New York to pick up some records I'd be so thrilled to get these records, I'd go to maybe 10 record shops and buy one record from each place, whatever I could find and I thought I could learn from, I'd bring these things home and I'd put them on the little old-fashioned wind-up phonograph, slow them down and I'd figure out the chords from the record, and I'd try to analyze these things, where the piano player played. I'd listen to it and hear it and try to find it on the piano. Then I'd try to break it down and I said, now, what is this he played, let me analyze this, what do they call this chord, and I learned a lot like that.

RJG: *Well, sure, with the blues thing, if you got hung up in the middle of the boogie-woogie thing you know the pattern on which it was based, you could go and do any darn thing and come out alright.*

HS: That's right.

RJG: *How are your hands, have you had any more trouble with your hands?*

HS: No, my hands have been doing very well, thanks to my doctor, I have a wonderful doctor. He's a chiropractic doctor and a physiotherapist, and I have a lot of faith in chiropractic doctors, specially this one anyway, a lot of people put him down, but this doctor's a very wonderful doctor and aside from being my doctor he's my friend too. He's around 71 years old. He's from New Haven, Connecticut. His name is Dr. Dwight Hamilton. He's about 71 years old and he was born on the same day I was and we're both Virgos, September 2nd's our birthday, and he's a friend of mine as well as my doctor. I've learned a lot from him about health. I've become very health-conscious through him and reading health literature and I had this, they thought it was arthritis at first, in my right hand, but it turned out to be a thing called tendonitis.

It's a sprained tendon and I had an overacid condition which was keeping it from getting well. I had about three times as much acid in my system than I was supposed to have and he got rid of that for me, and it took about eight months of treatments, little by little, to get rid of the thing, but I'm completely straight with it now, my hand is fine and I try to keep this acid thing down. But I have nothing but praise for him. He's a very wonderful person and for a man of his age a very studious man. I admire him so much, because I look at him at his age, he's so agile. He looks like he's about 49, and he's 71. Climbs the stairs two at a time. Rides downtown on his bike every morning for the paper and all of that and he's one doctor that's really interested in his patients, which most doctors today are not. They don't take an interest really, but he takes time with you and he's always studying something, he studies hypnosis, he studies graphoanalysis. He's a heck of a guy, a very interesting guy.

RJG: *What things do you have now in your mind that you want to do in the next few years, what challenges are you setting yourself?*

HS: I'll tell you, the things that I have record-wise, we have to do two albums a year, record-wise, what I have planned for this year is the things that we're rehearsing now. I've planned for a live date in a club in New York, I don't know which club, but some club in New York, we're going to record a live session, and secondly, a trio album which I haven't done in quite a few years, that's what I have planned for this year. And after that, maybe something with a big band or semi–big band or strings, I don't know exactly, something maybe a little different. Also I have something else in my mind for this year. I have been thinking in terms of trying to reach more people, a bigger audience with my music. I've been asking the booking agency to try to get us jobs in places that we haven't been before. We have no trouble playing all the major cities and all of that, but I'd like to get to some of these places that we've never played before. I mean foreign countries, we've been abroad, but there are some of the countries we haven't played before. Some of the smaller cities that we haven't played before, like Kansas City, we've never been, I think we're going to go there, and Milwaukee, Minneapolis, little places like that. Even if it means taking a little less money, I'd like to get to some of these places and present my music to a wider audience.

RJG: *Well, you got a lot to experiment with there. If you want to get around to those smaller places. Because most of them don't get jazz groups.*

HS: That's true. Rochester, New York, that's one, they have a club up there now. 'Fact, I think Jon Hendricks' brother is part owner in the club.

RJG: *Jimmy?*

HS: Yeah.

RJG: *Well, crazy, I look forward to hearing the trio album.*

HS: Well, it's my continual aim to try to improve my playing and my writing. I stay pretty busy, specially in New York because I never realized before I became a leader what work is involved in it. A lot of people probably don't realize, certainly the side men don't realize because it's a heck of a lot of responsibility. Aside from trying to keep up my instrument and trying to do the writing, arranging, there's so much business details to be taken care of, you got to get with your contracts in the office and publicity and all kinds of things, taxes, and it never stops. I'm always running around, never have enough time to complete anything. When I get back to New York now, I'll have been away for about three and a half weeks, and my mail box will be bulging with stuff to attend to.

RJG: *It's kind of interesting that you should have started out interested in boogie-woogie and end up on Blue Note because that was the daddy of the boogie-woogie labels.*

HS: Yeah.

RJG: *Give my regards to Alfred [Lion] and Frank [Wolff (founders of Blue Note Records)] when you get back.*

HS: I will, they're wonderful people.

RJG: *I knew them when they started.*

HS: They've given so many people, that label, Blue Note label's given so many people a chance. They still continue to do so, too, they're always giving guys a break.

Edward Kennedy "Duke" Ellington

JULY 10, 1960

■

Duke Ellington, the most esteemed composer and band-leader in the history of jazz, spent more than a half-century in the limelight as a star performer. In a rare conjunction of commercialism and artistry, he managed to sell millions of records even as he created some of the most ambitious rule-breaking compositions in the history of popular music. Yet even as he enjoyed the perks of stardom, Ellington guarded his private life. When dealing with journalists, he was invariably polite, but could be cautious or vague in his responses.

But Gleason had a close relationship with Ellington. A few years after this conversation, the two would collaborate on *Love You Madly*, a documentary about Ellington, and a film of the bandleader's cele-brated Sacred Music Concert at San Francisco's Grace Cathedral—projects that would earn three Emmy Award nominations. The rapport between the musician and journalist is immediately evident in this in-terview. "I feel like I'm on the same level as you," Ellington remarks a few minutes into their conversation, "because you have proven you are a great listener."

At this point in his career, Ellington was enjoying a second wind as an elder statesman of jazz. Just a few years earlier, his ensemble had struggled to find work as the American public's tastes shifted away from big bands to pop ballads and rock and roll. But Ellington's huge suc-cess at the 1956 Newport Jazz Festival had stirred up new interest in the band, accompanied by a *Time* magazine cover story and record contract with Columbia. Ellington was 61 years old at the time of the interview, but still filled with new plans and unfulfilled ambitions. Over the next few years he would record dozens of albums, collaborate with everyone from Frank Sinatra to John Coltrane, launch his Sacred Concerts, and almost win a Pulitzer Prize (the award jury picked him for the honor, but the Pulitzer board vetoed their decision!)—all while touring constantly with his band.

■

RJG: *I'm Ralph Gleason. This is* Jazz Casual *and you've been listening to the music of America's foremost composer, Duke Ellington, and if I had to identify him to you as a pianist there's something wrong with our educational system. The bassist is Aaron Bell and the drummer is Sam Woodyard. Duke Ellington is here with us . . . Duke . . . ?*

DE: Thank you very much.

RJG: *Duke, what was the name of that song?*

DE: That is "Happy Go Lucky Local."

RJG: *I thought that was "Night Train."*

DE: Oh, they do sound alike, don't they? Well, as a matter of fact, they are identical. Through some strange coincidence this came about . . . we did this in 1946 and it seems along about the same time, in 1951, the other one was written. So this is purely coincidence, you know.

RJG: *Well, it shows the influence that pure coincidence has on popular music in America.*

DE: Ah, coincidence. Yes. It's strange, isn't it?

RJG: *Duke, as such a prolific composer, it has frequently occurred to me, looking at your itinerary going around the country night after night in concerts and nightclub appearances, when do you have time to compose?*

DE: Compose? Oh, anytime. I just composed something a while ago while I was waiting for . . . [Laughter] . . . After the director said "30 seconds . . ." [More laughter] . . . I just composed something . . . very interesting, too. Well, I had the plan for quite a little bit of development, there, on a certain theme that I stumbled upon . . . that's a good piano, I like that.

RJG: *I'm glad you do. We hoped that you would.*

DE: This is a lovely station, here . . . KQED, I like this.

RJG: *It's very interesting . . .*

DE: Everything, yeah, it's wonderful. I mean, it's, you feel as though that you're here performing on the plateau of culture.

RJG: *That is why we have the columns in the background . . .*

DE: Yeah. Well, it's . . .

RJG: *. . . vista . . .*

DE: . . . couldn't be more apropos.

RJG: *Is it a very difficult thing to . . .*

DE: I was thinking of . . . shall we discuss the station?

RJG: *Alright.*

DE: Normally, I mean, if I was kidding, I'd say, like, "Ralph, you know, the station likes you so much they have named it after you," like, K-R-A-L-F or something like that, you know, but they didn't do it, you know, this time. They should, though, I mean, you're a great . . .

Duke Ellington

RJG: *Well, I feel very let down that they didn't . . .*

DE: You know, you and I, I always feel like—in the same category . . . we're . . . I feel like I'm on the same level with you because you have proven that you are a great listener. And, as always, I know the only thing I do in music is listen. Not the only thing, maybe, but the big thing I do in music is listen.

RJG: *How do you mean the big thing you do in music is listen?*

DE: Well, that's it . . . I mean, listening is the most important thing in music.

RJG: *Of course it is to the listener. But there must be sounds to be produced to listen to.*

DE: Oh no, because before you can play anything or before you can write it you'd have to hear it. If you can't hear it then it's a mechanical thing, it has no . . .

RJG: *Then the composer is a listener, primarily?*

DE: Well, I should say so, in music. Yeah. Because it has to do with the ear, you know. And no matter some of the prettiest things on paper come off very, very drab.

RJG: *When you listen, even without the sounds, which of course poses the philosophical question of when a tree falls in the forest and there's no one there to hear it does it make a noise, nevertheless when you do listen, without the actual sounds, do you then transform the talents of the various men in the orchestra with whom you have to function to correspond to what you have heard prior?*

DE: Yeah, well, this is where the listening becomes doubly important. Because, in listening, I mean, you hear, you imagine, you see a note, on a piece of paper, at the same time you hear it. And then, when you add the character of the tone that comes with a certain musician behind a certain instrument, then you get a specific sound. You not only get the pitch, or the timbre of the instrument, but you get the tone personality that comes with the combination of this particular performer.

RJG: *Does that pose a problem, over the course of years, as certain elements alter, and evolve and change, in the body of an orchestra?*

DE: Well, problems are funny things. I think if I had never had a problem in music, I never would've gotten into it. You see . . . I enjoy my problems. My problems come to me as opportunities . . . sometimes they're a challenge. So, I mean, it's like going big game hunting . . . when you get a big problem, you know, you say, well, here's a guy who uses a certain mute on a horn and he can get only seven good notes out of it, you know, and so, the problem is to employ these seven good notes so that they come off effectively and accomplish the dramatic aim of the sound and so forth or whether they blend with another instrument which of course is almost equally as limited. Now, when I say only seven good notes on an instrument, I mean, this can be misunderstood, of course, because on a cocked valve trumpet, I mean, Rex Stewart found out that he had much less than seven good sounds when he did "Boy Meets Horn," you know . . . and personalized writing is very, very important. It is to me, anyway. If I didn't know who I was writing for I wonder what I'd write.

RJG: *What has been the greatest problem you have faced writing?*

DE: Problems? Well, problems like that. I mean there are no problems. Actually, they don't come off as problems. Problems aren't problems. They're opportunities.

RJG: *Well, then, would you recall an opportunity that was more out-standing than others?*

DE: Oh, yeah . . . because an opportunity which was a problem at first . . . when we were recording "Black & Tan Fantasy" and using the two squingee-phones, you know, the plunger and the mute in-side of it, this tone, two of these instruments in the microphone, the trombone and the trumpet, they caused a mic tone. And so, we had to tap, oh, I mean I don't know how many masters, because every time the guy . . . and everybody was very sincere about it . . . and we wanted that sound. But in order to get it we had to get the mic tone with it. And so as a result, I mean, you know how strict they were about those things, way back then, when I was five years old. So we threw out all these masters and so finally we got one through with a minimum of mic tone.

So, when I was writing "Mood Indigo" I decided to use these mic tones, you see, so to create this mic tone with the two in-struments, the trombone and the trumpet, and add another note down a couple octaves below, I thought that this might centralize the mic tone and give it an imaginary specific pitch. Which I understand it did. But of course, this is only for the listener. Of course, everybody who puts a record on a machine doesn't nec-essarily listen to it.

It's very lucky that we encountered this problem, for instance, with the two horns and the mic tone, because if we'd never had the problem there . . . it would never have occurred to me to em-ploy the mic tone. There are many people who've accomplished this. I don't know if they set out to do it in the beginning or not.

RJG: *Is this problem an electronic problem which is solvable outside of the studio?*

DE: Well, I don't think it even exists anymore, because they've cleared up so many things, now, even some of the record companies have machines now where they take old records and they run them through this machine and it comes out with high fidelity and all of the noise is scratched off of it and everything. They don't have that anymore. You can do anything in a microphone now.

RJG: *It has occurred to me also, that, with such things as the G.I. Bill, producing a generation, several generations of young people who are musically schooled, producing them in quantities, that this suggests the possibility of jazz forms that will be more completely written than they have been in the past. Is there any . . . do you see any possibilities in this?*

DE: Well, I feel that the American audience generally is becoming more and more musically mature. That's been coming on for quite a while. We . . . I think we've had an opportunity to see this more so than anyone else, and over a longer period because we started doing these long, unknown works, you know, as far back as 1932, we did, what is it, "Creole Rhapsody," and then in what is it, '35, we did "Reminiscing in Tempo" and in '38 we did "Diminuendo" and "Crescendo" and then in '43 we did "Black, Brown and Beige," and then every year after that, we did one that they did for the premiere at Carnegie Hall.

RJG: *Is the fact that the American audience is becoming . . .*

DE: Incidentally, we used to find audiences everywhere who would listen to it and I think this is the great thing. When you play something that's totally unknown to an audience and they sit and listen to it, it isn't like, say, for instance, you come in and say to the audience, we're going to play "Tea for Two," everybody says, oh yeah, well I know "Tea for Two" and so I'm going to hum along with it, you know, but this is something they don't know, and it's long, you know, and this has nothing to do with the geographical situation of the audience, either. This does not mean that this is true only in one of the two cities of the United States. We find these people everywhere, all over the United States.

RJG: *That is on the plus side, then?*

DE: Yeah, way up. We played, let's see, we've been doing those things . . . we always did them in all the concerts up in the, where, the University of Iowa, because, you know, you go to the University of Iowa, if you listen to the, you know, bad comments of people who don't know, you'd get the idea, well, I mean you're going to have to play something that's not so fancy.

RJG: *"Tea for Two."*

DE: Well, "Tea for Two" is a terrific number, you know. Now, I mean, don't let's get "Tea for Two" mixed up. Vincent Youmans wrote some of the great things. But when you get there, this was back in the early '40s and we played things like "The Tattooed Bride" and all that and long things with no theatrical or anything added to them.

RJG: *Does the rising sophistication of that audience enable you to en-large your horizons, perhaps?*

DE: Oh yeah . . . I mean this is a point of encouragement because I'm the type of writer who says, well, I never look at money, you know, I never look at the royalty checks so I have no idea what my monetary status is. I only go by those who listen. If I go some-place and there are two people who are listening to what I've got to say, then this is it, this is enough encouragement for me to go on and do what I want to do. But it isn't like, say, for instance, you depend upon the record company coming back and say-ing, well, listen, you sold two million copies of so-and-so, so you should do that same thing over again. I'm not guided by that, unfortunately. I should be.

RJG: *Well, fortunately for us you aren't.*

DE: I never concern myself with the size of the audience. I don't even want to know whether they're listening or not. I mean, I'm sometimes annoyed when I suspect that possibly an audience is analyzing. I don't appreciate analysts of music. Analyzing . . . if you're busy analyzing you don't have enough time left to listen. And if you don't listen you can't analyze anyway. I mean you have no foundation. I mean a listener is one who listens, and if they once listen they always listen. They never change from a listener to an analyst. Never.

RJG: *They also enjoy it.*

DE: Yeah, that's very important. Listen and enjoy. Yeah.

RJG: *I would like to ask you if it would be possible for us to have the opportunity to listen to and enjoy some more of you on this program. Would you honor us?*

DE: Hey, what happened? I thought Strayhorn was going to be here.

RJG: *I don't know what happened to him. I looked for him.*

DE: Strayhorn was supposed to be playing the piano while we were talking. Do you suppose he's a listener?

RJG: *Perhaps he is.*

DE: Hey, Billy Strayhorn, where are you? Billy Strayhorn, you know, is my writing and arranging companion, ladies and gentlemen, and we've been together since 1940 and he wrote our theme, "Take the A Train," and he was supposed to have been playing while Ralph and I were conversing. He sort of likes to sneak in, come in with no fanfare, but it looks like he has to have the fanfare.

Les McCann

NOVEMBER 17, 1960

■

Pianist and singer Les McCann was still in the early stages of his career when he participated in this interview with Ralph Gleason. McCann's first taste of fame came when he appeared on *The Ed Sullivan Show* in 1956, as a result of winning a Navy talent competition. By the end of the decade, McCann was building a fan base in southern California, initially by focusing on his funky piano playing but gradually gaining recognition for his gospel-ish vocals.

At this juncture in American history, many listeners objected to the combination of the sounds of the sanctified church with secular themes—especially lyrics about love and sex. At the same time that McCann was building a following, Ray Charles found himself banned from many radio stations for a similar combination of gospel vocal inflections and earthy romantic lyrics. Such songs, according to one critic, "started in church and ended up in the bedroom." But McCann refused to change his style in the face of these attacks, and they didn't seem to hurt his popularity—which would skyrocket during the years following the Gleason interview.

In 1969, McCann would enjoy his greatest hit: the funky social protest song "Compared to What," recorded with saxophonist Eddie Harris at the Montreux Jazz Festival. This single sold more than a million copies, and the *Swiss Movement* album that featured it went gold. In the aftermath McCann became more than a jazz star: he was also a role model in the world of soul and R & B music. Not only do his old songs continue to find new fans in the current day, but they are often frequently sampled by hip-hoppers and beat-makers.

■

RJG: *Les, when you started playing the piano, did you ever anticipate any such a hullaballoo as this?*

LM: No I didn't. I didn't feel that I was doing that much of a different-type thing, as far as playing some music that people, seem like people never heard before.

RJG: *Did you think you're doing something different now?*

LM: Well I feel that in a way we are because we're bringing, maybe not different in the sense of something new, but something in the sense of bringing a kind of a swing back that hasn't been heard for some time—where musicians enjoy playing. Musicians that we play with, they feel like we're doing something different. But it's not that I'm trying to be different. I just really want to play, that's all. And maybe that alone can be different.

RJG: *Sure. In the way that you're playing now, is this something that you developed over a period of time or is this the way you have been playing all along?*

LM: Well basically this is the way I've always played, but at the same time I started like, it's just like anything else, I couldn't do all the things—

RJG: *Yeah.*

LM: It just had to mature and we're just now getting a touch of what I really plan on going into. This is the sense of a rhythm. I feel that the bass player Herbie has just now realized what we're really trying to do, so when we get back to Los Angeles we're going to try to get into it more.

I don't know, for us it's been kind of hard to rehearse like we always do. When we was in Los Angeles we used to rehearse no less than three or four times a week. But the thing was with Leroy [Vinnegar] and Ron [Jefferson], we all felt the same way about everything. With Herbie [Lewis] at first it was a little difficult because he was more, like he's kind of young and he wants to, you know, he experiments quite a bit so when he finally got his experimenting into the same realm of what we were doing, I think he understands what we're trying to do now and it's more of a group thing now.

RJG: *How long have you been playing professionally?*

LM: Well, let me see, three or four years, I think.

RJG: *Were you working at any casuals or anything when you were up here in the navy?*

LM: Well, then I was just trying to learn how to play the piano. I used to sit in on intermissions at the Blackhawk. I really didn't know what I was doing, I knew what I wanted to do—but I didn't know anything really about music, I could play the blues then.

RJG: *Yeah.*

LM: But when I was in the navy the bands that came to the base, the guys would show me chords and what you call this kind of chord and all that, so actually I didn't really get into anything until I went to Los Angeles and went to a school which I hate to mention, Westlake.

RJG: *You're another Westlake grad.*

LM: No I'm not a Westlake grad but I went there—I know, they use my name for everything now but I, the school doesn't teach me a thing, except one teacher, I had a very good teacher there.

I learned how to read chords and then I was offered a job and I think I only knew at the most four or five songs—at the Purple Onion—and I stayed there a year and three months and by the fact that I had to have a trio when I was playing piano I had to learn a few more songs, but—

RJG: *Any other musicians in your family?*

LM: No, there's nobody, I have four brothers and one sister and I come from a very large family. Very large family as far as cousins and everything, nobody plays. My sister took up piano in school but it's never something she, you know, went into.

RJG: *How did you happen to, then?*

LM: Well, when I was in high school I was always in the choir, I've sung in the choir ever since I can remember.

RJG: *Where was this, in Lexington?*

LM: Lexington, Kentucky, yeah, Shiloh Baptist Church. And we had a little singing group, around five guys, we'd sing rhythm and blues things and we'd sing gospel music, you know, we had all, both sides covered just in case. Who was right? But we'd sing around the churches and sing on little shows at school and things like that, but I went into the band, I wanted to be a drummer, I still have a desire for drums and bass, and I was always showing off and beating on things when I shouldn't be. So I got kicked out of the band. So the band teacher told me if I wanted to come back in the band I would have to play what he wanted me to play. So he taught me how to play the sousaphone, the big tuba. So I played that when I was in high school and I, I became assistant band teacher, you know, director of junior bandleader and all that, and we had a piano at home and I, I used to try to get things going. I had piano lessons when I was younger, me and my little brother, my little brother could really play, you know, but every time we'd go out to perform some place at a church or a meeting or something, they'd have us there, young kid, he'd start crying, the show would be called off or I'd have to play by myself so it just worked out, you know, but it's, a teacher we had, she taught us for 35 cents, you know, we could afford that. After she died it was all over.

RJG: *Is your family still back there?*

LM: Yes, my brother, my sister, she lives in Philadelphia, she just got married not too long ago. My brother, he saved up, little brother, he saved up his money he's going to Tuskegee to be a veterinarian, and my other two younger brothers, they're still in high school, I'm the oldest, I have one brother in the army. But I went to see them when I was in Chicago, I had two days off, I dropped down. I called up my band teacher and he says, I'll call you right back. So he called me right back and he says, yeah, we're going to have a concert tomorrow at school at one. Just like that. So all night long he was trying to find a bass player, they had a very good bass player, little kid about 15 years old, plays around and it was the most, I don't know how to describe it, but the audience was, they enjoyed it so much. I just got the greatest feeling of self, you know, they just went wild and I signed autographs for every kid in the whole school, the teacher finally had to tell them to stop. And the guys that were playing with me, like, he said nobody ever knew me before but now look at me. But, it was a very good thing. Teachers who didn't like me like me now.

RJG: *Sure.*

LM: People who never spoke to me speak to me now. And there was this girl there that I really liked, I used to go to her house all the time. Her father, he'd speak to me, but nothing and so this girl finally got married and she got pregnant, had a couple of kids. Come to find out he was a big gangster someplace, the FBI caught him. And I mean these are respectable people, supposedly. So I go back, I told them, I says, "I told you you should have let your daughter marry me." He said, "Well why don't you call up tomorrow, here's the phone number. In fact I'll call you up tonight." Boy, he was coming on. I had a very good time there. I was looking for it to be a very depressing, completely depressing thing, but that made it much, you know, something to remember because I hate Kentucky, in the sense that I can't see how people, I can see how, but I, when I hear a person say, like, I asked how's so-and-so doing and they say, he's got a chauffeur's job, best job in town, you know, I can't stand to hear things like that. I had a teacher who always told me, like, "Whatever you do when you finish school just get out of town." So, lotta guys, they took her advice and those that did are, they become something.

RJG: *How did you happen to make that first album?*

LM: Well, I never even planned on making a record then. I always had it going around that, after I had the few jobs that I said about four years from now I'd like to make a record which would be like '63 or something like that. And, but everybody had told Dick Bock, seems like everybody, I know more people in L.A. than you can imagine, I went to City College and I was, I could have been school president and all that but, took up too much of my time so I canceled out on that.

RJG: *Los Angeles City College.*

LM: Yes. But they all, everybody was always telling Dick Bock or some other record company man to sign him up and there were always people who would come up to me and tell me that they were trying to get up enough money to record us, you know, back us up, and there was, the club owner, they all tried to get up enough money and it was just a group, I had one group they call Concerts, Incorporated, now. And they tried to do a lot for us, this was when I was really very young in playing, but I didn't feel I was ready to record then. But when people started telling Dick—every time Dick come around I would be, like, playing songs I never played before or something like that so Dick, he'd never say anything, well he'd say, well, okay, we'll see you know, and so finally I guess so many people had told him he should go ahead, you know, we had a friend of mine working in the office so he called me and we signed the contract. Then this, at this time I had the group that, that I felt I never would want to record with really because we had made a record for this club owner which he had put up all his money for us but this club owner was a kind of a gangster-type character. I really didn't want to be involved with him, but, and he never, I had, we had a singer with us named Gene McDaniels, you ever heard of him?

RJG: *No.*

LM: Well he's a very, he's on tour with Dizzy Gillespie over in Europe —Australia, someplace, but he was with us and that club was packed every night of the week, every night. We were open and, like, we'd ask him for a raise and he'd say I'm going to give it to you, you know, but all he was doing was opening up more clubs. He finally had like three or four clubs in his own name. Nobody was getting a raise, I was making 40 dollars a week for six nights' work—under scale, and I'm in the union too, and the drummer would come, he wouldn't hire the drummer, I'd give the drummer half of my money. The bass player was making about 40 dollars a week so he'd be making more money than anybody, and so one night I just said if we don't have a raise by tomorrow night you'll never see us here again. I made this announcement to the people, I bought everybody drinks and, because I know he wasn't going to give us the raise and I said it would be nice if you would support us like you always have and not come back, you know, unless whoever they hire here next, they do pay them scale. And they opened and so that night I told the guy that was there and like they for about a month and a half they tried to put different groups in there, they put names and everything, but nobody would come and so they finally closed up. So—with the group that I had I felt that I didn't want to make a record really with them, not that they wasn't, I don't mean to put them down but it was more than that I wanted to do to make a first record, you know, and even when we made the first record I didn't want to make it then because we were, we'd only been together two weeks, me and Leroy [Vinnegar], but what happened, I told the guys if they wanted to go with me, alright, they'd have to rehearse much more and that if I wanted to travel they would have to drop out of school and I knew they wasn't going to quit school so that was my way out. So I told them okay, after this week, you know, we get a new group, so I got Leroy and Ron [Jefferson]. So two weeks after we got together, that's when we made that record. So then for seven months we stayed out of work. We just did like one-nighters once in a while or a dance or booked some horn players and it was like Ron working here and I'm working here, but every day, every morning nine o'clock we'd go rehearse and leave about eight at night. So this new club owner, called the Bit. They'd rebuilt it and enlarged it, and we was supposed to work there for two weeks, three nights a week, and it was so crowded that first night and next three nights, next two nights, that they de-cided to open up five nights a week, then six nights, then a Sun-day afternoon session. So we stayed there 25 weeks, that was it.

RJG: *Willard Alexander books you now?*

LM: Yeah, he came out to hear us one night, he signed us up right away. But no, he didn't sign us up right away because there was a big hassle going on between him and GAC, they wanted us to sign with them. They'd been sending their guys in every night trying to get in good with my manager.

RJG: *Who is your manager?*

LM: Her name is Olga James. This is not the singer, this is another woman, but I figured Willard, for what I wanted, would be much better. Because I would go over there to GAC, me and Dick went together and I would say, well, what, what kind of places would you book me. He'd say, well, you know, well, all the jazz places. I'd say, well, just name one. He says, well, you know, like in New York. I said where? Well, and they, but they never would say anything, I says no, well, later, so—

RJG: *As a result of these, let's see, how many albums is it now, total of—*

LM: Two of our own, one with Teddy Edwards.

RJG: *You got the whole jazz world split right down the middle.*

LM: Got the whole jazz, what do you mean by that?

RJG: *Well, I mean the reaction is either pro or con.*

LM: Oh yeah, I know what you mean.

RJG: *There's no in-the-middle reaction.*

LM: No, there's no, no, no, and I, in fact, I think that's the way it should be really. I'd rather for you to dislike us completely or like us, you know.

RJG: *Well, now, why do you think that the music that you've, that the records that you've, well this is an awkward question because the group doesn't sound the same in person as it sounds on records at all but why do you think that what is on the records upsets people so much?*

LM: Well—now, which record are you talking about, both of them?

RJG: *Um-hmm.*

LM: Well I've been trying to figure that out myself and I think it's the combination of the names of the songs, the way they're played, and what they think they are supposed to represent, as far as this is supposed to be gospel music. See, I've never said I was playing gospel music, but I say this. If it sounds like it, I'm very happy, because I love gospel music and I mean that's, I mean if you live next to a church all your life what are you going to play? Some people don't, some people do, I mean, there are people that play church music, I mean in the same sense of like what you would call jazz in a way that I've heard that I wish I could come close to that's much more far, but this is just the music I like, to me when I hear a choir or, the gospel choir, it just really does something to me.

RJG: *Well how would you describe the music you play, then?*

LM: Well I would describe it, this as being the music I know how to play, that's all it is, just as simple as that.

RJG: *But when you went to the man at GAC and you asked him to tell what clubs he was going to book you in, so you come to a club and the man says to you, what music do you play, and you say, well.*

LM: Well, I told him this. I always tell people all I'm trying to do is play good music in the sense that, I don't, you don't have to put any tag on my music, you know, but if you like it you like it. If you don't, you don't, that's all. So, because—I doubt if I would even, you know, get into a technical thing about what I'm doing as far as, because it really doesn't mean that much to me as far as that it's just this is the way I like to play, you know.

RJG: *Now, when your albums came out and talked about the truth and soul and so on, how do these terms apply to music?*

LM: I think there's a big misconception of soul and all those terms, which are tagged to music. Now, soul music can be anybody's music, but it just so happens that the Negro has used this word to themselves more than any other race, so you can't say it's not soul music because it is soul music, because it's their soul. Now if you played, you'd be playing your soul music, but your soul music hasn't been tagged as soul music. You see what I mean?

RJG: *Well Martin Luther King talks about soul force.*

LM: Of what?

RJG: *Of soul force.*

LM: Yeah, well, see—it's like a feeling of, you know, like, what do they have on the downbeat, a racial, something fight back or something—

RJG: *The soul, funk and yeah—*

LM: Yeah, well in a way you know, soul is a big word in the church, it's as used. We must use our souls, you know, take our souls and this. This clings more to the Negro people I think as far as to use. Now, there's no soul on any of my records I don't think, I've never used that word. And, but—I think that the word is definitely overused now.

RJG: *Sure, it is.*

LM: But whether the word is overused or not it still can be true, and as far as the word "the truth," the title didn't mean we were playing the music. It meant that this is one of the songs on the record *The Truth.* We thought about that at first, but Dick said, well, I think they will understand, because I think they wanted to play, they wanted it to be the other way at first. I said no, I don't ever, ever want to say that, I know a lot of, like, I feel that people like, but like Ornette Coleman feels that his way of playing is it. And I have a guy—a friend of mine in Los Angeles—who teaches music, who teaches a form of rhythm and things like that and he tells them, "This is the only way." But I don't believe that. I think of all the music jazz is supposed to be the widest and there's every person's way, you know, this is the whole thing but it is still true. There's more than one way. This is our way of presenting some music and there's the gospel side, there's the hard swing side, there's a delicate side, we try to show all that—and there's no, I don't, I wouldn't never like to think of myself as being only to play one way because I think even just thinking about the rest of the fellows in the group there are more sides of us than the one way, we all couldn't be exactly that one way. That's it.

RJG: *Obviously you view the music you play seriously?*

LM: Oh definitely, I, this is the only way I want to play, that's what I mean, definitely—see, I think the people think because we laugh and we sing that that means we're not serious, but when we laugh and sing we's laughing and singing about the thing, we're being serious in that laugh as far as that, I'm laughing about something I want to laugh about. Now on the record *The Shout*, people are laughing when we play this gospel thing, you know what I mean, and Don DeMicheal say, well I doubt the—what's the word?—authenticity, and I said, well I won't tell you what I really said, but what I meant was, well, I asked him if he knew anything about Negro music and he said no, no, and I said, well, I'll talk to you some other time, but what I mean is that when people laugh now in a club, half these people haven't been to church in years and they hear this, man, it's like, oh yeah? It's like—to some it's funny to think that you could play it here, but I feel if the music is good and this is what you play well then you like it if I'm playing church music I can play this music anywhere. If I'm supposed to be playing to an audience. Wherever I have an audience that's what I got to play regardless of what it is, so if I play something that reminds them of something that's going to naturally laugh or they are going to get mad and say what the hell is he doing, you know. It's the same reaction.

RJG: *Well you know curiously enough, now, speaking of this, the afternoon at Monterey, the Sunday afternoon with Jon Hendricks' "Story of the Blues," now that was a mixture of gospel music and blues music. In other words the, in other words, religious and secular music, and we had Big Miller singing, and Jimmy Witherspoon singing, and we had four girls from the Ephesian church in Berkeley singing gospel songs, and I mean they were, this is the first time they were ever in any scene like that, I mean they were right out of the church into there. They were only 11, 12 years old, you know, and some people took this wrong, and actually there was nothing wrong about this at all.*

LM: Well, see, that's what I'm saying.

RJG: *Precisely the same thing.*

LM: In L.A. they have a club called the Renaissance, and they have a group there they call the Gospel Girls. They sing the greatest and they are more exciting, really lift your soul, man, I mean just makes you feel like, I mean everybody just goes into the groove, oh I mean it's just a happy moment, you know, like they sing this song the "Shout," that's where I got the song.

RJG: *That's where you got that.*

LM: And each one sings a little phrase. "Meeting Night on the Old Camp Ground" and everybody just goes wild, they just, I think, if you have a feeling for something you should react to it. Get right out there and shout right along with them. And a lot of people thought that this wasn't, but they could never say why, you know, then, well I just don't feel that this should be done in a club, why? Well they could come up with some kinda reason, and it really to me didn't sound too sound, but if you sang a certain way and you want to sing for people and you sing where the people want to hear you—

RJG: *Well there's a group that's on the, church, that's been on the air in San Francisco on Sunday night for years that I've listened to that sounds like the Count Basie brass section, shouting the same way, singing different songs, but the thing is the same.*

LM: That's right. It's all the same and—

RJG: *Do you think, Les, that a prior acquaintance with gospel music and music of the Negro people would make someone's reaction to your music quicker and easier?*

LM: Well, not maybe as much as I mean, that would help, but just the desire, the willingness to say, wait a minute, let me try to understand this, you know what I mean, in the sense that I'm trying, see, you can say this, and, like, if everybody says we playing gospel music, now you hear some church choir or sing, well that's not gospel music they're playing, what is that. That's all, that's phony, you know, so naturally there's going to be some argument there, but we're all of us are people who play like this, or only playing like what has rubbed off on them as far as what they can bring out, you know.

RJG: *That's what Nat Adderley says.*

LM: When I hear a choir, I go home sometime and I just can't stand it because in some way I want to re-create that whole feeling of how they get them things going where one person's just holding the thing and the other one is, like on the song a "Little Three Four for God," I try to get the feeling of a choir, because, see, a lot of them, gospel music, they just keep repeating a phrase over and over, somebody else to be singing, it's just the greatest jazz in the world. Jazz is improvising, that's what they're doing, they making up their own melodies and it's—I've tried it, you know, I've heard people say they want to go to a Negro church and they go there and they sit there. What am I supposed to hear? Well, I say, well you wanted to come so you decide for yourself, you know and they, they don't, you know—

RJG: *Well, there's great difference between church music in various churches.*

LM: That's what it is. That's the way it is with different musicians, it's all the same thing, see, and, well, people have gotten on me about the titles of songs. When I was at home a man told me he says, "Don't name any more songs 'Fish and Chitlins,'" you know, and I says why, he says, "Oh," I said, well, I just named one "Hogs and Guts." And he says, "Did you really?" He says, oh, I say he, but he was embarrassed you know, I say, well, I don't feel there's anything to be embarrassed about. I feel like chitlins, you want to write a song about chitlins you write it.

We used to play *The Truth* in, say if I played it in a mixed audience at school, well I see some Negro students slide back in their seats, oh no, you know, what's he doing, you know, and I found out that they were kind of embarrassed because they weren't really, a lot of, a lot of them felt embarrassed because I don't think they were as proud of their music as they could be or should be. It's all like the old story of the slaves, they see the white man eating white bread and they're eating dark bread. Now dark bread's better for you but why can't we have that? And finally they get that and they find out that you know, that wasn't, you know, really the right groove as far as you know what they should, you know, they knew they had it first. I think all of the students finally came on around and said yeah, well, you know, because they found that some of them, the other side they wanted to like and understand, so okay, maybe we do have something.

RJG: *You know it's an interesting point to me, I mean, about all the things that are happening in jazz today, no Negro jazz musician who is 24, 25 years old or older, all of them come from—or at least*

99 percent of them come from—a family that was involved with the church. So this is a common experience, this is not true of the white musicians at all. But now in the future, because of the sociological changes that are occurring all over the country with everybody regardless of race, you're going to have musicians come up who are Negroes who come from families that are not involved with the church. The Negroes are leaving the churches too, just like everybody else, this whole thing is going on.

LM: Well, soon, I mean for that same reason what you just said, I don't think any person should say a pianist or a musician doesn't have any roots, he's too young to have those kind of roots. You know what I mean. Because, okay, say if everything was changed here. Say if this was a white musician playing and he's going to a church that just sings all Negro-type songs. Now he's getting all involved in this and he comes out playing like this. Now he's supposed to be a phony. Why, because he couldn't know anything about that. But yet he went through the same scene as everybody else is supposed to have gone through to get the same thing.

RJG: *Well, if you put it on any other basis all that you're doing is making out a logical case for racial characteristics which we all know aren't true.*

LM: See they, it's—

RJG: *It's environment that does it.*

LM: It's not, it's not a one-time thing, the one thing I hate is to hear a musician who plays horrible and he's a Negro, yeah, oh we got something ain't nobody got, you know, yeah, he's right. He's got something nobody wants, either. You know, he's by himself. I don't know if he's talking about we, him and his wife maybe.

Les McCann

RJG: *How far do you think this thing is going to go for you? What else do you want to do?*

LM: Well I don't feel very great about this thing being the soul era? You know, because like I said and you've heard us play, there's more to us than that and seem like every time there's a blindfold test, only songs they play are supposed to be the gospel songs or when they bring up our name they talk about those songs, but they never bring up "I'll Remember April" or something like that.

RJG: *Well you have come to represent this whether you wanted it this way or not.*

LM: Yeah, well, I wanted to represent this, but I wanted to represent completely what I am instead of just a fourth or a half, and, well, that's alright, we'll just have to develop more on what we're popular on I guess because and everything we play because we still enjoy what we are doing, and to me that's a big important thing.

RJG: *Who are your favorite jazz piano players? Let me put that another way: Who are your favorite piano players?*

LM: Well—I couldn't name you any piano player that plays in church, but the few that I've heard that were, that oh, I'll just put in that there are certain ones that I've heard that have impressed me more than any other kind of pianists. But as far as all of the survivor-type jazz of today, I like, well, I like Oscar Peterson, I think, and I like most of these people in person, Erroll Garner and let's see, who can I think of, I like Carl Perkins. I like C.P. for more than his playing. I think—when he talked to me he used to make me feel that whatever I wanted to do in life to go ahead and do it, musically, you know. Because I was always asking him about why he plays like that, you know, I was always asking him about why he plays like this, you know, I was always asking questions like, well, doesn't this hang you up here and you do this? No, you know, like if you can do it you can do it whatever way you attempt it, like, say I'm playing my drumsticks and somebody walks up, you're holding your sticks wrong, yet I'm doing what I'm trying to do. I have some people come up and say you have no technique. I say, what do you mean? Well, I say, you mean I don't play the notes very clear or something? And he says, no, I don't mean that; I mean your fingering. I said, well, what kind of technique are you talking about? Well, you know, in school they teach you this. I said, well, I had all that and for me that doesn't work, you know, right now it doesn't. Maybe some other time I might see where that might be, but for what I'm playing now, it doesn't, you know, and—

RJG: *Well, Carl Perkins was important to you then.*

LM: In a very, in a very strange sense he was. See, I didn't know him that well but I talked to him a few times when I went to see him and he was always wanting me to come over, he'd show me things, but we really never got together, you know, but I like his playing an awful lot. I felt that he, he filled out something like it was completely music—you know, on his ballads, oh, I just felt if I ever was to copy somebody, if I couldn't copy him I wouldn't play, because he, oh, he just seems to have, ballads, I mean I love to play slow songs, but the way he does them they filled up with just, it didn't seem like they were too overcluttered with all kinds of things—you know what I mean, where they're a drag, but things that were just completely beautiful.

RJG: *Have other musicians been important to you like that?*

LM: Miles Davis, the ever popular one, and, but I mean, I ain't sup-posed to mention Miles' name because, you know, like, you get put down for that too, but he has, Miles is, I think his, whether he knows it or not I think he has a very great natural sense of rhythm that's not heard on the everyday one, two, three, four type of rhythm, you know, I think he has a two, four feeling and like you hear a lot of people talking about two and four. I don't think there are very many people that play on it in the true sense of playing on it because everything leads right back to that one again, but I mean this is in more detail I would tell you a lot about it, but Miles plays in a way that I like to hear music played.

RJG: *Philly Joe talked about Miles' sense of rhythm like that.*

LM: Yeah, well, he, he has a, and the last time I heard him I couldn't believe the way he played. In Chicago I thought that was the greatest and Miles was smiling, laughing and friendly. I mean, I know him, but I mean to other people, man, he was just nice and when I was sitting out in the audience he was walking off the stage and he, hey, just like that, everybody didn't believe it, man, you know, the whole band was just having a good time. Think happiness is coming into music and that's what they have in the church. The happiness is a big thing, man.

RJG: *Absolutely.*

LM: When you hear, have you ever been to a Negro church where they really get into something, I mean, that kind of, everybody's just laughing when the song's over, say yeah, amen, and the preacher man he's so happy himself, man, he's so proud of his choir, he doesn't know what to do, he goes in competition with them way back there, when I speak this Sunday go on sing some more, you know.

RJG: *Sometimes I think I'm, I get worried about it because I've been listening to those churches on the air since about 1939 and in New York they used to have meetings, revival meetings, up in the ball-*

room that they since tore down, it was up past the Savoy ballroom with Georgia Peach and the Dixie Hummingbirds.

LM: Oh yeah.

RJG: *Sister Ernestine B. Washington.*

LM: Brother Joe May? You remember him.

RJG: *—John Brody, Rev. Brody from New Jersey.*

LM: I get the deepest feelings of all like as far as love, as far as prettiness, as far as death when I listen to this choir, I never, when I, when I heard a song they were singing, I heard the Wings Over Jordan sing a song called "Going to Get My . . ."—I think it's "Going to Get My Long White Robe"—oh, "Trying to Get Ready"—I think that's the name of it. I never felt like any person would be that close to death, you know, I just, I don't know, to me that's what I got the feeling of, man, I'm, I'm all so shaken, man, like this was it.

RJG: *Ernestine Washington did a song once called "I Walk thru the Valley of the Shadow of Death," scare you, terrify you.*

LM: That's the way this was, man.

RJG: *Well that's what Jon Hendricks did Sunday afternoon at Monterey. I mean he had everybody sitting there crying and wanting to cry and hug everybody.*

LM: That the way it is, man. I, you know, the main thing, I don't want to sound conceited or anything, but when we play, man, at a place, people all want to come up and hug us and love us. They never met us before, shake our hands, just like they do in church.

And it's getting to the point now where people tell me you look like a preacher and I hate that, oh man, you know, but—

RJG: *Any preachers in your family?*

LM: My cousin is a preacher, he's very young, but he just started, I think. But it's, to me, man, it's a great feeling, I don't know, this guy misconstrued the whole thing in this last issue, time before this about the guy coming up teaching me, did you read that? See, well, the whole thing was this guy had, he goes to see a psychiatrist three times a week. So he told, he used to come to the club and hear us and he says, when I come up here, he says, I never, he says, this is the only place where I feel like I have no troubles, no problems, he says, I'm really healed when I walk in this door, and that's what I told John. So this guy come back and say I'm healing somebody. Not John, but the guy from Canada. I never said I healed anybody, you know. A lot of people have told me that, but I, you know, as far as, he can be healed in more ways than one. He can be healed as far as coming in being mad and walking out being happy and—

RJG: *You got your mind all straightened out.*

LM: That's right. You can be, you know, getting ready to divorce your wife and you hear something that in music that you feel maybe you can sit down and free your mind as far as, think about something you never thought about before and walk out and say, yeah, there you are, well, let's try this again.

RJG: *It's a great tranquilizer.*

LM: It is, you know, if it's something you like. I don't, I won't sit anyplace and listen to music if I don't like it. Unless I just can't get out. The aisles are blocked.

RJG: *Well that's the worst chore in my job and I've, I've walked out of the Workshop, I mean, and the Black Hawk too in the last couple of months there have been groups I just couldn't stand it, it made me too nervous to sit there.*

LM: Well, lots of groups make me very, very nervous, the tension is so high and I get needles and things feel like I, you know, and—

RJG: *Donald Byrd and Pepper Adams drove me right out of the room.*

LM: Yeah.

RJG: *I don't know what was going on in that group but, well, 'fact they later did have a battle and Donald Byrd hit Doug Watkins, but so I know there was something to it but I got like this I was so tense.*

LM: Well, see, all that—and I don't mean it like sometime we go up on the stand, we don't feel the best, you know, but we still, even if we don't say anything to each other, we trying to play group-wise or bring out something from us that we really, I know, I can hear this from a fella like the bass player and the drummer, they really want to give something, I know this. I get so happy sometime to think that this really happens like that, and, like, Herbie the bass player, he, I just feel like, man, he has so much to give, he's just trying to give it all now, you know, he's just so enthused about giving.

RJG: *What's your reaction when somebody comes up to you like that kid did the other night and says you play with the soul of Jesus?*

LM: See what I mean. See, I forgot all about that. They say that, man, all the time things like that. They call me God in circles in L.A. Here comes little God and, man, I get so embarrassed, but see that guy the other night he was so sincere, man, he had, I don't know what his conception of Jesus is, but you could tell it was something good in his eyesight.

RJG: *Oh, he meant it well.*

LM: That's what I mean, I mean, you know, see, but if I was to say something about that, who do he think he is, you know, who am I kidding. I got people come up, old women, man, all they want to do is just touch you, son, and said that I've seen you. This happened to me at home too, like people in Chicago, man, I, the people were so, the people just come there and sit and they'd sit all night, man, but they wouldn't go, they were there, they'd bring back people. Everybody inviting us over to their house for dinner. I know you like chitlins, that's what we'll have, I know it's out of season but we'll have them anyhow, you know, and I don't know, I just sometime—in a way it's kind of depressing from a sense that—people like this are really real and why don't, why aren't they believed in?

RJG: *Are you a religious person?*

LM: Well—honestly I would say I am in the sense that I believe in religion, but I'm not a person that goes to church every Sunday and like that because I don't like that because I don't, I mean, there are churches I could go to every Sunday if I were there. But for what places I've been I don't get anything out of the church, and if I don't get anything out I won't go—and I'd like to get religion, I mean as far as more things about it from other people who talk about it who I feel are sincere and are, whether they, they can be kidding and you find out something else, yeah, well, he's had a reason for his kidding, you know, I'm just saying all these things that relate to this.

RJG: *Do you see your music as having a religious significance?*

LM: Yes, in the fact that this is the way we want to play and it's no jiving and shucking, it's like I say, when people put me down for their writing "Little Three Four for God," they'll never play it on the radio. I say, well, who cares, you know, I mean, that's not even, I didn't write a record, I'm making a record so they'll play these songs on the radio. Well I did it 'cause I, I really at that time I had a feeling of, like I, you know, I feel like whatever it has been so good to me to allow me to play this I want to dedicate a song to him and that's the way I, I like, I want to do a lot of tunes like that, but I want to get that same feeling when I write the song again though, you know, it's not I'm just going, I never sit down and say, well, let me see, let's think of a song and do it like this. I never write a song like that. A lot of people can and I'm just, I'm not saying it's a far out way of doing it, but this is the way I do it.

RJG: *Sometimes you talk to Dave Brubeck about this, he has some of those same feelings.*

LM: Yeah? Oh I, that's it for me.

RJG: *Comes out in a different way, you know—in his way.*

LM: Oh, I wasn't putting that down, I was just saying the thought is to me, that's the thought, the right thought you know for us.

RJG: *You like Ray Charles?*

LM: Yes, I do, I, I think Ray Charles is really misunderstood too.

RJG: *Why?*

LM: Well—I don't think that a lot of people really think that he's sincere either, you know what I mean. They think this is a, he's monopolizing on the way he learned how to sing in church and which is what he really is doing and this is the way he sings.

RJG: *He couldn't possibly be shucking with that.*

LM: That's what I'm saying.

RJG: *Couldn't do it like that if he didn't mean it. How could he?*

LM: Well, that's the same way I feel about our group, you know, and like I tell you this in a sense that Herbie, I bring his name up again, when he first started playing with us I would always say, come on, man, get into this, you know, but Herbie's never lived that type of, he has to play the way he knows, so I finally found out that with what he knows and what he feels from us his thing works just as good so I had to leave him alone and let him get in, you know, like bring his own things in and let's see if that fused in with what we were doing, and it did. See, now, Leroy and him are two different people, two different kinds of bass player, but there are a lot of people like Herbie much more than they like Leroy, but—

RJG: *Did you hear Mahalia Jackson's record with Duke?*

LM: "Come Sunday." One of the most beautiful things I ever heard. I heard that one Sunday. They have a show down L.A. called *Jazz Goes to Church* and they played that.

Jon Hendricks

MARCH 9, 1959

■

Jon Hendricks is best known as one of the inventors of *vocalese*, a style of jazz singing based on creating new lyrics and attaching them to existing jazz melodies and improvisations. Many fans embrace vocalese as the most jazzy style of singing of them all. After all, what could be more authentic then singing an actual solo by Count Basie or Miles Davis?

The first genuine hit of the vocalese movement dates back to early 1950s, when King Pleasure and Eddie Jefferson enjoyed great success by adding words to James Moody's improvisation on "I'm in the Mood for Love." But Hendricks brought this approach to the next level in his collaborations with singers Dave Lambert and Annie Ross. Their celebrated 1957 album *Sing a Song of Basie* took intricate big band charts and translated them into elaborate vocal numbers. This recording not only expanded the horizons of jazz singing, but also showed the potential for overdubbing of vocal parts in jazz music.

At the time of this interview, the trio Lambert, Hendricks & Ross was consistently winning jazz polls, and drawing capacity crowds to their engagements. The following year they would enjoy great success with "Twisted," Annie Ross's vocalese version of a solo by saxophonist Wardell Gray that would win a Grammy and become a jazz cult classic.

In 1962, Annie Ross left the band, and in 1966 Dave Lambert died in an auto accident. Hendricks reinvented himself as a solo artist and impresario. His project "Evolution of the Blues Song" started out as a special feature at the Monterey Jazz Festival but turned into an acclaimed stage show. At the end of the 1960s, Hendricks relocated to London, and developed a new following in England and on the continent.

In a strange twist of fate, Hendricks moved to California in the mid-1970s, and began writing jazz criticism for the *San Francisco Chronicle*

—replacing Ralph Gleason, who was then focusing much of his efforts on the recently launched *Rolling Stone* magazine.

■

RJG: *You can't read or write music?*

JH: Never learned. Every time I go to learn, as soon as I *hear*, the notes don't mean a thing!

RJG: *Do you play a horn?*

JH: No. I played drums for about 15 years. Trombone for about a month. I learned the scale and then my front teeth got bad, had a bad embouchure. So I had to quit. I grew up listening, though.

RJG: *Listening to what?*

JH: Art Tatum! Lived five houses from him. And I used to play up on his front porch, you know, I used to hang around with his little brothers and sisters and we'd be sitting out in the swing, out on the front porch, laughing and hollering and whooping and yelling and Art would be practicing, you know, and so his mother would come through the kitchen and say, "Stop that noise. Can't you see Art is practicing"? He said, "They don't bother me." So finally I started listening, you know.

RJG: *How early did you sing?*

JH: I was singing since I was seven. And whenever I forgot the words to a song I would make up words that I thought would fit and I got to the point where—I used to sing in places where they'd throw me money—every time I'd sing "Pennies from Heaven" people would throw me pennies—I forgot the words, I'd just put in my own words, I found out that as long as they rhyme, people didn't know whether they were my words or the real lyrics.

RJG: *You were doing this just off the top of your head?*

JH: Yes. Those were the first I ever wrote. The first original was a funny song called "Just Because I Kissed the Bride." I was working with a group in my hometown and I was late for work and the fine for being late was 10 dollars. So I couldn't spare the 10 dollars so I went to the leader, I said, "Look, man, like, I can't spare 10 dollars," and he says, "Then write an original song for tomorrow night." So I said okay and I come up with this "Just Because I Kissed the Bride." A very funny song, that was the first thing I ever did. I was about 24. I was working in Toledo with the Mainstemmers with a guy named Harold Jackson, played bass with Ellington, we had a guitarist you might know of, Bill Jennings— left-handed guitarist—had a piano player named Buster Hawkins, he was around New York for years, a big-eyed guy. And me, and I couldn't read and so they'd have to get the arrangements and I'd listen to them and I'd learn and I was playing drums and singing with the group.

RJG: *How old are you?*

JH: Thirty-seven. No other musicians in my family. My mother used to sing in church, and I sang in a choir.

RJG: *When did you first start to write words to instrumentals?*

JH: When I heard "Moody's Mood for Love." Opened up all the doors. What in the world is this? So I got right busy and wrote "Four Brothers." I was in New York working in a wholesale paper house and I used to spend my lunch hours in Washington Square Park and that's where I wrote the song about the wine, have you heard that song that we do? "Gimme That Wine"? A funny song. I wrote that there. I was busy looking at some winos, listening to them talk and my, they told a funny story. "Four Brothers" was the first record. I made that with Dave and eight voices. When I got ready to do this "Four Brothers," this guy, Teacho Wiltshire, he says, "There's only one guy that can do this for you: Dave Lambert." So I said, "Oh, yeah, be an honor. Will you introduce me?" And that was it and we been together ever since. Dave had to fight me all the way, he kept telling me, "You should put words to Basie." Do you know how much work that is?

RJG: *How do you do it?*

JH: Well, I listen. The main thing—I figure—this is true of anybody, if you listen long enough, you'll hear it finally. And when you hear it and you can get it to the point where you can hum it on the subway or walking down the street, then, after a time, words begin to come to you, whatever the horn is saying, they just form themselves, some of the phrases, like that on "Let Me See," that just screams, "How d'you do there?" It shouts, just like what he was saying.

RJG: *Did Pres [Lester Young] ever hear this, do you know? What was his reaction?*

JH: Well, he looked and then he looked away and he said, "Y'know Pres—I don't go by eyesight, I use my ears, and you got a nice sound." So I knew I was in.

RJG: *Does it take you long to do these things?*

JH: No, if I can just get it all heard, you know, after I play it a couple of weeks or so, while I'm around the house, I get it in my head so I can hum it, the words come in no time. Seems like I got more words than anything else. I got a lot to say. I been quiet a long time.

RJG: *Do you take off from the title of the tune?*

JH: I never change the title. 'Cause I think most guys who name songs, they had something in mind, y'know, when they named the song and I like to stick with that, that usually just gets me to the story quicker. I had a little trouble with "Shorty George." I didn't know who this guy was. So I go to Basie and I say, "Hey, Base, who *is* Shorty George?" And Basie looked at me, looked me up and down and turned around and walked away and said, back over his shoulder, "That's the cat that comes in the back door!" So I'm standing there like, "Oooooooh yeah?" So I got into the whole story.

RJG: *Do you think of these things, when you write them, as little dialogues?*

JH: Oh yeah! 'Cause I always wanted to write short stories and plays—in fact, that's what I went to New York to do. When I got there, wheeee! The panic was on. Everybody told me, "That's a good way to starve to death." So I looked around and ran into this. Looks like this is it. A whole new idiom.

RJG: *You've appeared with Basie at Birdland and where else?*

JH: At the Apollo. We did a week there. He watched us every show. Standing back, you know, and moving his whole body with us. When we make one of those nice old riffs, you know? Move around.

RJG: *Where have you appeared outside New York?*

JH: We did the Red Hill Inn in Camden, New Jersey, and we were paid a high compliment by Buddy Rich. You know, we don't play behind singers. So when we got to Red Hill we were worried about what we were going to do. Who was going to play behind us. And he said, "Man, I been looking forward to this, I wore out two albums already!"

RJG: *What was the hardest one to write?*

JH: "Jumpin' at the Woodside." Because it has one phrase that repeats and repeats and repeats and repeats and repeats and repeats and repeats and repeats, and to think up something different every phase—whoooh!

RJG: *Do you change them around much?*

JH: I'd like to, but once they're recorded I can't.

RJG: *Before they're recorded?*

JH: Sometimes, not too much. Usually the first draft is the one.

RJG: *Do you ever alter them when you're singing?*

JH: Sometimes it comes out accidentally that way. Like I came in different one time on "Let Me See"; I sang something different, I forget what it was.

RJG: *You said one night you had done something that had gassed you?*

JH: That was on the Oscar Pettiford thing, "Swinging till the Girls Come Home." I played a little thing that, *unh*—if only I had a fiddle in my hand!

RJG: *Would you like to play a horn?*

JH: Oh yeah! I'm a frustrated horn player. I'm thinking about a bass now. If it hadn't been for Roy Haynes, I'd have kept on playing drums. I heard him and quit. He sounded like everything I wanted to do. This was in 1952 in the Apollo Bar at 126th Street with Bird and Gerry Mulligan and Bud Powell and Tommy Potter. That shook me up something *awful*. I haven't played drums since I told Roy, "You messed up a promising career!" So much taste. We had him in Chicago. We had Roy, Ike Isaacs, and Nat Pierce.

RJG: *When you work with Basie, do you just do the tunes from the LP?*

JH: Unh-unh. We do the others, all of them. Frank [Foster] wrote some charts while we were at the Apollo with the band, you know, and I guess we'll do the same thing at the Crescendo. People were just gassed. At the Apollo, you could feel the love coming over the footlights.

RJG: *You've used that term a couple of times speaking of music, Jon. Is that the way you see music?*

JH: Oh, yes.

RJG: *When is this feeling of love strongest with you?*

JH: When you're singing it . . . right. And you *know* it's right. When *you* know it sounds good. Then it's a beautiful thing. But that's seldom though, at least with me. Seldom do I think that what I did was beautiful.

RJG: *Are you very critical of your own work?*

JH: Oh yes. Sometimes I think people can't hear. When they say it's marvelous and I know the clinkers I made, you know, and I know the things I should have done and didn't do, if you accept what people say at those times, you'll never improve. I learned that from Wardell [Gray]. Never accept praise when you know you didn't do good, 'cause that's the way you stop. I learned a lot from him. I was with him for six months. He was in my hometown. I used to go by and wake him up, you know, I'd get him breakfast and everything. I was learning. That's the way I learned music. Hanging around musicians. Listening all the time. I never did say too much. I hadn't anything to say. I was always listening. I heard a lot of things.

RJG: *You must have plans?*

JH: Oh, I'd like to do a jazz play, jazz music, jazz-based music, real jazz-based music, with real honest characters, as depicting musicians as they really are, some I've known, you know, just their story, their lives, those who were married, how they struggled to keep decent in an indecent environment. Just real good jazz musicians . . .

RJG: *This thing about music and love. Is this the feeling you'd get when you'd hear bands?*

JH: Oh, yes. I'd get so thrilled I couldn't say anything—just look if I met somebody I couldn't even talk! Like when I first met Ray Nance. I was *thunderstruck*. I couldn't say a word. He gasses me. Ooooooooweeeeee!

RJG: *Do you think jazz draws this happy feeling from audiences more than other music?*

JH: No. I think that jazz has a harder time doing it, because peoples' minds aren't opened to jazz. Jazz is—I make a claim—people say jazz has made so many strides, so much progress, I claim that in essential areas, it ain't made no progress at all. Back when it was first beginning to form, you know, that music was centered in the houses, you know, the picturesque houses, and in a sense it's still there. Now they got licenses, whiskey licenses, but it's the same kind of environment. Hasn't changed a bit. And this discourages a lot of people, you know, people who regard themselves as socially prominent and decent, you know, to look down on jazz, where at the same time they'll go to hear somebody like Jascha Heifetz who they don't understand anymore, but they'll do it with an open mind and they'll get something out of it. If they did the same thing with jazz, they'd get the same feeling. But they don't open their minds to it because of the social evil.

RJG: *Don't you think that's improving?*

JH: Oh yes. It is improving because the status of jazz itself is improving. Its acceptance abroad has done a lot to help it over here. And musicians have become more aware of their place in society, too, incidentally. They finally realize that they don't have to be characters. The more they do it, it helps a lot. In general, it's getting a lot better.

RJG: *You spoke the other day about how long it's taken jazz to get back out from under the movement towards classical.*

JH: Yes, it's the key to what's been happening the last 10 years.

RJG: *How did it get sidetracked?*

JH: Big record companies, you know, the big labels, have a hand in it. They don't like to recognize anything they can't take over— you know, and call their own. Like they took what used to be called race records and, later, rhythm and blues, and they have this attitude, you know, "Eh, I'll condescend to recognize it, but first I must cleanse it," you see, and this sterilizes it, takes out all the grit and, you know, there's nothing left but vapid, vacuous, boneless adolescence. And the same thing happened with jazz. In this country, it is difficult for people to regard something as a cultural art form that came from a people they regard as inferior, you see, so they have to change the source of it to something they regard as socially alright. And this is what I think affected it. A lot of people got sucked in, a lot of musicians got sucked in, a lot of musicians *knew* they were getting sucked in and sold themselves. Now they're trying . . . they got rich, but they lost their souls. What profiteth a man, you know. . .

RJG: *How did Annie get in the group?*

JH: Annie was on the Patrice Munsel show, dancing and once in a while a walk-on and a line. And Dave and I had hired 13 singers, the Ray Charles singers, people who could read anything. This was for *Sing A Song*, so we go to the studio and they sound like Walter Schumann singing Basie. So there was $1,200 and I was going to go out and kill myself! We figured, oh well. So we just happen to have an A&R man with a lot of soul. Boy, this guy says, "Throw that out and just start from scratch"—Creed Taylor. So we dig Annie, you know, because she seems to be the only one who could do it, even then we had no idea about going out like this, you know.

RJG: *How long did it take you to do that album?*

JH: It took us about, oh, we recorded for about three months. We wrote for about three months, Dave and I. That's about seven, eight months. I went to the hospital after the last date. Went right out. Just that last date, I staggered out to the taxicab to Bellevue, got operated on the next morning. I didn't have any money. Stone broke. So I had to go in as a charity patient and they operated on me the next morning. I had a fatty tumor on my rib. And when I started getting well, the album started to take off. So we figured, you know, let's sing around New York and make ourselves some little extra money. We ain't been in New York since!

RJG: *Do you read poetry?*

JH: I used to. I was studying poetry and I read Shelley and Byron and Keats and it seemed to me all those cats did was invent pictur-esque ways to say "I love you." I was saying, what was happening during the time they were living, you know? What was going on? It seemed to me they didn't say anything had any significance at all and I start writing my own things. I was on the newspaper at

University of Toledo and they gave me the poets corner and I was supposed to pick a poem and just run it, you know, but I started writing my own and I was saying some *funny* things, man! I did one about getting up in the morning that was called "Awake Is What I Wish I Wasn't So Why?"

RJG: *Do you think music offers a solution to some of the world's problems?*

JH: Yeah, I do. Well, it already has. You remember that cartoon in one of the *New Yorkers* that showed these guys around a conference table in Washington and the guy is saying "It's a serious situation, we don't know whether to send John Foster Dulles or Satchmo." It already has made such an impact, that's why there's so much attention being paid to it by the State Department. It's not that they love it any more, it's that everybody else has made them aware that "This is your only native culture, never mind coming over here telling us how to live and what to do, just send us some of your jazz and be cool." I was overseas during the war. Three and a half years. I got within 14 miles of London. And I went through Paris in a big convoy early in the morning about dawn and I looked around and that's all I saw of that and I hope to get back there. I like it in Europe.

RJG: *Was this trip you just made to London very exciting?*

JH: Oh, my, yes! Indeed. So much happening. In the first place, we went over there for an organization called the Christian Action and we arrived on a Sunday and it was sunny, like here, beautiful sunny day, everybody was so happy . . . after the concert it rained. It rained the night we left.

RJG: *Other jazz groups on it?*

JH: Johnny Dankworth, Ronnie Ross.

RJG: *How did they come to pick you for this?*

JH: We don't know exactly. They sent to Willard [Alexander], they wanted Lionel Hampton, who had been there last year, he couldn't make it so they asked Willard who he had, so he said, Lambert, Hendricks & Ross, and they said, "Who the devil are Lambert, Hendricks, and Ross?" So he says, "The greatest trio going!" So he sent over the contracts and they said come ahead. It was a very important benefit—the South African trials. Next day, 26 were killed in Nyassaland.

RJG: *How do you pick a tune to do?*

JH: I listen for one that sings to me. All of them sing to me, but one that sings to me very clear, you know, most lyrically. "Doodlin'" was a cinch. That piano solo!

RJG: *Does it happen often?*

JH: Oh yeah. I find it happens every time. Miles' "Round About Midnight." That sings. In fact, I got a theory: singin' and dancin'. Every musician is either a singer or a dancer. All guys who play drums are dancers. All horn players are singers. Still ain't nuthin' but the voice and the feet.

RJG: *Do you work at a studio?*

JH: No, I do them at home. In fact, I can't work anywhere else. Now, if I get in a studio, I find that it's like work and I never like to regard it as work, you know, because I get very unemotional about work 'cause it reminds me of the other end of the business. The songwriting field that I was in for a while, the pop field, so I like to write from warm feelings which I can feel better at home than in any studio. In fact, I feel cold in a studio. I like to record at home. We'd like to record on the job at the Crescendo.

RJG: *When you work up a lyric, do you write it on the typewriter?*

JH: I print longhand. A typewriter I can't make. I find I get so involved in the mechanics of getting words down that by the time I
get the word down, it ain't the word I had in mind.

RJG: *Is it difficult to make them scan?*

JH: No, I just write by phrase. I write by each phrase the guy plays.
There's never any trouble. As long as I hear the phrase, it'll turn
out alright. I find sometimes, though, that when I write them out,
it's hard to sing them, because I stop in the middle of the phrase
and go to the next line, and it throws you off.

RJG: *They didn't arrange those lyrics right on the album.*

JH: A certain critic who shall be nameless invited us up to his pad
to hear the album and when we got there, he thought that I was
singing all the solos. He didn't know me from Dave Lambert
and Joe Williams. And Joe sounds altogether different. He always gassed me. He always looks like he was saying a prayer. And
there'd be nothing moving but his left foot. And I notice, too,
the same thing about Mr. [Jimmy] Rushing. Nothing but his left
foot. He might be swaying, but he's not swaying right on, you
know, the rhythms, but his left foot is steady going . . .

RJG: *When was the first time you worked with Basie?*

JH: We did "Every Day" at the Apollo when he was there once. We
came up, you know, out of the audience and sang it and when he
was down at Birdland, we went down and did two things. Then
we did a week at the Apollo . . .